T0215181

Peripheral Methodologies

How does peripherality challenge methodology and theory-making? This book examines how the peripheral can be incorporated into ethnographic research, and reflects on what it means to be on the periphery – ontologically and epistemologically. Starting from the premise that clarity and fixity as ideals of modernity prevent us from approaching that which cannot be easily captured and framed into scientific boundaries, the book argues for remaining on the boundary between the known and the unknown in order to surpass this ethnographic limit. *Peripheral Methodologies* shows that peripherality is not only to be seen as a marginal condition, but rather as a form of theory-making and practice that incorporates reflexivity and experimentation. Instead of domesticating the peripheral, the authors engage in (and insist on) practicing expertise in reverse, unlearning their tools in order to integrate the empirical and analytical otherwise.

Francisco Martínez is Associate Professor at the School of Humanities of Tallinn University, Estonia.

Lili Di Puppo is Assistant Professor of Sociology at the National Research University Higher School of Economics, Moscow, Russia.

Martin Demant Frederiksen is Associate Professor at the Department of Anthropology, Aarhus University, Denmark.

Anthropological Studies of Creativity and Perception
Series Editor: Tim Ingold

The books in this series explore the relations, in human social and cultural life, between perception, creativity and skill. Their common aim is to move beyond established approaches in anthropology and material culture studies that treat the inhabited world as a repository of complete objects, already present and available for analysis. Instead these works focus on the creative processes that continually bring these objects into being, along with the persons in whose lives they are entangled. All creative activities entail movement or gesture, and the books in this series are particularly concerned to understand the relations between these creative movements and the inscriptions they yield. Likewise, in considering the histories of artefacts, these studies foreground the skills of their makers-cum-users, and the transformations that ensue, rather than tracking their incorporation as finished objects within networks of interpersonal relations. This series is interdisciplinary in orientation, with the concern of the titles always being with the practice of interdisciplinarity: on ways of doing anthropology with other disciplines, rather than doing an anthropology of these subjects. Through this anthropology with focus, they aim to achieve an understanding that is at once holistic and processual, dedicated not so much to the achievement of a final synthesis as to opening up lines of inquiry.

Titles in series
Design and Anthropology
Edited by Wendy Gunn and Jared Donovan

Making and Growing
Anthropological Studies of Organisms and Artefacts
Edited by Elizabeth Hallam and Tim Ingold

Reflections on Imagination
Human Capacity and Ethnographic Method
Edited by Mark Harris and Nigel Rapport

Craftwork as Problem Solving
Ethnographic Studies of Design and Making
Edited by Trevor H. J. Marchand

Exploring Atmospheres Ethnographically
Edited by Sara Asu Schroer and Susanne B. Schmitt

Attention in Performance
Acting Lessons in Sensory Anthropology
Cassis Kilian

Peripheral Methodologies
Unlearning, Not-knowing and Ethnographic Limits
Edited by Francisco Martínez, Lili Di Puppo and Martin Demant Frederiksen

www.routledge.com/Anthropological-Studies-of-Creativity-and-Perception/book-series/ASHSER1315

Peripheral Methodologies

Unlearning, Not-knowing and
Ethnographic Limits

**Edited by Francisco Martínez, Lili Di
Puppo and Martin Demant Frederiksen**

LONDON AND NEW YORK

First published 2021
by Routledge
2 Park Square, Milton Park, Abingdon, Oxon OX14 4RN

and by Routledge
52 Vanderbilt Avenue, New York, NY 10017

Routledge is an imprint of the Taylor & Francis Group, an informa business

British Library Cataloguing-in-Publication Data
A catalogue record for this book is available from the British Library

Library of Congress Cataloging-in-Publication Data
Names: Martínez, Francisco, 1982- editor. | Di Puppo, Lili, editor. | Frederiksen, Martin Demant, 1981- editor.
Title: Peripheral methodologies : unlearning, not-knowing and ethnographic limits / edited by Francisco Martínez, Lili Di Puppo, and Martin Demant Frederiksen.
Description: Abingdon, Oxon ; New York, NY : Routledge, 2021. | Series: Anthropological studies of creativity and perception | Includes bibliographical references and index.
Identifiers: LCCN 2020048368 (print) | LCCN 2020048369 (ebook) | ISBN 9781350173071 (hardback) | ISBN 9781003103646 (ebook)
Subjects: LCSH: Ethnology--Methodology. | Knowledge, Theory of. | Ontology.
Classification: LCC GN345 .P46 2021 (print) | LCC GN345 (ebook) | DDC 305.8001--dc23
LC record available at https://lccn.loc.gov/2020048368
LC ebook record available at https://lccn.loc.gov/2020048369

ISBN: 978-1-350-17307-1 (hbk)
ISBN: 978-0-367-75762-5 (pbk)
ISBN: 978-1-003-10364-6 (ebk)

Typeset in Times New Roman
by SPi Global, India

Contents

List of figures   vii

List of contributors   viii

Foreword: Between village and bush   ix
PAUL STOLLER

Introduction: Welcome to the corners of the peripheral   1
FRANCISCO MARTÍNEZ, MARTIN DEMANT FREDERIKSEN AND LILI DI PUPPO

PART I
Suspension of clarity   **15**

1   **At the core, beyond reach: Sufism and words flying away
    in the field**   17
    LILI DI PUPPO

2   **Shadows of meaning: Rethinking social dramas through absurdist
    theatre in a Georgian wedding**   31
    MARTIN DEMANT FREDERIKSEN

3   **'This parenting lark': Idiomatic ways of knowing and
    an epistemology of paying adequate attention**   45
    SEVASTI-MELISSA NOLAS AND CHRISTOS VARVANTAKIS

PART II
Unlearning   **61**

4   **Desiring the absence of knowledge: On knitting ethnography
    and navigating diaries**   63
    LYDIA MARIA ARANTES

5 Acquiring mētis in ceramic production: Patterned changes
and peripheral participation   81
   EWA KLEKOT

6 Hammering on the edges: Thresholds of un-knowing
in Santa Clara del Cobre, Mexico   94
   MICHELE AVIS FEDER-NADOFF

PART III

Absence of knowledge   **113**

7 Isomorphic articulations: Notes from collaborative
film-work in an Afghan-Danish Film Collective   115
   KAREN WALTORP AND ARTLIFE FILM COLLECTIVE

8 Here, there and nowhere in provincial outskirts
and haunted houses   131
   KIRSTEN MARIE RAAHAUGE

9 Fooled into fieldwork: Epistemic detours
of an accidental anthropologist   146
   FRANCISCO MARTÍNEZ

   Conclusion: Catching a glimpse of peripheral wisdom   165
   LILI DI PUPPO, MARTIN DEMANT FREDERIKSEN AND FRANCISCO MARTÍNEZ

   Afterthought: Notes on the peripheral, in a plague year   176
   ROBERT DESJARLAIS

   (Un-)Index   183

Figures

6.1 Maestro Jesús Pérez Ornelas. Three doves. Hammered,
    engraved and forged copper. 2000. (This illustrates
    the Photograph M. Feder-Nadoff.)   98
6.2 Maestro Jesús Pérez Ornelas. "Las sirenas". Hammered,
    engraved and forged copper. This piece illustrates
    the late middle-period work. Photograph Leah Solkoff Pohl   99
6.3 Maestro Jesús Pérez Ornelas. Three owls. Hammered, engraved
    and forged copper. 2014. This illustrates the later works created
    the year of the maestro's death. Photograph M. Feder-Nadoff   102
6.4 "The dance of agency". Maestro Jesús Pérez Ornelas (center)
    forging the round tejo, copper ingot with his sons, José Sagrario
    Pérez Pamatz (left) and Napoleón Pérez Pamatz in the
    family forge, Santa Clara del Cobre, 2011. Photograph M.
    Feder-Nadoff   106
9.1 Sergey Shamba. Francisco Martínez   148
9.2 Ochemchira. Francisco Martínez   149
9.3 Nik. Francisco Martínez   154
9.4 A group of young emigrées. Francisco Martínez   156
9.5 Chirikba. Francisco Martínez   157
9.6 Me and the ping-pong guard playing. Alex Bieth   158

Contributors

Lydia Maria Arantes is Assistant Professor, Department of Cultural Anthropology and European Ethnology, University of Graz, Austria.

Robert Desjarlais is Professor of Anthropology, Sarah Lawrence College, US.

Lili Di Puppo is Assistant Professor of Sociology, National Research University Higher School of Economics, Moscow, Russia.

Michele Avis Feder-Nadoff is an artist and scholar.

Martin Demant Frederiksen is Associate Professor, Department of Anthropology, Aarhus University, Denmark.

Ewa Klekot is Assistant Professor at the Institute of Design, University SWPS, Warsaw, Poland.

Francisco Martínez is Associate Professor at the School of Humanities of Tallinn University, Estonia.

Sevasti-Melissa Nolas is Senior Lecturer in Sociology at Goldsmiths, University of London, UK.

Kirsten Marie Raahauge is Professor WSD at The Royal Danish Academy of Architecture, Design and Conservation.

Paul Stoller is Professor of Anthropology, West Chester University, US.

Christos Varvantakis is, Research Fellow in Sociology at Goldsmiths, University of London, UK.

Karen Waltorp is Associate Professor at Department of Anthropology, University of Copenhagen, Denmark.

Foreword: Between village and bush

Paul Stoller

Cimi fonda: a ga cuu
Truth's path is tall (and long)
Songhay saying
We see the straight highway before us, but
we cannot take it because it's permanently closed
Wittgenstein, Philosophical Investigations (1953)

During my long apprenticeship to Adamu Jenitongo, my mentor of things Songhay would often send me into the bush to look for medicinal plants. He lived at the edge at the bush far from the centre of Tillaberi, a town nestled along the east bank of the Niger River. Leaving his compound of three two-room rectangular mudbrick houses and two conical straw huts I'd exit the 'village' and walk into the bush.

The first time he sent me on such a mission, Adamu Jenitongo asked me to look for curative plants.

'How do I know where to go? How do I know what to look for?'

The old man smiled at me. 'Follow the path', he said, 'and you'll find your way.'

I, of course, worried that I'd wander off to some godforsaken place and never seen again.

Adamu Jenitongo seemed unconcerned. 'Be careful in the bush', he told me. 'It's a dangerous place.' He chuckled. 'You'll be fine.'

Taking every precaution, I embarked on my first plant-seeking foray into the bush. With an empty burlap sack slung over my shoulder, I trekked east and south along vast laterite plains that pancaked to distant buttes that rose majestically in the Sahelian heat haze. I followed paths that cut through patches of scrub and crossed shallow wadies shaped through powerful rainy season runoff that cut through clay and sand. In a particularly broad and deep wadi, I found plants growing in moist sandy soil—a trace of the now-distant rainy season. Having 'found my way', I'd returned with a sack full of medicinal plants.

'We'll dry these plants and use them to heal people', Adamu Jenitongo told me. He was a short slight man who usually dressed in black – a black tunic, black drawstring trousers, and a black turban that framed the tight leathery skin of his aged face. 'It's good you returned before darkness. The bush', he reminded me, 'is dangerous'.

Adamu Jenitongo, who died more than 30 years ago, was a *sohanci,* a healer who traced his descent patrilineally to Sonni Ali Ber, the great 15th-century Songhay king who was renowned for his power of sorcery. Knowledge of his powerful practices has long been passed down through the centuries to Sonni Ali Ber's descendants, including, of course, Adamu Jenitongo.

As a sorcerous practitioner who can heal and harm people, the *sohanci* is a figure who lives at the existential edge of things. He is the intermediary between village and bush, between the social and spirit worlds, between health and illness, between life and death. The *sohanchi*'s familiar is the vulture (*zeyban*), a creature that partakes of the dead to live in the present. The vulture is a black bird of substantial power and mystery; it flies high and travels great distances. To emulate their familiar, *sohanci*, who have been known to fly great distances in the dark of night, also wear black. Like the vulture, they present themselves as mysterious beings who are feared and respected (see Rouch 1960; Stoller and Olkes 1987; Stoller 2008).

Like his father and his father's father, Adamu Jenitongo always lived at the edge of the village. No one wants to live close to a *sohanci* for fear of her or his over-abundance of power, a force that can burn those who get too close. And so, the *sohanci* is a peripheral figure par excellence. He or she lives a life filled with what John Keats long ago called 'negative capability', the capacity to live with incompleteness and contradiction (See Dewey 1929) In the arena of negative capability, you are compelled to pay attention and accept the experiential state, of 'not knowing your front side', to quote a Songhay incantation, 'from your back side'. In such a place you brutally confront the limits of comprehension.

Consider a 'not-knowing-your-frontside-from-your-backside' event that I experienced at the edge of the bush in Tillaberi, Niger. I had been living in Adamu Jenitongo's dune top compound for almost two months. My mentor had been teaching me about the curative properties of plants, knowledge he would only convey to me in *cino bi,* 'the black of night', which meant that I often felt sleep deprived. One night after a 'black of night' session, braying donkeys and howling dogs woke me from a fitful sleep. As I got up from my bed, the brays and howls grew louder, heading in my direction. I approached the closed door. I heard footsteps and high-pitched vocalizations – some kind of strange gibberish. Then came screechy scrapes of fingernails on corrugated tin – my door. Frozen in place, I wanted to open the door but lacked the courage to do so. The screechy scrapes continued followed by a high-pitched whine that sounded like a child's voice. Slowly the sounds moved away, as did the donkey brays and dog howls. Stealing all the courage I could muster, I opened the door. A ribbon of dawn orange stretched across the eastern horizon. At the edge of the bush, I saw dogs leaping the in air.

Moments later I woke Adamu Jenitongo's son and asked him if he had heard anything.

'No, I didn't hear anything', he said.

I needed some kind of verification. I approached my mentor and told him what I had experienced.

'You heard it, too?'

'Yes, Baba, what was it?'

'The Atakurma came to visit.'

'The little people – guardians of the bush?', I asked.

'You heard their squeaky little voices, and the dogs and donkeys?' He paused. 'The dogs and donkey get excited when they come.'

Adamu Jenitongo explained that on Sundays, a day of the spirits, he'd take a bowl of honey or milk into the bush and leave it for the Atakurma. 'It's been some time since I last brought them an offering. They came for honey or milk.' He shook his head. 'You heard that?'

++++

What I heard brought me to the limits of comprehension.

Had my senses betrayed me? Had I been dreaming?

Could the Atakurma be more than a sleep deprived hallucination?

In the immediate aftermath of that turbulent situation, I remembered that Adamu Jenitongo had once told me that human beings, who live in the village, cannot control the wild forces of the bush. To understand the bush, he counselled, you have to surrender to it and let it penetrate your being – a transformative process fraught with personal risk and existential vulnerability. Faced with a similar kind of philosophical incomprehension the great 19th-century philosopher Friedrich Nietzsche offered some advice about how to absorb the disturbing particularities of not-knowing. He wrote that the mission of science:

> …Is to make existence intelligible and thereby justified… Socrates and his successors, down to our day, have considered all moral and sentimental accomplishments – noble deeds, compassion, self-sacrifice, heroism… to be ultimately derived from the dialectic of knowledge and therefore teachable… But science, spurred on by its energetic notions, approaches irresistibly those outer limits were the optimism of logic must collapse… When the inquirer, having pushed to the circumference, realizes how logic in that place curls about itself and bites its own tail, he is struck with a new kind of perception, a tragic perception, which requires, to make it tolerable, the remedy of art.
>
> (Nietzsche [1876] 1956: 93)

In my own work, I have tried to follow Nietzsche's sage advice. No matter the subject of my texts, I have attempted to fuse of art and ethnography – the art of ethnography in which the writer or filmmaker crafts stories that evoke themes of anthropological import. Is this tack not one way to confront the imponderables of ethnographic experience?

For me, the contributions that comprise *Peripheral Methodologies: Unlearning, Not-Knowing and Ethnographic Limits*, a collection of stunningly creative and thoughtful essays, all evoke the 'remedy of art' to probe the indeterminate 'gray light' that illuminates the spaces between things (Martínez, Frederiksen, Di Puppo, Nolas and Varvantakis). They evoke 'the remedy of art' to highlight the process of unlearning on the path to artisanal mastery (Arantes, Feder-Nadoff, Klekot). They underscore 'the remedy of art' to confront ethnographic reality in the absence of knowledge (Martínez, Raahauge, Waltorp).

Between the lines of these elegant essays, brilliantly brought together by Francisco Martínez, Martin Demant Frederiksen and Lili Di Puppo, it is clear that the contributors understand what it takes to know the bush, to comprehend artisanal skill, and to describe an ethnographic event or film an ethnographic scene. They demonstrate that deep listening and deep comprehension comes not from disembodied theorisation but from opening their bodies to the world in much the way that a painter, uses body and being to create a tableau. In his book, *Le monologue du peintre*, Georges Charbonnier had a conversation with Andre Marchard during which the latter underscored sentiments that Paul Klee often expressed in his lectures:

> In a forest I have felt many times over that it was not I who looked at the forest. Some days I felt that the trees were looking at me. I was there, listening... I think that the painter must be penetrated by the universe and not penetrate it... I expect to be inwardly submerged, buried. I paint to break out.
> (Charbonnier 1959, cited in M-P 1964: 31)

Indeed, 'the remedy of art' takes its cue from the phenomenological thought of Maurice Merleau-Ponty (M-P), who, in his magisterial work, *Eye and Mind* (1964), wrote authoritatively about an artful approach to being in the world. M-P believed that the painter is our guide on the path to what he called the 'there is'. The painter savours the life that resides in the inner dimensions of things. Indeed, the painter, like other artists, feels the 'reverberations' that can create awareness in the eye and mind of the person who confronts the sensory splendour of the world. But M-P's writing about art is not some vague mystical journey into the unseen or the sensory unconscious. In *Eye and Mind*, M-P suggests that artists are our guides to the 'there-is' because they open their being to the world. 'Indeed, we cannot imagine how a mind could paint. It is by lending his body to the world that the artist changes the world into paintings' (M-P 1964: 16). Put another way, the act of painting is a metaphor for sensing the world from the inside.

++++

If you follow a path that winds its way. between village and bush, if you wander in the spaces between things, your head clears. At that point you are able to sense the world from the inside. Like the authors in *Peripheral Methodologies*, you also realise that stories are a powerful way to bring into relief the irreducible complexities of peripheral wisdom.

There are elements of good storytelling in the essays that comprise *Peripheral Methodologies*. The prose in this anthology features the elements of craft that make for a good story: the sensuous evocation of space (see Badkhen 2018), the idiosyncrasies of dialogue (see Behar 1996) and the depiction of character (see

Chabon 1995). These are necessary, but not sufficient conditions for crafting a good story. In the end, recounting a good story is certainly about technique and artistry but also about how you conduct your research and how you live your life.

> Do you live in the moment?
> Do you have confidence on your path?
> Do you 'open your ears' and listen deeply to wise elders?
> Are you willing to enter the stressful arena of representational vulnerability?

These existential practices implicate human beings in social relations, including, of course, the implication of ethnographers among their others. They empower us to tell a good story, which, in turn, enables us to better understand not knowing, unlearning, and the absence of knowledge. In the end, the contributors to *Peripheral Methodologies* show us how to move towards the destination of peripheral wisdom, a felicitous destination for the future of anthropological practice.

++++

During a televised interview the documentary filmmaker John Marshall posed a question to the inimitable Jean Rouch.

'Are you a filmmaker or an anthropologist?'

Rouch smiled broadly. 'When I am with anthropologists, they consider me as a filmmaker, and when I'm with filmmakers they consider me as an anthropologist, which means… I am Gemini by birth which means I am in two places at the same time' (Gardner 1980).

Being in two places at the same time put Rouch in a netherworld. He became an always already sojourner on the periphery. As he navigated the turbulence between bush and village, between Niger and France, and between filmmaking and anthropology, he led the life of a person who was neither here nor there. In search of peripheral wisdom, Rouch's indeterminate vantage inspired his inventive creativity, a creativity that produced a visionary body of work in film and text that will long remain open to the world (Henley 2009). Such is the anthropological reward of coming to grips with the suspension of clarity, states of unlearning, and the absence of knowledge (Stoller 1992, 2020).

References

Badkhen, Anna 2018. *Fisherman's Blues: A West African Community at Sea*. New York: Riverhead Books.

Behar, Ruth 1996. *The Vulnerable Observer*. Boston: Beacon Press.

Chabon, Michael 1995. *Wonder Boys*. New York: Picador.

Charbonnier, Georges 1959. *Le monologue du peintre*. Paris: Julliard.

Dewey, John 1929. *The Quest for Certainty*. New York: Minton, Balch and Company.

Gardner, Robert 1980. *Screening Room: Jean Rouch*, color 64 min. Watertown: Documentary Educational Resources.

Henley, Paul. 2009. *The Adventure of the Real: Jean Rouch and the Craft of Ethnographic Cinema*. Chicago: The University of Chicago Press.

Merleau-Ponty, Maurice 1964. *L'Oeil et l'esprit*. Paris: Gallimard.

Nietzsche, Friedrich [1876] 1956. *The Birth of Tragedy Out of the Spirit of Music*. Garden City, NJ: Doubleday (Anchor Books).

Rouch, Jean 1960. *La Religion et la Magie Songhay*. Paris: Presses Universitaires de France

Stoller, Paul 1992. *The Cinematic Griot: The Ethnography of Jean Rouch*. Chicago: The University of Chicago Press.

Stoller, Paul 2008. *The Power of the Between: An Anthropological Odyssey*. Chicago: The University of Chicago Press.

Stoller, Paul 2020. Imaging Knowledge: Anthropology, Storytelling and the Quest for Wellbeing in a Troubled World. *Swedish Journal of Anthropology* 3(1): 11–20.

Stoller, Paul and Cheryl Olkes 1987. *In Sorcery's Shadow: A Memoir of Apprenticeship Among the Songhay of Niger*. Chicago: The University of Chicago Press.

Wittgenstein, Ludwig 1953. *Philosophical Investigations*. New York: Macmillan.

Introduction
Welcome to the corners of the peripheral

Francisco Martínez, Martin Demant Frederiksen
and Lili Di Puppo

From fringes to knowledge

How does peripherality challenge methodology, theory-making and the porous relation between the two? And in which ways can we approach the peripheral as a generative condition? The guiding inspiration of this book is to explore the manners in which the unarticulated, the edgy and the unknown can be considered a form of thinking about problems, questions and evidence, which also entails reflecting upon what it means to be on the periphery — ontologically and epistemologically. We start from the premise that the peripheral is not just a location or a feeling, but also a form of knowing as well as an unconquered knowledge (previously thought as non-knowable). Our project is an inquiry into the kinds of knowledge that are hidden, counting as not counting, not easily transformed into data and information, or simply belonging to the realm of the non-measurable, as this quote from Mary C. Bateson illustrates:

> Ambiguity is the warp of life, not something to be eliminated. Learning to savor the vertigo of doing without answers or… making do with fragmentary ones opens up the pleasures of recognizing and playing with pattern, finding coherence within complexity... Improvisation and new learning are not private processes; they are shared with others.
>
> (1994: 9–10)

Here we seek to materialise methodological experiments on the edges of knowledge-making, and to get beyond the rigidities of the academic format and language in order to provide an original catch of something more in the flux of life. The main novelty brought by this collection is therefore to approach the peripheral not only as a representational issue but also as an methodological one: generative of new epistemic directions, unforeseeable knowledges and questions out of the visual field. We provide different re-imaginings of the peripheral, as an epistemic effort to reckon with what we cannot fully understand or represent – with the possibilities of relating to the unknown and the extraneous. Within this frame of peripheral methodologies, the vague, contradictory, unfinished, superficial and eccentric are seen not as flaws to banish through iterative polishing, focusing, rightening and re-centring, but as a valuable source of creativity and evidence in their own right (with the capacity to reorient the limits of the knowable). We also explore how to access to the infra-knowledge, to what is there before or under anthropology, at the gates of scientific research, as distinct minor types of understanding such as inner dialogues, embodied imagination or the revelation of immaterial aspects of life.

Based on decentred methodological experiences, we propose a grammar that makes it possible to put into words the uncontrolled, elusive and opaque aspects of the field. Here, they are taken as constitutive of knowledge production, instead of as an unintended outcome or side-effect. In doing so, we critically question what constitutes ethnographic work and the field itself, providing not just diverse perspectives, but also different ways of looking at the same issue, and therefore of knowing reality. For instance, we pay attention to how our fieldwork might be in the periphery of someone else, and something else, that has not yet been brought into question, but which could indeed be the object of our study.

We do this by letting the periphery to break through, by maintaining things unsettled, by stepping into the unspoken and incomplete, simultaneously inside and outside, taking the direction lacking a clear path. By assuming that the periphery is a zone of challenges and questions, empirically multiple, emergent, mysterious, conflicted and ambiguous, methodologically non-coherent and excessive (Plows 2018), we set out to engage with a series of empirical and theoretical issues such as:

–   What is the centre and the periphery of what we do? And what is its surface and core?
–   How to represent infra-knowledge – what lies beneath the threshold of verbal reasoning, or does not respond to the criteria for widely recognised types of knowledge?
–   What is the place in social sciences for the unfinished, vague and messy?
–   How can we apprehend modes of knowing that open up to an invisible realm?
–   How can the peripheral theorising be integrated into anthropological training?
–   Which are the consequences of the immediately unknown on our ethnographies?
–   And what kind of incubators are peripheries?

We aim to open up a space for these and similar questions and thoughts at and on the edge that are often segregated out by academic works. We believe that the notion of peripherality might help us to transcend some conventional divides, such as between reason and the senses, design and accident, or analysis and aesthetics, generating other modes of being attentive to the world. We are aware of the intrigue and risk that this term implies, bringing to the fore, at first glance, knowledge that has been marginalised, excluded or suppressed. Even if we appreciate the bottom-up critical connotations of the term, elaborated for instance by Immanuel Wallerstein in his World System Theory (1974),[1] our main interest is in discussing how, in moments of epistemic and socio-political crisis, peripheries hold the potential to disrupt established ideas and to push methods beyond their traditional disciplinary limits.

Peripheries have long been intertwined with the production and also the reception of anthropological knowledge, discussing how peripherality involves questions of difference and modernity. Likewise, peripheral knowledge has been produced as a critique of hegemonic ontologies and epistemologies connected to various notions of 'core', placing the empirical in contrast to the 'centres of calculation' (Latour 1987). In anthropological studies, peripheries and margins have often been presented as imbued with a sense of ambiguity, and often as being misinterpreted by a centre. Likewise, peripheries tend to be hidden in the process through which things are made to seem clear, bounded and fixed (Green 2005). A focus on peripherality thus gives access to the minor key (Ingold 2017), to what can be only accessed at the corner of the eye, looking sideways (see Raahauge, also Waltorp and ARTlife Film Collective, in this volume).

Being in the periphery has several existential repercussions, as people often get pulled by different centres and in different directions. Peripheries may be seen as spaces of marginalia, ex-centricity and renewal (Stewart 1996), whereby the fantasy realm finds its physical location (Scott 2000). As such, peripheral wisdom appears as a form of sensed information, generally known, but hard to articulate verbally; part of the ongoing negotiation between what is known and what is not known; an engagement with 'what goes missing when one looks for meaning' (Frederiksen 2018: 1), and, overall, the realm of the fringe – a dimension of the experience that disappears with normative articulation (Crapanzano 2014). Hence, we do not seek to provide a precise definition of periphery or the realm of the edgy, but rather to account for what is pushed out of sight to make something else appear clear – the shadows, opaqueness and vagueness encountered in the social world, the ambiguities and the unfinished quality of ethnographic knowledge and the roles of the unspoken and implicit phenomena.

Suspension of clarity

Besides approaching the peripheral as a contemporary problem space, we reflect on the constitutive presence of uncertainty in the field and how the undefined areas of our fieldwork challenge our own epistemological and ontological assumptions and methodologies. We invite readers to rethink how the unarticulated can be incorporated into ethnographic research as a generative condition to build in turn a peripheral methodology. In doing so, we argue that peripherality should not only be taken as an unfinished space, a marginal condition, or that which is excluded from the hegemony of vision, but rather as a form of making theory and practice, deploying an eventful sensibility and (in)attention.

Hence, we move aside from traditional approaches in anthropology that put the focus on marginal people, subversion, the subaltern, suburbs or novel forms of connection between peripheries (Martínez 2019a). In such cases, the object of research and the core are already formed on a more normative basis in opposition to what is established, accepted, dominant etc.; hence, one cannot exist without the other. Yet if already constituted as an object of research and in opposition, then it is no longer ontologically peripheral, and one can study it with the same usual methods. In our view, it is the mode of being available, (in)attentive, and open to getting lost that makes the peripheral appear to us and as a way of stay-ing with the trouble (Haraway 2016), even if we 'fail' or reach certain limits of comprehension. Perhaps we should not talk of being centred in the field, but rather of standing fringy, engaging with the outside, which always remains as an unordered, ungraspable space of multiplicity and indeterminacy.

We approach the periphery as a zone of uncertainty wherein traditional meth-odological codes fail to guide our action. Peripheries are sites of experimenta-tion and path-finding, yet they are always a pathless path – a methodological orientation to be walked through. The urban sociologist AbdouMaliq Simone foregrounds that the periphery should not be approached as a stabilised whole: 'Rather, it is an ongoing deformation of systemic entities' (2019: 9). The periph-eral shies away from the light clarity of social categories and does not adhere to any script or definitive conceptualisation; it refuses to be represented in some 'right' way and rather operates, or oscillates, within the opaque, indeterminate and diffuse.[2] Such fields demand particularly methodological considerations or innovations, as well as particular forms of analysis and representation (Frederik-sen 2020; Taussig 2018).

During fieldwork, we encounter things and phenomena that we cannot com-prehend to the end, at the limits of what can be perceived or comprehended (Des-jarlais 1997). We do not encounter these things as fixed and clearly delineated, we make them so through our analytical deskwork. What if we resist the urge to extract meaning and assemble fragments into a whole? Some things cannot be known in the very moment of encounter – just felt, or sensed, because these things cannot be directly related to our experience, and, hence, apprehended. Moreover, peripheral wisdom is not about some *other,* subversive knowledge, but rather it is related to the ups and downs of living, to moments of hesitation, of feeling lost, of not knowing, of being vulnerable, and also of contemplating overwhelming beauty and the significance of un-systematised ways of knowing. All these are intimate aspects that we encounter during field research and also in the process of writing, as noted by Robert Desjarlais in his afterword.

Most often the peripheral goes into the infra-knowledge folder. Social accel-eration and the neoliberalisation of academia are further foreclosing collateral explorations, diversions and imaginings, reinforcing in turn calculative and cor-porative discourses. We propose a challenge to this in methodological terms, by staying with the unexpected encounter without being intimidated by the com-plications that may arise in doing so. Despite the trouble involved, we hold that doing so has its benefits. Staying in the in-between fringe allows us to 'breathe in the creative air of indeterminacy' (Stoller 2009: 4); that is, to work 'beside the point' away from preconceived meaning (Frederiksen 2018), examining places, situations, experiences or conditions that remain asymptotes of social reality, even if they never fully come together or reach the points they curve towards (Dunn and Frederiksen 2018).

By caring for and preserving moments of suspension of clarity and not-knowing, we might find a language to write the incomplete or invisible (Mittermaier 2019), and to carve out a poetics of peripherality that opens up for the otherwise and he not-yet-known. Peripheral wisdom is related to temporal openness to as yet unknowns and not-yets (Dalsgaard and Frederiksen 2015), and to idiotic techniques proposed for enabling alternative thoughts of action and perspectives (Nolas and Varvantakis in this volume).

In the field of STS, peripheral methodologies have been approached as a speculative mode of action that withholds an idiotic component (Farías 2017; Gaspar 2018; Guggenheim, Kräftner and Kröll 2017; Stengers 2005). The idiot puts hegemonic notions of the useful and the sensical in suspension or standby, a proactive disruption that helps us understand 'what we are busy doing' (Michael 2012). The idiot stays beside the point, reminding us of decentred potentials and that there are different ways of being through time and space. Indeed, *through time and space* directly pertain to peripheral conditions, which brings to the fore elements of heterochronia, epistemic multidirectionality and lateral ways of noticing (Irving 2017). Suspension also brings reflection. These moments of apparent unproductivity go hand in hand with accessing distinct types of knowledge and to know without knowing.

Through peripheral methodologies, we rescind relevance and purpose to the minimum to access infra-knowledge, challenging, in turn, late-modern paradigms of innovation and the need for everything to be useful. We propose to gather data by preserving the moments of suspension and surprise, by embracing experiences that lead to not-knowing, and by defending the qualitative time of doing nothing (Martínez 2019b). We are indeed motivated by not-knowing,[3] as a learning process that magnifies our awareness of the outer limits, of what remains unknown – hence it becomes a resourceful component of knowledge-making and not only disruptively, but also generatively and with a methodological potential.[4]

Ex-centricity

In this anthology, we explore the kinds of knowledge that peripheries deliver. This term finds its etymology in the ancient Greek *peripheres*, meaning an outer surface, or a line around a circular body. One may fruitfully consider this in relation to Tim Flohr Sørensen's call for staying on the surface. Writing on the archaeology of the contemporary, he notes how 'the modernist dogma dictates that it is superficial to remain on the surface, but this rests on the contention that the surface is singular and impenetrable, covering up things that are otherwise unknown, forgotten, repressed or subconscious' (Sørensen 2014: 12). This suggestion to stay on the surface is, in many respects, a suggestion to stay within the peripheral; that is, to not work one's way towards a perceived idea of a core or a perceived idea of knowledge as solid fact, and instead consider wisdom as a form of 'seeing without knowing' (Downey 2007: 231). Hence, wisdom is not confined to cognitive aspects; rather it is a form of embodied and shared knowledge.

In this volume, the intent is to engage with the limits of interpretation and representation by intentionally reaching aspects beyond clarity and precision, escaping dualisms and resisting the linearity and rational predictability of modernity (Savransky, Wilkie and Rosengarten 2017). It sets out to open a new conversation about the need, in some instances, to operate with a limited understanding of what is going on, for concealment, lack of transparency, accountability and exposure, keeping things in the dark as they originally are (Strathern 2000), or as Édouard Glissant asserts for the right to opacity (1997), letting things be in their obscure otherness and interrupting the central modern gaze, taking opacity as a project, as a figure for diversity.

Yet when it comes to knowledge or rather wisdom, we are not looking for other forms of knowledge as constituted in opposition to modern Western habits and representations. It is more about learning to value our periphery and rethinking the knowledge acquired there, which, in some cases, comes about through an intense emotional engagement, and in some others, through forms of being away despite being present (see Nolas and Varvantakis in this volume). Further, it is also about embracing a mode of attention that does not disturb things and the unfolding of events. We become attentive because we understand that, at any moment, the thing that we suddenly feel can disappear, and this often takes place subtly so. We thus propose to be (in)attentive and account for knowledge that is not just conceptual and verbal, but also attitudinal; a knowledge that hovers between the actual and the potential (Crapanzano 2004), to what lays behind the visible arrangements yet still co-produces our way of being in the world. Such evocative, disordered knowledge still affects us, making certain forms of thought possible (and not others), and felt as an intensity that sticks in the mind (Berlant and Stewart 2019).

Wisdom unfolds relationally, in the space between us, linked to open attentiveness to the world, rather than in the assumption of cognitive mastery, to the point that our attempt to reason it or be conscious about it often leads to the end of the existential experience.[5] It is in this sense that we talk of a suspension of clarity. The wisdom that we might acquire can be understood not in relation to methodological tools and designs, but rather based on the helpless state that we enter. Since we are also acted upon (Mittermaier 2012; Rytter 2016), it is worth reflecting on what things do to us in a state of staying on the boundary, testing the limits and engaging with the outer lands and the suspension of clarity. In this anthology, we invite readers to also acknowledge that things can be vague and elusive per se, and that the suspension of clarity is also a social fact; so, accordingly, we can also let vagueness remain vague (Sørensen 2016).

Attention to the unclear or the peripheral may well erupt from not knowing exactly what to look for.[6] Here, we not only propose to move along this epistemic limit but to also remain in or on it. This may be in terms of what Kathleen Stewart refers to as 'an effort to dwell in the uncertain space of error or gap (and) displacing the premature urge to classify, code, contextualise, and name long enough to imagine something of the texture and density of spaces of desire that proliferate in Othered spaces' (1996: 26). Or, if reflecting on the limits of capturing and on what goes almost unfelt – engaging with things that can hardly be methodologies – we might decide to include the centre or not, as something that is irrelevant to our endeavor.

In its classical sense, the notion of eccentricity refers to a deviation from a customary practice or character, standing out of the normative way. We use it here in a dual sense, both as a question of peripherality in terms of that which either resides away from or moves away from a centre, and as a question of form – that which as a representation is irregular, peculiar or erratic precisely because it seeks to convey empirical aspects of the peripheral. Although eccentricity and unclarity may be seen as a challenge to conventional approaches within social sciences such as anthropology, there are other disciplines in which the notion has been central. In this regard it is worth remembering death and, in particular, the role of *memento mori* in the Renaissance and onwards, as well as the ways in which visual ambiguity increasingly became an aspect of fine arts. A case in point is Hans Holbein's painting *The Ambassadors* from 1533, a composition that at first sight appears simple and clear. Two figures – the ambassadors – stand almost symmetrically in an interior space, leaning against a set of shelves where instruments of knowledge contemporary to their times have been arranged, such as globes and astronomical instruments. The viewer's gaze on the composition, however, is disturbed by a grey shape that cuts diagonally through the lower part of the painting, conspicuous yet indistinct. The viewer can only make sense of it if he or she stands in just the right spot to the lower left of the painting. From that point the indistinct shape is foreshortened and reveals itself to be a human skull, an encoded *memento mori*. Although we do not have Holbein's own explanation of the reason for this visual ambiguity, it is probable that one intention was to ensure that, when standing in front of the painting for the first time, the viewer stares directly at death without recognising it; and secondly, that this inscribed form of vagueness actually demands the viewer's intensified attention.

Locating wisdom

A key to this project resides in testing the applicability of 'peripheral wisdom' as a concept and setting the general framework for studying the corners of knowledge. In our research, however, we do not discuss whether the centre is dependent on or relevant for the periphery. Instead, we aim at learning to pay attention to things laterally, attending to what we observe, accessing to a fruitful space and time of infra-knowledge. Hence, we place an emphasis on reconfiguring the epistemological presuppositions of anthropology to include the eccentric, the invisible, and the vague, as constituting different forms of being in the world, as well as the imaginary outside, away from the scientific city walls. In this sense, we show that the stuff of the unknowable is also an ethnographic object of inquiry and not part of the academic neglect (Bendix 2005; Berglund and Kohtala 2020). Moreover, we intend to not just make the peripheral present and sensible in our research, but also to reshape some of our frames of reference and learn in ways that might be considered wrong by some traditional perspectives.

In this anthology, the peripheral carries multiple functions and meanings, ranging from epistemological and disciplinary concerns, to hierarchies of knowledge production and the situated condition of any methodology. We are aware that knowledge is built through places and embodied relations that are situated in particular locations and times, 'bound up in one way or another with the world' (Harris 2007: 1). In *Wisdom Sits in Places* (1996), Keith Basso studied how members of the Cibecue Apache community in the US think and imagine their geography in correlation to wisdom. Both landscapes and place-names were associated with particular manners and morals, passed on generationally by being in that place.

As some of the members of the community emigrated, they lost their wisdom and the capacity to hear their ancestors speaking. At the end of the book, Basso asks rhetorically, 'What is wisdom?', and Dudley, one of his informants, replies that 'Wisdom sits in places. It's like water that never dries up. You need to drink water to stay alive, don't you? Well, you also need to drink from places' (1996: 127).

This mirrors the difference between the notions of knowledge and wisdom; Whereas the former implies questions of education, scientific reflection, reasoned or logical thought, confident understanding, and having clarity of facts and truths, the latter relates to intuition, skills and abilities – to an intangible quality gained through personal experience. Although we speak of knowledge production here, it is the notion of wisdom that forms our point of departure, along with its position alongside peripherality. We asked a series of authors to explain what the anthropological application of peripheral methodologies would be, and to explore how peripheries might be the metaphysical location of the contemporary moment. We can indeed view this volume in contemporary methodological terms, yielding themselves as specific ways of knowing and seeing (Grasseni 2007). Practicing ethnography entails creative invention and not merely writing and description. Moreover, we agree with the recent criticism raised claiming that anthropology has been too verbal and rational, and insufficiently graphic and sensorial (Ingold 2014; Kuschnir 2016; Taussig 2011).

The challenge, however, is to identify the instances in which we have to liberate ourselves from the glasses of positivist, logic reality in order to make certain phenomena comprehensible or knowable, and how to do so. Also, in this project, we assume certain ethnographic limits and the impossibility of always getting there, while we also accept that we sometimes cannot go far enough with reason alone. This ethnographic thinning is not necessarily a surrender, and it does not have to entail a 'failure of nerve' (Ortner 1995: 173), as it maintains the effort to communicate social life, albeit in a different way. Thus, we aim to reconsider the affective relationship to knowledge practices and at extending the possibilities of ethnographic play by taking up idioms, failures and vagueness as being generative of wisdom. In this project, we aim to contribute to contemporary discussions about the experiential and experimental character of anthropology. We draw on the assumption that peripherality is a form of making theory (Roy 2011; Simone 2010), one that involves thinking-doing and is not afraid of failing in and falling into fieldwork (see Martínez in this volume).

Conversations at the periphery can sometimes be sweet, but they can also be tense and bitter. This project is rich in fragrance in itself, but it is not free of tensions. It underlines aspects and phenomena 'that don't just add up but take on a life of their own as problems of thought' (Stewart 2008: 72). The emphasis is put on carving both chances and skills for learning about those phenomena that are visibly invisible by linking analytical and sensuous approaches. This is done to develop our perceptual capacity for studying the depth of the visible, and our capacity to bridge interiority and exteriority in different stages of the research process. We thus draw on the assumption that certain things can be learned only from a partial perspective (Strathern 1991). As we hold, through this oblique approach, we can address issues of knowledge and method, as well as reconsider the relevance of situated ways of seeing in a world that often feels like a digital panopticon.

Ethnographically, the set of chapters of this anthology interconnect various accounts from diverse settings to explore how peripherality is not simply a condition or space, but instead a way of theory-making and a mode of attention. Moreover, the volume seeks to generate new forms of thinking theoretical and empirical experiences of what it means to be on the edge. The move towards the periphery allows us to recover a sense of fertility and openness that lacks at the centre. We aim to broaden our sense of what is relevant and what counts as knowledge, by using peripherality as a way to explore alternative modes of doing research and to open up new ways to approach social phenomena. As such, it is a project (and an attitude) that deliberately goes against the grain of seeing only the empirically admissible as being worthy of scientific investigation (Crapanzano 2004). In this vein, we want to explore the possibility of whether, in some cases, clarity and fixity prevents us from approaching that which cannot be easily captured and framed into scientific boundaries, as in T.S. Eliot poem (1934):

> Where is the Life we have lost in living?
> Where is the wisdom we have lost in knowledge?
> Where is the knowledge we have lost in information?

Invent your own periphery

We do not know in which condition this book will be read. We are open to allow analytical questions to emerge from the edges of our own work and disciplinary training, accounting meanings and events as they are meant – vague, contradictory, unfinished, superficial, polluted. As Michele Feder-Nadoff notes in her contribution to this anthology, peripherality means 'I will see how it comes out!', and hence entails making mistakes, taking wrong steps, testing, and being out of the line. Feder-Nadoff has worked as an un-knowing apprentice or amateur artisan in a coppersmith workshop in Mexico, learning when to let things go. As her chapter concludes, 'the wisdom of an artisan is more about reach than grasp, more about extending, than holding fast'. We have to think more with the body, insists Ewa Klekot. In her chapter, Klekot considers how to integrate non-discursive knowledge of the body into ethnographical cognition. She describes her own practice of working on a potter's wheel and of casting porcelain ware, reminding readers of the situated character of *mētis* and how centring a lump of clay on the wheel is the very act that precedes all others.

In relation to her fieldwork among knitters in Austria, Lydia Arantes explains that peripheral wisdom also refers to translations, to a sensual attuning to a specific environment, in order for knowledge to be able to unfold. As Arantes observes, 'My body did not only play a mediator's role, it did not only connect myself with my field. Much to the contrast, it also came to be perceived as a problem for my research.' This is a chapter about the intricacies of transferring and translating embodied knowledge, starting by the ethnographer. Arantes had to learn how to distance herself from her embodied experience and knowledge – to learn how to unlearn, acquiring 'new forms of bodily perception to develop a novel understanding for materials and procedures'.

In his chapter, also Martínez discusses how we come to reshape our understanding of the field. Through a series of unfortunate episodes in Georgia, he reflects on how failures gave form to his fieldwork and whether the knowledge generated in field accidents might have any epistemic value despite not being part of a result-oriented ethnography. By exploring how accidents can become an element of learning and part of our maturation as researchers (instead of dirt that has to be sanitised from our ethnographies), he also ponders if we always remain an anthropologist-in-the-making.

If Martínez wonders whether his work qualifies as anthropology, Lili Di Puppo reconsiders her uneasy attempts to approach Sufism as an object of study in Russia. The elusiveness and incommensurability of her field necessitates practicing a form of ethnography that allows the unknowable to remain. Sufism in the Volga-Ural region can be approached as a visible social phenomenon, but it ultimately escapes attempts to be 'captured' as it points precisely to the limits of knowledge by opening up to a realm beyond the known. Di Puppo's own ethnographic 'failure', experienced during a ritual ceremony, leads her to feel that 'the more we strive to reveal and expose, the more we hide'.

Drawing on fieldwork experiences with children in Athens and in London, Sevasti-Melissa Nolas and Christos Varvantakis reflect on the relationship between ways of experiencing and modes of knowledge. They do so by asking what we miss if not always trying to pay attention in the field, and what kind of knowledge is created by being methodologically absent, engaging in play instead of following the original research strategies and plan. Kirsten Marie Raahauge also reflects on the consequences of being defocused in the field, or rather seen through the corner of the eye, as a methodological short-cut through which the vague, the uncontrollable and the unexplainable aspects of the periphery can be accessed.

Equally, Martin Demant Frederiksen invites readers to pay attention to 'that what goes on at the fringes' of what is going on, even if they do not always feel or understand what is actually happening. His chapter reflects on systems of non-meaning and shows how human worlds can also be based on not-knowing. Frederiksen questions the centrality in the research of the notion of meaning and the way anthropologists tend to attribute coherence and transparency to the world, even in instances when there is nothing but ambiguity and doubt. As Karen Waltorp and the ARTlife Film Collective propose in their chapter, 'let knowledge unfold'. Waltorp's collaboration with this Afghan-Danish film collective shows that peripheral wisdom is to be found in the in-between, as a form of greyness that dismantles polarised binary logics. For that, she recommends practicing methodological unlearning, keeping open matters of relevance and concern open, and resisting premature analytical closures.

This book is not a quest for categorical knowledge; rather, it engages with what does not admit a straightforward solution or datafication. Accordingly, it pays attention to the limits of meaning and to the epistemological value of the peripheral as a particular form of knowledge-in-the-making. Likewise, it shows that our research and the knowledge that we create are defined by our relationship with the unknowns of the field, as much as by the strategies and resources that we decide to employ. In our attempt to contribute to current debates on ethnographic epistemology, we propose not only moving along the boundary between the known and the unknown, but also remaining in it. By moving the periphery to the centre of methodological interest, we intend to understand how to proceed in situations where boundaries begin to blur and the research field loses its boundedness (McLean and Leibing 2017). This boundary is fleeting, unfixed, vague and more closely related to a state in which we enter than to a geographical space. In our account, there is no peripheral region – the peripheral is not where we are, but how we are where we are; it is an experience that occurs at the limit of knowledge; in other words, something gone through. The peripheral appears not once we arrive, but when we stay.

Notes

1 A macro-sociological perspective that tries to explain how the structural factors of capitalist economy (division of labour, differential flow of surplus and investment, capacity of political decision making...) produce a core-periphery relationship of dependency, domination and exploitation.
2 After paying attention to the everyday un-makings 'in an urban south', Simone presents the periphery as 'a space for multiple compensations' (ibid.: 116) in which things do not always make sense and are characterised by tentative recalibrations and insufficient understanding.
3 For Georges Bataille, non-knowledge (non-savoir) can be a generative, fruitful resource and an epistemic expenditure (2004). Bataille was himself inspired by French surrealism and Plato. For him, destruction, waste and expenditure (luxury) characterise the human work more fundamentally than simply production, concluding that excess is a necessary by-product of growth; yet when limits to growth have been reached, the excess must be sacrificed (Bataille 1988).
4 Reading Bataille's concept of *non-savoir* has led Taussig (2011) to argue that disciplinary professionalism ruins the possibility of accessing non-formal knowledge, by sacrificing ambiguity and attempting to explain and reduce the unknown into information – the known. From Taussig's reading of Bataille, one could infer that sacrifice is on the side of mastery, anticipating outcomes and colonising the world (if not depredating it). And on the side of non-mastery, we find living with excess, participating in the world like an initiate, embracing the unknowns and accepting how to work with what we do not understand.
5 For a discussion on intuitive knowledge, see Klekot's discussion on the Greek *mētis* in this volume, or Ingold's observations on the wisdom that exists as a form of movement among hunters (1992).
6 In Gabriele Schwab's terms, this is a question of focusing on 'what it means to explore something new and unknown and insisting that research is a search that moves along the boundary between knowledge and the unknown' (2012: 3).

References

Basso, Keith H.. 1996. *Wisdom Sits in Places. Landscape and Language among the Western Apache*. Albuquerque: University of New Mexico Press.
Bataille, Georges 1988. *The Accursed Share*. New York: Zone.
Bataille, Georges 2004. *The Unfinished System of Nonknowledge*. Minneapolis: University of Minnesota Press.

Bateson, Mary C. 1994. *Peripheral Visions: Learning Along the Way*. New York: Harper Collins.

Bendix, Regina 2005. 'Introduction: Ear to ear, nose to nose, skin to skin—The senses in comparative ethnographic perspective'. *Etnofoor* 18: 3–14.

Berglund, Eeva and Cindy Kohtala 2020. 'Collaborative confusion among DIY makers ethnography and expertise in creating knowledge for environmental sustainability'. *Science & Technology Studies* 33: 102–119.

Berlant, Lauren and Kathleen Stewart 2019. *The Hundreds*. Durham: Duke University Press.

Crapanzano, Vincent 2004. *Imaginative Horizons: An Essay in Literary-Philosophical Anthropology*. Chicago: University of Chicago Press.

Crapanzano, Vincent 2014. 'Must we be bad epistemologists? Illusions of transparency, the opaque other, and interpretative foils'. In *The Ground Between – Anthropologists Engage Philosophy*. V. Das, M. Jackson, A. Kleinman and B. Singh (eds.) Durham: Duke University Press.

Dalsgaard, Anne Line and Martin Demant Frederiksen 2015. 'Out of conclusion: On recurrence and open-endedness in life and analysis'. *Social Analysis* 57 (1): 50–63.

Desjarlais, Robert 1997. *Shelter Blues: Sanity and Selfhood among the Homeless*. Philadelphia: University of Pennsylvania Press.

Downey, Greg 2007. 'Seeing without knowing, learning with the eyes: Visuomotor 'knowing' and the plasticity of perception'. In *Ways of Knowing*. M. Harris (ed.) New York: Berghahn, 222–241.

Dunn, Elizabeth Cullen and Martin Demant Frederiksen 2018. 'Uncanny valleys – *Unheimlichkeit*, Approximation and the refugee camp'. *Anthropology Today* 34 (6): 21–24.

Eliot, T. S. 1934 *The Rock*. London: Faber and Faber.

Farías, Ignacio 2017. 'An idiotic catalyst: Accelerating the slowing down of thinking and action'. *Cultural Anthropology* 32 (1): 34–40.

Frederiksen, Martin Demant 2018. *An Anthropology of Nothing in Particular*. Winchester: Zero.

Frederiksen, Martin Demant 2020. 'The wind in the mirror: Some notes on the unnoteworthy'. In *Anthropology Inside/Out*. A. Andersen, A. L. Dalsgaard, M. L. Kusk, M. Nielsen, C. Rubow and M. Rytter (eds.) Wantage: Sean Kingston.

Gaspar, Andrea 2018. 'Idiotic encounters: Experimenting with collaborations between ethnography and design'. In *Experimental Collaborations*. A. Estalella and T. S. Criado (eds.) Oxford: Berghahn, 94–113.

Glissant, Édouard 1997. *Poetics of Relation*. Ann Arbor: University of Michigan Press.

Grasseni, Cristina 2007. 'Good looking: learning to be a cattle breeder'. In *Ways of Knowing*. New York: Berghahn, 203–221.

Green, Sarah 2005. *Notes from the Balkans – Locating Marginality and Ambiguity on the Greek-Albanian Border*. Princeton: Princeton University Press.

Guggenheim, Michael, Bernd Kräftner and Judith Kröll 2017. 'Creating idiotic speculators: Disaster cosmopolitics in the sandbox'. In *Speculative Research*. A. Wilkie, M. Savransky, and M. Rosengarten (eds.) London: Routledge, 145–162.

Haraway, Donna 2016. *Staying with the Trouble: Making Kin in the Chthulucene*. Durham: Duke University Press.

Harris, Mark (ed.) 2007. *Ways of Knowing: New Approaches in the Anthropology of Experience and Learning*. Oxford: Berghahn.

Ingold, Tim 1992. 'Foraging for data, camping with theories: Hunter-gatherers and nomadic pastoralists in archaeology and anthropology'. *Antiquity* 66: 790–803.

Ingold, Tim 2014. 'That's enough about ethnography!' *HAU: Journal of Ethnographic Theory* 4 (1): 383–395.

Ingold, Tim 2017. 'Evolution in a minor key'. In *Verbs, Bones, and Brains*. Agustín Fuentes and Aku Visala (eds.) Notre Dame: University of Notre Dame Press.

Irving, Andrew 2017. *The Art and Life of Death. Radical Aesthetics and Ethnographic Practice*. Chicago: HAU Books.

Kuschnir, Karina 2016. 'Ethnographic drawing: Eleven benefits of using a sketchbook for fieldwork'. *Visual Ethnography* 5 (1): 103–134.

Latour, Bruno 1987. *Science in Action: How to Follow Scientists and Engineers Through Society*. Cambridge, MA: Harvard University Press.

Martínez, Francisco 2019a. 'An expert in peripheries. Working at, with and through the Margins of European anthropology'. In *Changing Margins and Relations within European Anthropology*. F. Martínez (ed.) *ANUAC. Journal of the Italian Association of Cultural Anthropology*, 8 (2): 167–188.

Martínez, Francisco 2019b. 'Doing nothing: Anthropology sits at the same table with contemporary art in Lisbon and Tbilisi'. *Ethnography* 20 (4): 541–559.

McLean, Athena and Annette Leibing (eds.) 2017. *The Shadow Side of Fieldwork Exploring the Blurred Borders Between Ethnography and Life*. Malden: Blackwell.

Michael, Mike 2012. '"What are we busy doing?": Engaging the idiot'. *Science, Technology and Human Values* 37 (5): 528–554.

Mittermaier, Amira 2012. 'Dreams from elsewhere: Muslim subjectivities beyond the trope of self-cultivation'. *Journal of the Royal Anthropological Institute* 18: 247–265.

Mittermaier, Amira 2019. 'The unknown in the Egyptian uprising: Towards an anthropology of al-Ghayb'. *Contemporary Islam* 13 (1): 17–31.

Ortner, Sherry 1995. 'Resistance and the problem of ethnographic refusal'. *Comparative Studies in Society and History* 37 (1): 173–193.

Plows, Alexandra (ed.) 2018. *Messy Ethnographies in Action*. Wilmington: Vernon Press.

Roy, Ananya 2011. 'Slumdog cities: Rethinking subaltern urbanism'. *IJURR* 35: 223–238.

Rytter, Mikkel 2016. 'By the beard of the prophet: Imitation, reflection and world transformation among Sufis in Denmark'. *Ethnography* 17 (2): 229–249.

Savransky, Martin, Alex Wilkie, and Marsha Rosengarten (eds.) 2017. *Speculative Research: The Lure of Possible Futures*. London: Routledge.

Schwab, Gabriele 2012. *Imaginary Ethnographies – Literature, Culture and Subjectivity*. New York: Columbia University Press.

Scott, Julie. 2000. 'Peripheries, artificial peripheries and centres'. In *Tourism in Peripheral Areas*. F. Brown and D. Hall (eds.) Clevedon: Channel View, 58–73.

Simone, AbdouMaliq 2010. *City Life from Jakarta to Dakar: Movements at the Crossroads*. New York: Routledge.

Simone, Abdoumaliq 2019. *Improvised Lives*. London: Polity.

Sørensen, Tim Flohr 2014. 'The outermost boundary'. In *A Superficial Issue*. A. Baader, M. D. Frederiksen and K. Stadler (eds.) Skanderborg: A.R.T.

Sørensen, Tim Flohr 2016. 'In praise of vagueness: Uncertainty, ambiguity and archaeological methodology'. *Journal of Archaeological Method and Theory* 23 (2): 741–763.

Stengers, Isabelle 2005. 'The cosmopolitical proposal'. In *Making Things Public*. B. Latour and P. Weibel (eds.) Cambridge, MA: MIT Press, 994–1003.

Stewart, Kathleen 1996. *A Space on the Side of the Road*. Princeton: Princeton University Press.

Stewart, Kathleen. 2008. 'Weak theory in an unfinished world'. *Journal of Folklore Research* 45 (1): 71–82.

Stoller, Paul 2009. *The Power of the Between: An Anthropological Odyssey*. Chicago: University of Chicago Press.

Strathern, Marilyn 1991. *Partial Connections*. Savage: Rowman & Littlefield.

Strathern, Marilyn 2000. 'The tyranny of transparency'. *British Educational Research Journal* 26 (3): 309–322.

Taussig, Michael 2011. *I swear I saw this. Drawings in Fieldwork Notebooks, Namely My Own*. Chicago: The University of Chicago Press.

Taussig, Michael 2018. *Palma Africana*. Chicago: Chicago University Press.

Wallerstein, Immanuel 1974. *The Modern World System I: Capitalist Agriculture and the Origins of the European World-Economy in the Sixteenth Century*. New York: Academic Press.

Part I
Suspension of clarity

1   At the core, beyond reach

Sufism and words flying away in the field

Lili Di Puppo

> When I suppose that I have lost it, I find it and whenever I imagine
> that I have found it, I lose it.
>
> Shibli on wajd[1]

In this text, I assemble different fragments of my field research on Sufism in the
Volga and Urals. At the core of the text, I present a paradox: an attempt to convey
the experience of a ritual ceremony that cannot adequately be expressed in words.
While my narration of this experience forms the core of this chapter, it does not
say anything *of relevance* about my field research on Sufism. Indeed, this experience seems to defy all attempts to incorporate it into a work of research, inevitably remaining *out of context* (see the conclusion to this volume). My narration of
the experience takes a poetic form and resembles the movement we evoke in the
conclusion to the volume, that of *circling around* – a type of movement to which
peripheral wisdom leads us. Even if the experience appears to be *out of context*, I
begin by discussing Sufism in the Volga and Urals and reflecting on a parallel that
emerged during my field research: that between the attempt to frame Sufism as a
component of a local Muslim identity in the region's current Islamic revival and
the attempt to make it an object of scholarly research (along with the inevitable
limits of this enterprise).

Rediscovering Sufism in the Volga and Urals

When beginning my research on Sufism in the Volga and Urals, conversing with
scholars, Muslim officials and Sufi disciples, I noticed uncertainty about the phenomenon. Was it present or absent? Sufism can be approached as a visible social
and public phenomenon (in contrast to the image of a secretive and individualistic
esoteric practice, as noted by Simon Sorgenfrei (2018)), having permeated the
lives of Muslims in the Volga-Ural region for centuries (Frank 2001, 2012; also
Kefeli 2015). At the same time, Sufi practices gradually became marginalised in
the course of the region's Muslim history, in part as an outcome of Soviet anti-reli-
gious policies. The Soviet authorities were particularly inimical to Sufism, which
they regarded as backward and as a religious tradition that was bound to disappear
as a result of modernity's advances. Negative images of Sufism as 'backward',
which can still be encountered today in the Volga-Ural region, also date from the

time of reformist discourses promoted by Jadid theologians. In her discussion of the book *Extinction* by the reformist author Gayaz Iskhaqi and of the writings of Tuqay, Ross (2012: 358) notes that it was Iskhaqi who began 'to systematize young Muslim intellectuals' criticism of religious and mystical leaders and transform the criticism of individual shaykhs and 'ulama into the indiscriminate criticism of shaykhs in general'.[2] The term *ishanliq* (*ishanism*) came to be used to depict *ishans* (Sufi *sheikhs*) as enemies of national progress (Ross 2012: 359).

In his historical research on Muslim communities in Russia, Allen Frank (1996, 2001) observes that a particular interpretation of the history of the Volga and Urals was dominant among Soviet and Western historians, who tended to give prominence to nationalist and reformist readings. Sufism and religious practices such as pilgrimage and saint veneration were consequently downplayed. In reality, Sufism played a prominent role in the region's Islamisation and in the transmission and preservation of Islamic knowledge in difficult times. Sufi *sheikhs* appeared during the period of the Bolghar Khanate (Algar 1992: 112); Huseyn Bek, who played a major role in spreading Islam in the Urals, was a disciple of the Sufi *sheikh* Ahmad Yasawi. The Naqshbandi Sufi order became the most prominent in the region; the major Naqshbandi brotherhoods in the region are the Naqshbandi Mujaddidi and the Naqshbandi Khalidi orders, the latter counting the sheikhs Zaynulla Rasulev (1833–1917) and Muhammad Zakir Chistavi (1804–1893) among its members. Hamid Algar notes that the Naqshbandi Sufis fully dominated the religious and intellectual life of the 18th and 19th centuries (ibid.). Ravil Bukharaev (2004: 75) further argues that Sufism became an important way to keep the Islamic faith alive following the fall of Kazan and Astrakhan in the 16th century and amid official anti-Muslim repression.

Sufism currently holds a marginal position in the Volga-Ural region to the extent that few Muslims can be counted as Sufis and the Sufi brotherhoods in the region often have *sheikhs* situated outside the region (for example, in Dagestan, Central Asia or Turkey). Another aspect that might explain the phenomenon's lack of public visibility is the reluctance of certain Muslim officials to declare that they are themselves Sufis. This cautiousness can be interpreted as indicating the persistence of negative images of Sufism in the region and the lack of knowledge about it among many Muslims. On an official level, I also noticed the preference for a guarded, more restrained and private form of Sufism. This preference can be interpreted as an effort to portray Sufism as an 'intellectual' and enlightened tradition among Tatars and Bashkirs so as to distinguish it from its association with popular, 'irrational' and backward traditions (in the images that were created at the turn of the 19th and the beginning of the 20th centuries in the context of reformist discourses). In this image of an intellectual, guarded, private spiritual practice, we find an attempt to emphasise the enlightened dimension of the Sufi tradition in the Volga and Urals.[3]

The renewed interest in Sufism in the region has resulted in the publication of books, the diffusion of documentaries and the organisation of annual readings in honour of prominent historical Sufi figures, in particular Zaynulla Rasulev, a Sufi *sheikh* or *ishan* who lived in the city of Troitsk near the border with Kazakhstan at the turn of the 20th century. My conversations with local historians revealed that they are seeking to form an image of Sufism as it was practiced in past times, for example by studying the debates around 'correct' practices and correct ways of performing the *zhikr* ceremony, the remembrance of God. On an official level, the dominant image is that of the silent *zhikr* practiced by the Naqshbandis, which is portrayed as being typical of Tatar and Bashkir Muslims: a silent ritual practice that corresponds to the image of restraint, which certain Muslim officials view as characteristic of the local Muslim culture.

In a conversation with a young imam in a mosque in the Urals on the topic of Zaynulla Rasulev, the imam begins by enumerating the many ways in which the *ijaza* he gave to his students was preserved in Soviet times. He lists the possible figures to which Rasulev gave *ijaza*, a chain of transmission that extends to Dagestan. To the external observer trying to understand who he was, Zaynulla Rasulev, or Zaynulla Ishan, appears as a figure situated between different worlds. When asked about him, an older imam in a mosque recounts, in a fragile yet authoritative and certain voice, how the *ishan* would find water springs with his cane, how dogs would stop barking when he passed, how he could communicate with birds, and how he prevented the outskirts of the city of Troitsk from being flooded. Another imam recounts how Rasulev would suddenly throw the contents of a glass of water over his shoulder, thus extinguishing a fire in a faraway place.

Following our conversation with the older imam, some local scholars who are accompanying us refer to these stories as 'legends and myths'. Later, we are told by other local Muslims in the same mosque that Zaynulla Ishan recited verses of the Quran to heal; he would collect healing herbs in the remote and silent corners of his native Bashkir mountains, 'where no cockcrow could be heard'; he mastered hypnosis.[4] On a visit to the Troitsk historical museum, which contains a display with information on Zaynulla Rasulev and his family, the museum guide immediately refers to his healing powers in response to my question about the source of his authority in Troitsk. At the same time, the exhibition itself presents Zaynulla Rasulev as an 'enlightener' and praises the widespread prestige of his *madrasa*, in which he adopted the new Jadid educational practices.

Zaynulla Rasulev, learned imam and 'enlightener', promoter of reforms – Zaynulla Ishan, healer and master of 'hypnosis', who could intuit the problems and sorrows of everyone who came to see him (as we are told by an imam) – appears as a multifaceted figure. He seems to exist between different worlds: the city and the countryside; Jadid reformist thought and the 'irrationality' of rural customs and beliefs; enlightened modernity and Sufi tradition; Turkey/Europe and Central Asia; Bashkir, Tatar and Russian identities (he had disciples of various ethnicities and also healed Orthodox Christians). Each of our interlocutors, Sufi healers, scholars and Muslim officials emphasise a particular facet of his life and influence. When approaching Zaynulla Rasulev's grave in the old Muslim cemetery on the outskirts of Troitsk, we notice the porous surface of the gravestone. We are told that some Kazakh pilgrims break off small chunks from the surface, crush them, mix them with water, and drink the resulting substance. These practices suggest a lived connection to past *ishans*. They suggest a different mode of connection to Sufi *ishans* than the one we find in official celebrations and scholarly works on Sufism. In these practices, the *awliya*, or friends of God, are alive, emanating *baraka*, the divine blessings.

During a conversation with a young Muslim Sufi interlocutor, himself a healer (who insists that he is not only a student of Sufi healing but, more importantly, a *practitioner*), I ask: 'How did Rasulev heal?' He looks startled and responds: 'Exactly as he has just described regarding the different techniques of Sufi healing. How could it be different?' Even if he had filled in the details for me over our several conversations, the central dimension of the healing process appears to be beyond the reach of non-practitioners, healing constituting an opening to the invisible realm, or *al-ghayb* – the world of the unseen. This is also noted by Nils Bubandt, Mikkel Rytter and Christian Suhr: 'While al-ghayb is a marker of the unseen domains of reality, for the adept it signifies a supremely visible reality' (2019: 1). They observe how *al-ghayb* – and more broadly, the invisible – stands in an ambiguous and paradoxical position in relation to enlightened modernity and its assertion of the primacy of vision (Bubandt, Rytter and Suhr 2019). *Al-ghayb* refers to phenomena that are by their nature concealed, such as the past, the future and divine secrets. While this knowledge is only accessible to God, certain believers may experience glimpses of the Unknown. *Al-ghayb* is potentially dangerous, but it is also associated with healing and protection.[5] In the case of the Sufi tradition in the Volga and Urals, our Sufi interlocutors emphasised the importance of their practice in ensuring that the Islamic religion outlives any material power – including Soviet secular power (Di Puppo and Schmoller 2020). The *heart*, the subtle organ of perception reflecting the divine light, is the place where faith is preserved.

Sufism, as a path of initiation that brings the disciple closer to a hidden reality, poses a challenge to the traditional scholarly viewpoint, limited as it is to observable phenomena or those that can be made comprehensible. Certain anthropologists have acknowledged the inaccessibility of Sufism's central dimension, *taste* (*dhawq*), pointing to the fact that their research remains limited to the *exterior* of the practice, even if they have been able to glimpse the inner states of Sufi disciples based on conversations or participant observation in rituals (see Lizzio 2007; Rytter 2015). Nils Bubandt, Mikkel Rytter and Christian Suhr (2019: 11) thus ask: 'How can we approach unseen worlds such as that of *al-ghayb* empirically in our research in ways that do justice to invisibility and do not domesticate it within the orthodoxies of ocular-centrism?'[6]

Sufism can be approached as a mode of knowing or unknowing that leads the disciple to an *inner* realm of perception in a succession of states. The symbol of an almond's shell and its kernel is used to denote the existence of the world of appearance (*zahir*) and a hidden reality (*batin*). In order to experience veridical 'direct vision' (*shuhud*) (Knysh 1993: 58), the Sufi disciple polishes the mirror of the *heart*, guided by the Sufi *sheikh*, activating the organ's capacity to reflect the divine light. The scholar of Islam Alexander Knysh refers to the Sufi medieval scholar Ibn Arabi's doctrine of divine manifestations to evoke the *heart*'s capacity to reach higher knowledge:

> to discover the 'true' nature of God and His relationship with the World, the observer must renounce his rational outlook and give himself to the veridical 'direct vision' (*shuhud*) and intuitive 'direct tasting' (*dhawq*). This new,

higher knowledge can only be achieved by the human heart (*qalb*), an Arabic word whose lexical connotations point to 'motion', 'fluctuation' and 'transformation'. The heart 'moves', 'fluctuates' and 'transforms' persistently following the outward 'movements', 'fluctuations', and 'transformations' of the Divine Reality.

(Knysh 1993: 58)

The association of light with knowledge is also present in the enlightenment project and what Bubandt, Rytter and Suhr (2019) refer to as the modern 'empire of the gaze', with its ideals of visibility and clarity. In the enlightenment ideal, however, visibility and clarity are associated with a civilising process, a process of *domesticating* the invisible, as foregrounded by Rytter (2015). The effort to domesticate phenomena, to render them knowable and shape them into coherent representations, can be found in contemporary attempts to study Sufism in the Volga and Urals as a scholarly object and to incorporate it into the image of a local Muslim tradition. In official representations of the Sufi heritage, preference is given to a guarded, restrained and silent Sufi practice, seen as characteristic of Tatars and Bashkirs. Furthermore, Sufism is associated with images of enlightenment and of an intellectual and scholarly pursuit in reference to prominent theologians such as Shihabetdin Marjani. In these representations, the connection to an invisible realm that Sufism opens up and the mystical dimension of Sufi practices sometimes occupy an ambiguous position, as some may present the miracles attributed to figures such as Zaynulla Rasulev as 'legends and myths' or rural beliefs from more distant times.

In the following, I will describe my own experience of a ritual ceremony, which will lead me to adopt a more poetic form of narration.

Words flying away

The bird of thought cannot soar to the height of His presence
Nor the hand of understanding reach to the skirt of His praise

Saadi[7]

During one of my fieldwork stays, I attended a religious ceremony and would like to evoke the difficulty of understanding and naming my experience of this ritual. I omit certain details when relating this experience – an absence that can be interpreted as vagueness. This vagueness is at the same time purposeful and simply given. It is purposeful in the sense that I knowingly avoid giving too many details about the ritual itself. I want to maintain a certain vagueness about my experiences in the field in Russia.

This vagueness is also a given because my experience of the ritual simply escapes description. Vagueness is protection. This vagueness can also be understood as stemming from an understanding that richness and accuracy can conceal more than they reveal. A profusion of detail for the sake of accuracy, of showing that *I was indeed there*, can distract from my experience. These details can themselves serve as a cloak of vagueness behind which I might hide. In their accuracy, they can act as a weight, threatening to bring down the experience and change it, for the potency of the experience is precisely in its delicacy and lightness, in the certainty that it was, although it did not leave any trace.

In the space in which the ritual was held, the objects in their simplicity appeared to be prepared, waiting. I had come to a religious place where a ceremony was being held, a location to which a few people had pointed me and which had appeared by coincidence some time before on a virtual map when I was searching for another destination. Before the ritual started, I paid attention to the details of my surroundings: the objects, the people, the way they were dressed and their gestures. I also noted what was said at the very beginning of the ceremony. My 'observation', in a conventional sense, then stopped:

> We are told to open our hands and close our eyes. I close my eyes and realise that I cannot observe. I realise that I am already thinking about my notes, about some reflections during the prayer. It seems inopportune; it doesn't go well with the moment. The analysis fatigues me; it appears rather heavy, inopportune; it fills my head; it is not welcome, not appropriate. I want to feel the prayer for myself... to honour... I feel that I can draw closer... I feel a presence.

Following the ritual, I waited in a room below to meet with the imam. In my memory, these rooms were permeated with light, even though it may not have been a sunny day. I waited without looking at my watch. I was offered tea while I was waiting but politely declined. A young man asked me if I had read Derrida.

The imam entered surreptitiously; I hadn't quite seen him coming, and he suddenly sat next to me, joining in the small circle I had formed with the two other young men with whom I was intermittently chatting. I hesitantly asked him if I could record our conversation. He said that I did not need to record our conversation, not because the recording was unwelcome in itself, but because it was *unnecessary*. My little tools for approaching – somehow capturing, recording – things seemed useless, *unnecessary*. I had foreseen this in the sense that I realised I did not quite know what to ask. The encounter seemed enough. I was asked what religion I was. One of the young men asked where I had been in Europe, which place had felt the most spiritual to me. I asked a question knowing that there was no possible answer to it. How does one find the spiritual path? The imam spoke about there being a map for each person, how each must walk his own path. I asked about Sufism, but not once did my interlocutor talk about Sufism in relation to himself. A vagueness remained.

I attended the ritual again some days after our conversation. After this second experience of the ritual, I let some time pass before sitting down to write my notes. I had left my fieldwork site in the evening, waiting for a propitious time and place to write.

When writing my notes in a quiet place, I let the words come to me. Trying to remember the experience and knowing that I could not express it, words appeared to me and became interlaced with notes on the nature around me: a cloud passing by, leaves falling, trees bending in the wind. I wrote some words, interspaced with long intervals of silence. My writing took a poetic form, hesitant. These words appeared like passing birds in a vast space.

My eyes are closed and my hands open. I feel a touch on my head, I feel a sensation of light humidity, as if of moss.

I feel a presence approaching, a fragrance, I feel a touch on my head, stronger, more powerful
I don't remember

I'm a little troubled, on alert, I feel something powerful something happens something is taking place
I follow I let myself be carried taken
I feel flows entering me
I think
I feel powerless

Words stir inside me I feel a resistance light I understand that I need to let myself be carried by respect
I feel a light struggle
Words stir lightly
in me I am myself stirred
And then the calm the silence I feel defeated
Then flows
I am defeated I bend I feel like an old woman bending

I abandon myself
I am defeated

I feel something happening in me with the voices
Something happens in me

I am defeated the gift is big

I feel my hands getting bigger widening they are very sensitive
My feet leave the soil slightly I feel like I am lifted up
I feel the space

I feel defeated as if I were bending myself

I abandon myself

The voices

When slowly exiting the space, I call a taxi, my voice trembling. I look at my watch; not much time has passed, but it feels as though it lasted longer.

I come home. I feel a bit fragile, in love. I am gently stirred. I enter my room. I sit on a chair.

In the moments, days that follow, after I have left my fieldwork site, I try to preserve.

How can I reach this feeling? I realise that there is no thread.

I left in love the heart joyful the heart already sad to leave
Silence, subtle when leaving I feel the absence
A wave of presence and absence

I have no link
But what is the object?
In me
I am in love but with whom?
This is the answer to my question
Love

I want to keep but it's a breath
I am in my kitchen in the early morning
I drink tea from the ritual site I close my eyes when drinking face turned to the window
The soft light
I breathe when drinking

Then the sadness the loss the sadness breaks through

The flux and reflux
The branches of trees bend under the wind

The sweet secret

In the following days and weeks, I become more sensitive to silence. I keep some perfume from the ritual site in a corner of my home and smell it whenever I pass by.

I describe my experience of the ritual as a beautiful failure in the sense that conventional fieldwork methods beautifully failed to capture and relate it. This failure is beautiful because it resembles the moment at which the scholar-warrior, on a long journey, sets down his weapons and kneels. The fieldwork experience is always conveyed in the form of a recollection; the immediacy and puzzlement of some fieldwork experiences are attenuated when they are used in the construction of a greater edifice, the work of research. The experiences cannot breathe and diffuse their subtle knowledge, akin to a perfume, long after they have taken place, as they *are made to have passed*, to become incorporated in the work of research. They cannot enter into composition with new experiences and reflections formed outside of the field if the field is separated from life itself. But the liveliness of the experiences, their oscillation between the known and the unknown, between presence and loss, is what preserves their truth. Their truth appears lost in the work of the mind.

On the failure of photographic imagery to capture *jinn* possession, Christian Suhr (2015: 108) observes how it leads to a surrendering to the unknown and to an attitude of humility. The encounter provoked by failure is an opening to an invisible realm that withdraws and cannot be grasped (ibid.: 109). In the case of my experience of the ritual, I cannot but let this experience live on. Any attempt to explain and use this experience as material, as a brick, as a means of uncovering and unveiling something 'bigger' about my research, seems futile and *unnecessary*. The experience cannot be hastily made into something known, as its nature is more akin to a perfume. It is a trace that demands to be followed. It is a direction. I need to search for an answer where the question comes from, where the appeal resonates. Removing the experience from the unknown is futile, as the movement goes in the other direction.

The futility of trying to claim knowledge of the experience is linked to the very state that I intuitively felt should awaken in me during the ritual. This state was that of confessing to my unknowing, one of humbleness and of bowing. It was a sincere state of unknowing, the admission of utter powerlessness.

When the light resistance gave way to silence during the ritual, I felt words and thoughts ruffle inside me like birds and then fly away, in awe of an immense power. They flew away and left the space.

They left me behind. What are you without us? We are of no use to you here.

During the ritual, my hands became sensitive. They sensed something that I didn't know.

The image of the scholar-warrior came to me when I realised the exhaustion caused by my research, my search for meaning. I longed to sit and rest. Searching for meaning and looking at things and beings with piercing eyes, engaging in an *unnecessary* fight, hastily gathering notes and impressions and carrying these like a bag weighing me down.

When sitting and waiting, waiting to receive, having lost sense of time, my whole self was engaged. I sensed that I needed to follow a certain etiquette, *adab*, during the ritual. My mind was intrusive and an unnecessary guest in this space; it was staring too intensely, without knowing where to direct its gaze. My experience of the ritual was a gift, a gift of knowledge that required patience, knowledge unfolding like a subtle perfume. The experience seemed to teach me that delicacy is more potent, the delicacy of not rushing things, letting knowledge unfold or remain hidden. The urge to find meaning in experiences and encounters during fieldwork, to assemble the pieces into a whole, can be seen as resulting from distrust – distrust in the way the world presents itself to us.

During this particular fieldwork stay, a certain imperceptible atmosphere accompanied my encounters. It was the time of Ramadan, and it felt as if emotions were simmering under the surface. During my encounters, my interlocutors were fragile, making excuses for this weak state. I met two young interlocutors who were learning the Quran. One young man seemed hesitant to speak with me; he spoke in a whisper, almost inaudible, as if the words coming out of his mouth felt inadequate and he needed to compensate for this inadequacy by following each sentence with a long silence. He didn't trust words. He was folded into himself, as if trying to protect a secret from the conversation that was taking place. His face was light and fragile. I realised that I could learn more from the faces of my young interlocutors – dreamy, tired faces, as if illuminated from within – than from hearing what they said. They were making an effort to give me something, not knowing what I needed; I did not know either. Emotions came to the fore during a long conversation in a quiet classroom filled with light, when a woman interlocutor suddenly shed tears when talking about her faith.

Parallels

Much has been said about the impossibility of talking about Sufism. I have chosen to relate my fieldwork experience of a ritual in parallel with reflections on contemporary discussions about Sufism and attempts to frame the phenomenon in the Volga and Urals. These parallels emerged during my field research. I reflected on the attempt to take hold of the phenomenon, to frame it, to retain it. I also saw parallels in a certain fear of the phenomenon – fear, but also awe in the face of its beauty and power, its capacity to live on under the surface and to outlive any material powers.

The preference for a guarded, restrained form of religious practice as an image of Sufism that can be more adequately incorporated into a larger representation of Islam echoes academic, scholarly conventions demanding that we shape phenomena into coherent, meaningful representations. In both cases, a claim to knowledge is made; the representation of the phenomenon inevitably contains unknowns, however. These unknowns are hidden and masked. While anthropological research can be understood as an effort to *go beyond the surface*, the research that it generates itself veils the many unknowns contained in field experiences.[8] It is also a process of forming certain truths at the level of analysis and concepts. My experience of the ritual prevents me from engaging in this process, as it precisely reveals the limits of this enterprise.

By putting fieldwork experiences into *accurate* words, by turning them into material, one may lose one's sense of how alive they are and of their inherent secrecy. Constructing coherent representations of phenomena and events inevitably involves creating distance, as if putting objects behind a glass wall. These experiences cannot live on. If I were trying to recount my experience in detail and extract meaning from it, what I would try to preserve is not the experience itself but my analytical mind, the meaning. My mind is a mask behind which I hide. It may appear as a reaction of fear when faced with the unknown, a handle to hold on to. It suppresses the immediacy of the experience.

As an *unnecessary* guest in the space opened up during the ritual, my analytic mind cannot convey the experience. It will strive to reveal, expose and make intelligible what is beyond the intelligible. The more we strive to reveal and expose, the more we hide. I cannot put a name to my experience of the ritual, and nor would I want to; the moment I name it, I lose it. Naming the experience would break the subtle spell that it contains. I know that something happened in me, a power that made me bow; the experience is contained in knowing this, in knowing that I know nothing and in sensing beauty. A space opened up, a direction.

In the search for meaning, the puzzlement and wonder contained in the experience are reduced and lost. The filmmaker Andrei Tarkovsky says: 'If you look for a meaning, you'll miss everything that happens. Thinking during a film interferes with your experience of it. Take a watch into pieces, it doesn't work. Similarly with a work of art, there's no way it can be analyzed without destroying it' (cf. Strick 2006: 71).[9] The experience cannot be encountered by tearing it apart, examining the many details that constitute it. We can only encounter it in its totality, in its wholeness. The ritual opened up a space, one that demanded my whole self and that rendered the words and thoughts that remained in this moment futile. The words and thoughts were reduced, made useless.

Epilogue: The comfort of mystery

One day, a man stopped under a tree. He saw leaves, branches, strange fruit. Of everyone he asked what such a tree and such fruit were. No gardener could answer; no one knew their name or their origin. The man said to himself: 'I do not know this tree, nor do I understand it; and yet I know that from the moment I caught sight of it, my heart and my soul became fresh and green. Let us then go beneath its shade.' Jalal ad-Din Rumi

The comfort of mystery came to me as an association when reading Michael Taussig's words on the unknown: 'We strip the unknown of all that is strange. We show it who's boss, the basic rule of a university seminar. We tolerate neither ambiguity nor that which won't conform. The second and even greater misfortune here is that we thereby forget how strange is the known. This is why I have sought not for masterful explanations but for estrangement, the gift of ethnography no less than of literature' (Taussig 2006: 8). In a play on words, I thought that while mystery and the unknown escape any attempt to make them *conform*, they also appear as *comforting*. While the desire for estrangement drives us to engage in ethnography, I am also reminded of the soothing sensation of intimacy brought on by mystery.

My experience of the ritual ceremony was profoundly, startlingly intimate; I could not name it, however, and no *apparent* thread could lead me back to it. While knowledge is associated with clarity in the images conveyed by enlightened modernity, it also corresponds to distancing: we take a step away to *see* things. Knowledge seeks to make things, beings, phenomena known to us, and in doing so can be seen as bringing us to 'familiar ground', to a place where we know and can rest in the knowledge and assurance that we know. The experience I have tried to evoke is one of experiencing the intimacy of mystery. Mystery appears as a resting place, where a sensation of intimacy replaces comprehension as a source of knowledge. The longing for mystery, the way it feels both unsettling and intimate – it is this longing that makes us want to rest under the *shade of the unknown tree*, as in Jalal ad-Din Rumi's story.

In the weeks following my experience of the ritual ceremony, I became sensitive to silence. Silence suddenly felt alive, vibrating, inviting; I sat in my kitchen in the morning, listening to it. In his essay *The Lily in the Field and the Bird of the Air* (2000), Kierkegaard invites us to learn how 'to be silent' from the lily and the bird.[10] As he writes: 'There is silence out there. The forest is silent; even when it whispers it nevertheless is silent' (Kierkegaard 2000: 335).[11] Talking about divine speech in his text *The Sound of Silence*, the scholar of Islam William Chittick refers to the superabundance of God's light and speech as ultimately being a veil: 'the superabundance of God's light prevents people from seeing Him, just as the superabundance of His speech prevents them from hearing Him' (Chittick 2019: 21). An excess of light engenders *unknowing*, distinguishing it from an absence of light or ignorance.[12] Silence and unknowing are not absence or a lack; instead, they invite us to listen and acknowledge the limits of our knowledge, thus drawing us closer to the beyond, to the invisible.

I close this text with a story about another mosque, another town.

During a conversation on a summer afternoon, an imam in a mosque tells my travel companion and me that we need to turn to the light. The Quran is a lamp; he outlines the form of a lamp with his hands. He holds a key, which represents man, in his hand and shows us how man is situated between light and shadow. Man sees his shadow behind him; this is *dunya*.[13] If man turns to *dunya*, he will be controlled by it. The imam's aide, sitting next to him, says that in a sense there is nothing there but death. If man turns to the light, *dunya* will follow him; it will serve him. They say: this is how *sheikhs* accomplish miracles, *karamat*.

During our conversation, they ask us 'Where do the Sufi *tariqas* come from?' I answer, 'From the Prophet'. Hearing this answer, they rejoice; the imam says a prayer, as if something significant has been said. We are sitting next to a table, adorned with a beautiful deep purple tablecloth, in the vast space of the mosque. The imam holds prayer beads in his hand and moves them softly between his fingers, murmuring in a low voice, while we continue talking to his aide. I sense a shift in the atmosphere, deepening, as if something were affecting the surroundings. I write in my notes:

> I feel something delicate in this place, something eternal. Something emanates from the table around which we have gathered, conversing; the large window behind us opens up to a garden, suddenly appearing mysterious. I feel another place, an opening. A feeling that things are floating, suspended, sweet and calm. The large window lets the light pour in, filling the room; everything in the room is as if suspended. The objects are refined; they have their place. Everything has significance.

On our way back home, a woman runs, calling after us; she is holding my shawl in her hands; it had fallen without my noticing. That evening, a sensation grips my entire body as I fall asleep; I have a profound dream. My gaze is directed upward, following two rows of trees as if I were walking in a forest in the night. The two rows of trees form a line, pulling me in, opening up to a dark and profound sky and then to a trail of light, a path formed by the infinity of brightly lit stars.

Notes

1 *Wajd* is the mystical ecstasy experienced by the Sufi disciple. The quote is by the Sufi Shaykh Abu Bakr al-Shibli (861–945).
2 For a more nuanced account of the different gradations of criticism against Sufi practices over time and in the context of reformist discourses, see Di Puppo and Schmoller (2020).
3 For a more detailed discussion of the Sufi revival in the Volga and Urals and the question of its official representation, see Di Puppo and Schmoller (2020).
4 Our interlocutors used the term 'hypnosis'. A young Sufi healer used the term 'semi-trance' during another conversation to indicate the state in which certain patients find themselves during a healing session, as they are partially aware of what is happening.
5 On the danger involved in connection with the invisible realm, the young Sufi healer described to me in conversation the many techniques (consisting of the recitation of prayers and verses of the Quran and the exact placement of talismans on the body) that the healer needs to know in order to be protected from *jinns* (as *jinns* can seek revenge).
6 See Lizzio (2007) for a criticism of Western anthropologists' approach to the study of Sufi rituals. While Rytter (2015) admits that he did not directly experience the *taste* of Sufism, he recounts a dream visit in which he went into *wajd* after encountering a *sheikh* (whom he knew was special) and touching his hands. Kenneth Lizzio (2016) also notes the following regarding his experience of living with a Naqshbandi order in Pakistan: 'After so many months of immersing myself in the Naqshbandis' rigorous spiritual exercises, I knew I would soon be returning to the United States without ever having tasted that intoxicating wine I had so desperately sought.'
7 Saadi Shirazi is a Persian medieval poet, born ca. 1210 in Shiraz, Iran.
8 In his discussion of anthropology as the *mastery of nonsense* and of the parallel between the anthropological method and medieval witch trials, Richard Baxstrom (2013: 8) refers to anthropologist Bronislaw Malinowski in the following terms: 'One is on the lookout for symptoms of deeper, sociological facts, one suspects many hidden and mysterious ethnographic phenomena behind the commonplace aspect of things.' Going beyond the world of appearance to glimpse a hidden reality is what the Sufi path of initiation brings the disciple into; however, a condition for undergoing this process of transformation is the abandonment of any pretence of knowledge.
9 See Frederiksen (2020) for a reflection on Tarkovsky and the question of meaning.
10 The text is a commentary on the Sermon on the Mount, in which Jesus tells his followers not to worry about earthly needs by considering the lilies of the field and the birds in the air.
11 Commenting on his text in an introduction, Bruce H. Kirmmse (2016) notes that Kierkegaard saw in nature a reality that lay beyond it, making use of nature to allow 'the lily and the bird to point to something invisible but real that lay beyond the visible world – and indeed, what Kierkegaard pointed to was far more real than what is merely visible'.
12 The scholar of religious studies Arthur Versluis emphasises this distinction when considering Divine Darkness: 'The nether-darkness and the Divine Darkness are not the same darkness, for the former is absence of light, while the latter is excess of light. The one symbolizes mere ignorance, and the other a transcendent unknowing.' Arthur Versluis, footnote 1 to Dionysius the Aeropagite *Mystical Theology* op. cit.
13 The temporal, earthly world.

References

Algar, Hamid 1992. Shaykh Zaynullah Rasulev: The Last Great Naqshbandi Shaykh of the Volga-Ural Region. In J-A. Gross (ed.) *Muslims in Central Asia*. Durham: Duke University Press, pp. 112–133.

Baxstrom, Richard 2013. Knowing Primitives, Witches, and the Spirits: Anthropology and the Mastery of Nonsense. *Republics of Letters* 4 (1): 1–22.

Bubandt, Nils, Mikkel Rytter, and Christian Suhr 2019. A Second Look at Invisibility: Al-Ghayb, Islam, Ethnography. *Contemporary Islam* 13 (1): 1–16.

Bukharaev, Ravil 2004. Sufism in Russia: Nostalgia for Revelation. In D. Westerlund (ed.) *Sufism in Europe and North America*. London: Routledge Curzon, pp. 64–94.

Chittick, William C. 2019. The Sound of Silence. *Renovatio*, Fall 2019, 13–22.

Di Puppo, Lili and Jesko Schmoller 2020. Here or Elsewhere: Sufism and Traditional Islam in Russia's Volga-Ural Region. *Contemporary Islam* 14 (2): 135–156.

Frank, Allen J. 1996. Islamic Shrine Catalogues and Communal Geography in the Volga-Ural Region: 1788–1917. *Journal of Islamic Studies* 7 (2): 265–286.

Frank, Allen J. 2001. *Muslim Religious Institutions in Imperial Russia: The Islamic World of Novouzensk District and the Kazakh Inner Horde, 1780–1910*. Leiden: Brill.

Frank, Allen J. 2012. *Bukhara and the Muslims of Russia: Sufism, Education, and Paradox of Islamic Prestige*. Leiden: Brill.

Frederiksen, Martin Demant 2020. The Wind in the Mirror: Some Notes on the Unnoteworthy. In A. Andersen, A. L. Dalsgaard, M. L. Kusk, M. Nielsen, C. Rubow, and M. Rytter (eds.) *Anthropology Inside/Out*. Wantage: Sean Kingston.

Kefeli, Agnes 2015. *Becoming Muslim in Imperial Russia: Conversion, Apostasy, and Literacy*. Ithaca: Cornell University Press.

Kierkegaard, Søren 2000. The Lily in the Field and the Bird of the Air. In Howard Hong and Edna Hong (eds.) *The Essential Kierkegaard*. Princeton: Princeton University Press, pp. 333–338.

Kirmmse, Bruce H. 2016. Introduction: Letting Nature Point Beyond Nature. In Kierkegaard, Søren (ed.) *The Lily of the Field and the Bird of the Air – Three Godly Discourses*. Princeton: Princeton University Press.

Knysh, Alexander 1993. Orthodoxy and Heresy in Medieval Islam: An Essay in Reassessment. *Muslim World* 83: 48–67.

Lizzio, Kenneth 2007. Ritual and Charisma in Naqshbandi Sufi Mysticism. *Anpere* 1–37.

Lizzio, Kenneth 2016. Mubarak Sahib: A Firsthand Portrait of an Afghani Sufi Master. *Quest* 104 (2): 75–79.

Ross, Danielle 2012. The Nation that Might Not Be: The Role of Iskhaqi's Extinction After Two Hundred Years in the Popularization of Kazan Tatar National Identity Among the 'Ulama sons and Shakirds of the Volga-Ural Region, 1904–1917. *Ab Imperio* 3: 341–369.

Rytter, Mikkel 2015. The Scent of a Rose: Imitating Imitators as They Learn to Love the Prophet. In B. T. Knudsen and C. Stage (eds.) *Affective Methodologies*. London: Palgrave Macmillan, pp. 140–160.

Sorgenfrei, Simon 2018. Hidden or Forbidden, Elected or Rejected: Sufism as 'Islamic Esotericism'? *Islam and Christian–Muslim Relations* 29 (2): 145–165.

Strick, Philip 2006. Tarkovsky's Translations. In John Gianvito (ed.) *Andrei Tarkovsky – Interviews*. Jackson: University of Mississippi Press, pp. 70–73.

Suhr, Christian 2015. The Failed Image and the Possessed: Examples of Invisibility in Visual Anthropology and Islam. *Journal of the Royal Anthropological Institute* 21: 96–112.

Taussig, Michael 2006. *Walter Benjamin's Grave*. Chicago: The University of Chicago Press.

2 Shadows of meaning

Rethinking social dramas through absurdist theatre in a Georgian wedding

Martin Demant Frederiksen

Introduction

Surely, there must be more to it than that? This could be a standard phrase for any anthropological gaze on events, occurrences or utterances seen or heard in social lives and settings. And, surely, often there is. Untangling and clarifying 'the more that there is' is part and parcel of what takes place in the processes of both data collection and analysis, and it is often intricate and hard work. Luckily, we are armed with theories or comparative perspectives that can come to our assistance when carrying out this labour. Yet, as I will propose here, it is not necessarily easier when there is *not* more to it.

The main goal of the evening, it seemed, was to have it end in some kind of fight. It was also about Gia and Eka getting married and celebrating them at the wedding feast. But if it was to be a truly memorable wedding there would have to be a fistfight at some point towards the end of the feast – informal tradition called for that, I was told by Davit, a friend of the groom. Nobody knew, of course, what the fight would be about, what would cause it and who would be involved. Such things could not really be planned in advance. As it turned out, by hazardously messing with the ritual practices surrounding wedding gifts, Roma would inadvertently bring the reason.

In this chapter I depict a Georgian brotherhood, their participation in the wedding of one of its members, and the arguments, doubts and fights that erupted as another member brought a bigger wedding gift than he, according to his friends, was supposed to. Analytically, I depart from Henk Driessen's observation that 'whereas the cultivation of systematic doubt has been one of the tenets of scientific inquiry, events and experiences undermining certitude are often ignored in or eliminated from the canon of ethnographic fieldwork and writing' (2013: 149). I use this as a vantage point to examine an empirical case where informants cast doubt on each other's intentions, and subsequently an analytical doubt, or hesitation, about what it entails to either follow or not follow that doubtfulness. More specifically, through a description of events surrounding a wedding and a gift list, I examine what happens if we, while still describing the social and cultural contexts and practices surrounding a given ritual, trace everything back to the simple utterance of a key person involved in the event stating 'I had no intention'.

That is, if we focus on the hazardous and inadvertent, rather than the reflected and overt, actions of individuals as they partake in ritual practices.

In approaching the events unfolding around Roma's seemingly inappropriate wedding gift, I depart from anthropological analyses of ritual that take inspiration from literature. Since the publication of *Writing Culture* in 1986, numerous anthropologists have experimented with the boundaries between literature and anthropological writing and analysis (Clifford and Marcus 1986; Schwab 2012; Starn 2012). It is a particular aspect of this that I will focus on here. Or rather, it is a particular kind of literature, namely theatrical drama. The use of drama or theatre metaphors in the analysis of social lives and worlds itself has a long history within anthropology, both on a general level and in relation to the particular analysis of rituals (e.g. Bruner 1993, Geertz 1980; Goffman 1959; Hastrup 2004; Mattingly 1998; Schechner 1985; Turner 1975, 1985; Watson 2002). In what follows I take my cue from some of these insights while opening the door to another form of drama, namely absurdist theatre. As I will argue, deploying this in relation to the events surrounding Roma's wedding gift, along with rituals surrounding a subsequent funeral, allows us to approach the openness to interpretation afforded by rituals and the ways in which hazardous acts operate within them or on their fringes. The literary theorist Kenneth Burke, also taking inspiration from drama and performance theory, held that 'it is only through human motivated action that meaningful symbolic transformations of reality can occur' (quoted from Beeman 1993: 373). Here I argue that this is not necessarily the case in that hazardous, unscripted or unintended acts equally operate within social dramas, and with many of the same effects. I unfold this argument by elaborating on an elaboration. More specifically, I build on Richard Schechner's elaboration of Victor Turner's work on social dramas, and his argument that Turner's inspiration from Greco-European theatre may fruitfully be supplemented with other forms of theatre, literature and performance if we are to understand more fully how ambiguity, hazardousness and doubt operate within, and in relation to, ritual practices. In the final part of the chapter I relate these observations to recent discussions within anthropology on the role of meaninglessness and absurdity in social life.

In his introduction to a special issue on evidence in anthropology, Matthew Engelke writes that anthropologists are often seen as having a penchant for 'using a vignette or anecdote about what we observed one Tuesday morning in an open-air market outside Timbuktu eighteen years ago to explain the workings of political power in Mali, or African economies, or globalization' (2008: 12). Here, I am using an incidence that took place one Saturday afternoon outside a wedding venue in the Republic of Georgia. As such, it should be noted that this not an article about Georgian wedding rituals, but about a single incident that took place in relation to one, and about which forms of ritual-theory that may or may not be applied in giving an account of this incidence. Hence, it is about a stone in shoe that I use to explore two interrelated forms: Form in relation to ritual theatre and form in relation to analysis and meaning. My overall argument is not that applying classical theatre metaphors in analysing ritual drama is a question of getting it all wrong, but rather that it may, in some instances, be getting it a little too right.

Brotherhoods

In the middle of April 2009 Roma was released from prison after having served a two-year sentence for theft. He was 20 years old at this time. The first time I met him was only a few days after he had been released from prison and had returned to his hometown Batumi, a coastal city in the Autonomous Republic of Adjara in southwestern Georgia, where I was carrying out fieldwork at the time. It was Emil, who had been one of my key informants during this fieldwork, who introduced me to Roma, as they were old friends. They came to my apartment late one afternoon. They had brought chocolate and we went to the balcony to sit and talk. Roma was skinny, he had sunken green-brown eyes and dark blond hair and was missing his two front teeth. Emil said that there were running jokes about why he had lost his teeth (loosing fights, giving blowjobs in prison), but the plain fact was that he had lost them in a carousel accident as a child and had never had them replaced. The two of them had been drinking heavily over the last couple of days and Roma was clinging to a bottle of Fanta. We began talking a little about his life, and he agreed to let me record our conversation. 'My mother is Ukrainian', he began, 'but she was born here in Batumi. My father is Georgian but from another city. He left my mother and now I live with her and my sisters.' A little later I ask why he went to prison. 'I met these two boys who I thought were my friends. And they said let's go and steal a computer (which they did). After I left them, and I began working but they stole again, again and again, and the police caught them. They told the police that I was with them and then the police found me and I was sent to prison.' He went on to explain how exhilarating it had been to finally be released from prison. Doing time had been rough, but mainly it had been tedious, two years spent playing backgammon with his fellow inmates, and he had felt a rush of adrenaline as he left the prison.

I had heard many stories about Roma during the preceding months and, in many ways, he had been a missing piece within the brotherhoods that I had been studying since the previous summer. These included a group of 25–30 young men who knew each other to various degrees. Central to their relations was the concept of *dzmak'ats'ebi*, meaning 'brother-men'. This was a relation between two men who had either known each other over a long period of time or who had experienced something momentous together, thereby creating a bond resembling that of family, a form of spiritual kin not uncommon in the country at large (Bardavelidze 1984; Dragadze 1988; see also Muehlfried 2014: 36, and Manning 2015: xxxii). An ordinary friend or close relation was termed a *megobari* (literally 'one who eats from the same bowl'), but in terms of closeness and intimacy this was inferior to a brother-man relation. Given the closeness of the bond between brother-men a friend of one's brother-man would also be considered one's own friend, but only a *megobari*. Although the brother-man relation was most often a relation between only two people it thus often connected a range of people through it in a network of acquaintances (Bardavelidze 1984; Curro 2015; Frederiksen 2012; Zakharova 2010).

For the young men in whose lives I had been participating, the principle of brother-man relations, or brotherhood, was significant. From the early 1990s, when Georgia gained independence from the Soviet Union, the country had been marked by civil wars, economic stagnation and political corruption (Di Puppo 2015; Frederiksen and Gotfredsen 2017; Manning 2007). Although the situation improved for some following the revolution in 2003, large parts of the population still struggled to make ends meet. In a situation where it was difficult to achieve status as a man financially, for instance in terms of being able to provide for a family, it was extremely important for my informants to be good brother-men as this signified that a given person had long-term relations based on high moral standards, loyalty and trust, meaning that they could be considered *good men*, if not financially then at least socially. Further, brother-men provided each other with a social safety net in the sense that they helped each other with various favours such as small loans, getting off drugs (or providing drugs if desperately needed), steering clear of crime (or the police), finding jobs, contacting girls, and other occurrences that were prevalent and important in their lives. It was often referred to as 'a relationship of the hearts' and a relationship of practice meaning that it was not merely something one was but something one continuously *did* (Frederiksen 2012, 2013).

The young men usually had three or four brother-men, people with whom they were closest, and they would form the basis of small brotherhoods. There were no leaders in these brotherhoods but in larger gatherings it was usually always clear who were the 'best friends', or who had the strongest connection, and in this sense overlapping social hierarchies existed between the young men. Having learnt this during my fieldwork up until Roma's release from prison, I was curious as to what Roma's role and place within these brotherhoods would be after an absence of two years, and about how would he (re-)establish himself within them upon his return. The status of brother-man relations was rarely discussed publicly, making it difficult to just enter or negotiate one's way into a brotherhood. But in some instances the social hierarchies did become somewhat public. One such instance being Gia's wedding.

Roma at the wedding

Gia was one of Emil's other brother-men, and as an 'adopted' member of their brotherhood I had also been invited to his wedding. As Gia was the first within the brotherhood to get married, the wedding had been much anticipated, and the guest list numbered a few hundred people in total who were all friends and relatives of the bride and groom. I went accompanied by Emil, Roma and three of their friends; Davit, Magu and Beka. The wedding was held at a so-called 'wedding palace'; a large rented locale built for the purpose. Having arrived early, our small group gathered some chairs around a table in the yard outside in order to sit, talk, and wait for the bride and groom to arrive. Everyone was in a festive mood, cigarettes were put in a communal pile and chain-smoking commenced while correcting each other's hair and shirts, whispering comments about the female wedding guests and discussing the amounts of wine that was soon to be consumed. Another subject of discussion was the so-called 'list'. It is often uncommon at Georgian weddings to bring actual presents. Instead, the family 'makes a list' (*sias vzert*). Before entering the wedding reception each guest will put her or his name on this list and give a certain amount of money to a family member representing the bride and groom. This amount is then written next to the guest's name. The list serves as an account of reciprocity; if you have paid a certain amount of money at one person's wedding, this person is obliged to pay the same or more at your own future wedding. The amount of money paid signifies the extent of the relationship. Hence, very close relatives and friends are expected to pay a bigger amount than others. The same is the case for brother-men.

If Roma was to re-establish his relations and positions within the brotherhood after his long-term absence, this seemed to be an obvious opportunity. And sitting at the table in the yard outside the wedding palace he proclaimed that he intended to put 100 lari[1] on the list. This statement, however, caused immediate conflict. Emil, who was considered to be one of the groom's closest friends and who had already been disappointed by not being the groom's best man, had planned to put only 50 lari on the list. This in itself was a staggering amount that had been difficult for him to obtain as he was unemployed. 'I'm a brother-man (*dzmak'atsi*)!' Emil exclaimed angrily. 'You're just a friend (*megobari*), it will look completely wrong if you put double of what I put on the list!' Davit entered the discussion and took sides with Emil, scolding Roma for attempting to put himself in a higher position than what was right and for embarrassing Emil in that attempt. For a long while Roma insisted on putting his 100 lari on the list; he explained that he had gone to much trouble to get hold of the money (although at this point it was not explained exactly how he had gotten hold of it) and he was unwilling to change his position. 'I will pay whatever I choose to pay', he repeatedly insisted. Davit yelled at him even louder to the extent where Emil tried to calm him down by saying that it didn't matter anyway – in the end it was just a gift. Other arriving guests were casting glances towards our table, and the atmosphere had gone from festive to tense in a manner of minutes. Everyone was quiet except for Davit, who continued to throw verbal assaults at Roma from time to time. On his part Roma sat in silence, avoiding all eye contact. After some time, however, he got up from his chair and asked Davit to come with him. They left the yard without telling the rest of us where they were going and after a few minutes they returned. As it turned out, they had gone to change Roma's 100 lari bill into smaller bills. On their return, Roma handed Emil 30 lari, leaving himself with 70 lari. With the 50 lari that Emil already brought he now had a total of 80 lari, making him the one who would put the biggest amount on the list. 'I didn't intend to disrupt anything', Roma said as we went inside to put our names on the wedding list. He just wanted to give Gia and Eka a big gift. Two men were sitting by a table in the hallway. One was accepting and counting money while the other noted down names and numbers in a small booklet. To my horror I realized that all I had on me was a 50 lari note, which equalled what Emil had originally intended to give, but he nodded approvingly when I said that it was from both my wife, my son and I.

Once inside we were seated at the same table and as the bride and groom arrived the feast began. Waiters stacked endless amounts of traditional dishes on the tables, toasts were given, glasses were emptied and the dancing went on for hours. Throughout the evening Magu and Davit went outside to smoke weed or take pills, and while this left Magu increasingly calm and subdued Davit became more lively and agitated as the hours went by.

In the early hours of the next morning Roma, Emil, David, Magu, Beka and I left together. There hadn't been any fistfights during the wedding, but just as we were about to go in different directions at a traffic light in the city centre, one broke out between Davit and Roma, about the wedding gift. It was Davit who initiated it, restating his accusation against Roma despite the fact that the matter had already been settled. For his part, Roma restated that he had not intended to cheat or to look like a better friend than Emil because of his gift, and that in any case he had given money to Emil so that Emil could put a bigger amount on the list. 'Let's just go', Emil eventually said to me, and he, Magu and I left Davit and Roma arguing and fighting at the traffic light and went home.

I met with Roma a few days later and he reasserted that bringing the amount of money that he had was just a random decision. He had won the money gambling at a casino a few days before the wedding and had just decided to set it aside for the gift so that he would have something to give – most often be was broke, and he had been unable to find a job since he was released from prison. One immediate explanation for why Roma had acted as he did could have been that in the situation it had simply easier for Roma to lie and say that he didn't have any hidden agenda with the gift in order to avoid confrontation. But I spoke to Roma several times in the weeks and months following the wedding, and his version of the story never changed. Moreover, he was adamant about not cheating or being disloyal towards his friends, not least because it was exactly disloyalty that had caused his prison sentence, through his two former friends telling the police about his one-time participation in theft. He was fully open about the fact that he had committed a crime by stealing the computer, but friendship loyalty always took precedence over such acts (e.g. Frederiksen 2015).

Emil and the tombstone

The following year another event took place around which the question of money and friendship once again became an issue. It had been no secret that despite his young age Magu had been in bad health, mainly due to his excessive smoking and years of drug abuse and drinking. In the spring of 2010, around a year after I had concluded my fieldwork, Magu's body simply gave up and he was found dead in his bed one morning by his mother. Over the following weeks I was regularly in touch with Emil. It had not been possible for me to make it to Magu's funeral but around a month later I arrived in Batumi to visit his grave. Emil and I went there together. We had often before gone to the graveyard and we had spent many hours walking around to look at tombstones, particularly those with intricate engraved portraits which fascinated Emil. At one point we had even visited an engraver to see how the portraits were made.

Emil was keen to make sure that Magu would have a properly engraved tombstone, not least since Magu had been a tattoo artist and, in some sense, himself had worked with inscriptions, albeit on bodies not stones. But getting a tombstone engraved was expensive. Magu's family had no money and as a brother-man Emil had promised them that as an act of loyalty towards Magu he would raise the money and have the tombstone engraved. This, he told me as we sat by Magu's grave, had proved difficult – there was still no tombstone and many friendship-relations had been challenged due to arguments about who should pay what. 'Some people', he noted, had been unwilling to pay, although, in Emil's opinion, they were obliged to do so (Frederiksen 2013: 183). As a gesture, I offered Emil to either give or lend him the money needed. He responded by saying that it would be a respectful act on my behalf, but also that I would be taking upon myself a responsibility that ought to have been taken by others if I was to pay the main amount needed. Later in the day, I gave Emil an amount of money without specifying why or what for, although we both knew, none of us saying anything (ibid.: 184).

The reason for including the case of Magu's tombstone here is that it reveals something about Roma's intentions – or perhaps rather his lack of intentions – in terms of re-gaining a position in his brotherhood. What had struck me after my discussions with Emil about the tombstone was that if Roma had deliberately tried to re-assert his position within his old brotherhood via money during the wedding, then why didn't he try it now? Surely, he might have been afraid of more repercussions but given that I – as a much more peripheral figure in the brotherhoods – was allowed to give money, Roma was more than likely to have been allowed to as well. And it was well known that Roma had actually had money around this time, as he had recently won 1000 lari in a casino. He had soon lost them again, but the fact that he *had* had money at some point fuelled speculation among his friends.

Reasonable doubt

Davit, Emil, Beka and Magu had all voiced doubt Roma's reasons for bringing the wedding gift that he did. But was that doubt itself doubtful? As Mathijs Pelkmans writes, 'doubt denotes an active engagement with the world, and it is this engagement that affirms certainty about reality on other levels', thus turning epistemic crisis into epistemic affirmations (2017: 171). 'Crucially', he also notes, 'we need to ask how epistemic dispositions and probes are amplified, modified, and tempered by the affective ties between actors. We also must consider what stands behind the statements and available information' (ibid.: 171). If Roma was put on trial (which, in some ways, he actually was in the impromptu court by the wedding venue) one may ask whether it could be determined beyond reasonable doubt that Roma had the intention that was claimed. In many ways, the case of the wedding seems clear-cut. Roma attempted to re-establish his relationship by putting a significant amount of money on a wedding list. If successful in doing so he would place himself in a high position within a brotherhood because at some point the groom would have to reciprocate an equally big gift at Roma's future wedding, and although wedding lists are not public it would be known that they were close brother-men. But because there were other friends who, based on past relations, believed that they were better friends of the groom this became problematic. With brother-man relations being a relationship of practice, i.e. day-to-day support in terms of favours and assistance, Roma's gift made it seem as if he was short-cutting his way into a position that he, in the eyes of others, did not deserve. From their point of view, their day-to-day relations with the groom over recent years had been much closer than Roma's; for that reason they saw themselves as having the right to put more money on the list. As such, it was certainly reasonable for the others to doubt Roma when he said that he hadn't brought the gift in order to make it appear as if he was better friends with Gia than Emil was, because the wedding provided an arena for doing just that. In the courtyard-courtroom, the accusers-cum-jury quickly established that Roma's statement, that there had been no strategic thoughts behind his gift-giving, was dubious, that there was something *behind* the act, that it was not just random or devoid of any underlying meaning.

Nina Holm Vohnsen (2017) has rightly observed that the meaningless and the absurd has been a subject of little attention within anthropology, aside from being stepping stones from which to analytically make sense of things (see also Robbins 2006; Tomlinson and Engelke 2006). Yet there have recently been several contributions to the question of – or rather *questioning* of – the role of intentions and meaning in anthropological analysis, and I am by no means the first to raise the question of the coherence or meaning implicit in anthropological understanding. In an article from 1980, Dan Jorgensen explores the meaning of meaninglessness through an account of Magalim, a key figure in the cosmology of the Telefolmin people of Papua New Guinea. As Jorgensen notes, informants' accounts may often be experienced by a researcher as self-contradictory or fuzzy, something the task of ongoing fieldwork, interpretation and analysis is meant to sort out (Jorgensen 1980: 350). For Jorgensen, the figure of Magalim posed a problem of interpretation since the Telefolmin assert categorically that Magalim is without meaning but that he is nevertheless extremely important (ibid.: 349). Another figure, the female ancestress Afek, is the source and origin of all that is meaningful, yet she no longer plays an active in the lives of the Telefolmin, whereas Magalim does. Magalim is described as autonomous, capricious, non-reciprocal and without origin. 'Men who go about alone in the forest (…) may be tossed from mountaintop to mountaintop and be left stranded high up in the forest canopy for no other reason than that is what Magalim does' (ibid.: 353) – in the words of the locals, 'the meaningless one's meaning is meaningless'. He 'transcends the limits of human knowledge, is always just beyond the field of vision', yet 'he is continually manifest in the events of experience' (ibid.: 364). Magalim, Jorgensen writes, 'challenges the notion that coherence and transparency are attributes of the world (and) confronts humans with their ignorance – they may never understand him, but they must pay attention to him' (ibid.: 365).

Jorgensen uses this ethnographic example to criticise the (then) prevalent approach within anthropological studies of religion to look for coherence and meaning, approaches inspired, for instance, by the work of Clifford Geertz, and he describes how he, in his meeting with Magalim, was confronted with his own ignorance. That is, his ignorance towards meaninglessness. The figure of Magalim, Jorgensen notes in a later article, is something that simply 'happens' (Jorgensen 2002: 78). Of course, in the decades since Jorgensen put forth this critique, incoherence has become much more fashionable in anthropological studies of religion. Yet, as Matthew Engelke and Matt Tomlinson have recently noted, the notion of meaning has remained central. There have been numerous discussions about how 'meaning' should be defined and how to un-earth it through ethnographic work. However, amidst all these discussions and debates, we've forgotten to ask ourselves whether meaning is 'always a necessary or even a productive analytical category in anthropological work' (2006: 1, see also Frederiksen 2018).

A related example is found in Nils Bubandt's *The Empty Seashell* (2014). Providing an alternative to analytical perspectives that see witchcraft as explanations that offer certainty to ambivalence, Bubandt shows how in Buli witchcraft is surrounded by continuous doubt and uncertainty. Drawing on Derrida, he argues that this should be seen as an experiential aporia where believing and not-believing, certainty and doubt, and making sense and not-making sense continue to co-exist as part of social life. In a discussion of the book, Webb Keane asks whether Bubandt has simply replaced Geertz' famous allegory of 'turtles all the way down' with 'doubt all the way down'. Yet as Bubandt clarifies in his response, although Geertz' story 'became the allegorical justification for the claim that human worlds are based on meaning' (2016: 525), the image of depth that this implies does not necessarily capture what doubt is in the context that he himself describes, one in which doubt 'does not (necessarily at least) rest *on* something' (ibid., emphasis in original). While he agrees with Pelkmans (2011) that most doubts are put to rest, aporetic doubt 'continues to haunt and gnaw at the scaffolding of certainty and meaning' and is this an experience 'that is not domesticated by epistemic logic' (Bubandt 2016: 525).

Roma's return as a social drama

Engelke observes that 'one way in which anthropologists become convinced of getting it right (…) is through the recognition of patterns in the social life they observe' (2008: 9). He goes on to relate how Claude Lévi-Strauss 'admitted experiencing discomfort over how, when taken in isolation, the things humans do "are, or seem, arbitrary, meaningless, absurd' (ibid.). This may be eliminated by the discerning of patterns, by analytically carving out what the meaning of the meaningless is. In the empirical case at stake here, it may at first sight seem as if such analytical carving out could easily be done by taking inspiration from Victor Turner's depiction of how social dramas unfold. For Turner, a social drama consists of particular stages, the first of which is the occurrence of a breach, that is, a transgression of social norms. This may be the result of a cool calculation, a crime of passion, a political act or a mundane quarrel. In either case, however, it results in certain antagonisms being out in the open which forces members of the group in which it occurs to take sides or seek to create reconciliation. 'Thus', Turner notes, 'breach slides into crisis, and the critics of crisis seek to restore peace', this being done through certain forms of redressive action aimed at restoring pre-crisis-like-peace and eventually resolution or reintegration (Turner 1982: 10). The four stages, breach, crisis, redressive action and reintegration, all appear to be at play at the wedding: Roma transgresses a norm by bringing an inappropriately big gift in comparison to Emil's which results in a crisis, and as a critic of that crisis Davit seeks to restore peace through the redressive action of forcing Roma to give some of his money to Emil.

Yet, despite this all fitting very well, there are several factors that do not fit so well. Firstly, the event at the wedding connected not to one but two rituals – the formal ritual of gift-giving and the informal ritual of fistfighting at the end of the wedding. And secondly, there are two significant statements at stake: Roma's statement that 'I had no intentions' and Emil's statement that 'it doesn't matter'. Although Emil had initially been mad at Roma he actually accepted that the latter had not had any intentions of short-cutting his way back into the brotherhood, and Emil himself had not asked for any redressive action to take place. In effect, it was Davit who had caused the trouble, eventually forcing Roma to change his money and give some to Emil, despite Emil not demanding this. And it was Davit who later initiated a fight with Roma as the wedding had ended, founded on a situation that had officially already been solved – and a fight that Emil did not even bother watching. Rather than overcoming the crisis by restoring peace through redressive action, Davit had used Roma's hazardous gift-giving as a stepping stone to the informal ritual of fistfighting. Richard Schechner asks, in *Between Theater and Anthropology*, 'to what degree are performers of rituals (…) aware of the performing-arts aspects of their sacred work?' (1985: 4). In the case of Roma, we might say relatively little. At least, he did not seem to have a plot in mind, or to follow a carefully written script.

Through his work on social dramas Turner had been interested in the theatrical potential of social life, and the 'analogy, indeed the homology, between those sequences of supposedly "spontaneous" events which made fully evident the tensions existing in (Ndembu) villages, and the characteristic "processual form" of Western drama, from Aristotle onwards' (Turner 1982: 9). Throughout his career Turner explored and drew on a range of literary scholarship in the analysis of his empirical material, from the works of Shakespeare and William Blake over Dante´s *Purgatorio* to Icelandic Sagas (Turner 1990). Yet, as Richard Schechner notes on Turner's work, the Greco-European models of drama, on which the theory of social dramas as consisting of breach, crisis, redressive action and reintegration is based, does not necessarily suit all social dramas or ritual performances. 'It may be', he argues, for instance, 'that some social dramas are better looked at in Japanese aesthetic terms than in Greco-European ones' (Schechner 1985: 14). Schechner was interested in experimental theatre, an artform Turner also turned towards in the later years of his career. Yet although Turner does briefly mention the likes of Rabelais and Beckett as examples of playing with ideas, fantasies and words in order to 'transcend social structural limitations' (Turner 1982: 37), it does not seem to be their kind of experiments that underlie his focus on experimental theater. But perhaps it sometimes should, and this is where the *Theater of the Absurd* may be of help.

The *Theater of the Absurd* was a phrase coined by Martin Esslin as a way to depict a series of playwrights and directors who, from the late 1950s and onwards, began exploring and presenting instances in which there was no immediate meaning or plot (Esslin 2014). Taking cue from Albert Camus, Esslin described the absurd as consisting of individuals or groups being controlled by some outside entity that force them to act in ways that does not necessarily make sense to themselves, *The Myth of Sisyphus* being a case in point. Focusing initially on the work of playwrights such as Adam Adamov, Samuel Beckett, Jean Genet and Eugène Ionesco, with the later addition of Harold Pinter, Esslin notes how in absurdist theatre we see a devaluation of ideal and purpose, and a consequent breakdown (or absence) of the association between action and meaning most often found in Greco-European theatre (ibid.). William Beeman, in his review of theatre and spectacle in anthropology, provides an example of the latter by examining the work of Kenneth Burke, an author who inspired many scholars of performance theory, such as Victor Turner, in relation to a focus on the human intent to affect others through symbolic action by distinguishing between motion and action. For Burke, writes Beeman, 'things move, but human beings act, and it is only through *human motivated* action that meaningful symbolic transformation of reality can occur. Thus, a rock rolling down a mountain embodies no intrinsic symbolic transformation of reality. If someone throws the rock through the window of a house, then this becomes a symbolic act that will require interpretation and will have consequences for both the rock thrower, and for the persons into whose house the rock was thrown' (Beeman 1993: 373, emphasis in original). Yet, seen in relation to the empirical cases presented here, Roma didn't as much throw a rock as he simply dropped one. On the face of it, Roma and Emil were key-players in the social drama unfolding around the wedding. Yet none of them eventually saw it as being neither meaningful or transformative. This did not render it less of a drama, but a drama of a different nature, one built on hazardousness and a lack of intentions, one lying closer to absurdist theatre than Greco-European theatre.

Shadows of meaning and shadows of doubt

In her critique of interpretations of work of art, Susan Sontag wrote that interpretation is, problematically, based on erecting 'another meaning on top of the literal one. The modern style of interpretation excavates, and as it excavates it destroys; it digs "behind" the text, to find a sub-text which is the true one.' As such, she continues, 'to interpret is to impoverish, to deplete the world – in order to set up a shadow world of "meanings"' (2009: 4, see also Stoller 1994). Although it is definitely going a step too far to say interpretation should be avoided in anthropology, there may well be cases where digging for a deeper meaning does not necessarily add any further meaning. In lieu of Bubandt, sometimes there simply just may not be another turtle, or there may be indeterminable experiences at stake 'that is not domesticated by epistemic logic' (Bubandt 2016: 525).

Suspense in terms of postponement or judgement, writes Driessen, is necessary to preserve in ethnographic accounts as it allows for preserving ambiguities and complexities, and for taking into account that 'chance and serendipity, not to mention chaos, play a much larger role than we tend to admit' (2013: 151–2). In this perspective, there are grey areas of social life that require particular lenses in order to preserve rather than sort out the greyness (Frederiksen and Knudsen 2015). The danger of moving beyond the shadows of doubt in search for certainty is that this may, in the words of Sontag, lead to a shadow world of meaning. And beyond the shadows of doubt things are not necessarily less shadowy.

My own fieldwork experience around the time of Gia's wedding in many ways resembles that of Dan Jorgensen. There was a fuzzy nature surrounding the social lives that I was exploring that I wanted to sort out or make sense of – I wanted to figure out how Roma as a missing link within the brotherhoods would re-establish his former position by looking into his acts and motivations. Yet, as several anthropologists have recently pointed out, such explicit focus on doing, action, practices and meaning risks overlooking either the improvised, meaningless or outright absurd aspects of social life (Durham 2008; Frederiksen 2017; Harrison 2009; Ingold and Hallam 2007; Vohnsen 2017).

My last encounter with Roma was following the funeral of Magu. Emil had noted during those days how Roma had started gambling and that he 'doesn't even shower or get his hair cut anymore' (Frederiksen 2013: 184). A few years later, Emil moved to Moscow and although he remained in contact with most of his brother-men in Batumi, such as Gia, he eventually lost touch with Roma. I also lost touch with Roma, but I recently wrote Emil to ask him whether he remembered the circumstances surrounding the wedding. 'It was so long ago', he wrote back. Then as now, there was not really any way of knowing whether Roma had had the intentions that Emil and the others had claimed. On the one hand, it had seemed obvious that Roma had found a simple way to re-establish himself as a friend. On the other, Roma had always been adverse to people who cheated on their friends, particularly as that had been what at one point caused him to be arrested and imprisoned.

By reflecting on a gift list, a tombstone and a fistfight, my argument here has not been to say that rituals per se should be seen as either absurd or meaningless, or that social dramas are always a matter of absurdist theatre. Rather, it has been to establish that what goes on at the fringes of a particular ritual, such as among a group of brother-men waiting to enter wedding hall, cannot necessarily be read or understood with reference to whatever meaning the overall ritual might include. The drama, in this particular case, consists of occurrences where something 'simply happens'. And to reiterate, this is not a denial of Turner. Indeed, the case may be that Roma was simply a Beckettian character who stumbled into a Greco-Roman play where the audience expected to know the play in advance. And even absurdist theatre might bring too much epistemic logic into an event such as the one depicted here. But at least it comes closer to not getting it too right.

Note

1   100 lari corresponded to roughly 50 US$ at this time.

References

Bardavelidze, Vera 1984. The Institution of 'Modzmeoba' (Adoptive Brotherhood): An Aspect of the History of the Relations Between Mountain and Valley Populations in Georgia. In T. Dragadze (ed.) *Kinship and Marriage in the Soviet Union*. London: Routledge.

Beeman, William O. 1993. The Anthropology of Theater and Spectacle. *Annual Review of Anthropology* 22: 369–393.

Bruner, Edward 1993. Epilogue: Creative Personae and the Problem of Authenticity. In Smadar Lavie, Kirin Narayan, and Renato Rosaldo (eds.) *Creativity/Anthropology*. Ithaca: Cornell University Press.

Bubandt, Nils 2014. *The Empty Seashell: Witchcraft and Doubt on an Indonesian Island*. Ithaca: Cornell University Press.

Bubandt, Nils 2016. When in Doubt…? A Reply. *HAU: Journal of Ethnographic Theory* 6 (1): 519–530.

Clifford, James and George Marcus. 1986. *Writing Culture: The Poetics and Politics of Ethnography*. Berkeley: University of California Press.

Curro, Constanza 2015. Davabirzhoat! Conflicting Claims on Public Space in Tbilisi between Transparency and Opaqueness. *International Journal of Sociology and Social Policy* 35 (7/8): 497–512.

Di Puppo, Lili 2015. Marketing Reforms: The Dimension of Narratives in Georgia's Fight against Corruption. In Stéphane Voell and Iwona Kaliszewska (eds.) *State and Legal Practice in the Caucasus*. London: Ashgate, pp. 223–242.

Dragadze, Tamara 1988. *Rural Families in Soviet Georgia: A Case Study in Rural Georgia*. London: Routledge.

Driessen, Henrik 2013. Suspense in Retrospective Ethnography. In Mathijs Pelkmans (ed.) *Ethnographies of Doubt – Faith and Uncertainty in Contemporary Societies*. London: I.B. Tauris, pp. 149–163.

Durham, Deborah 2008. Apathy and Agency – The Romance of Youth in Botswana. In Jennifer Cole and Deborah Durham (eds.) *Figuring the Future – Globalization and the Temporalities of Children and Youth*. Santa Fe: School for Advanced Research Press.

Engelke, Matthew 2008. The Objects of Evidence. *JRAI* 14 (1): 1–21.

Esslin, Martin 2014. *The Theatre of the Absurd*. London and New York: Bloomsbury.

Frederiksen, Martin Demant 2012. Good Heart or Big Bellies: Dzmak'atcoba and Images of Masculinity in the Republic of Georgia. In Vered Amit and Noel Dyck (eds.) *Young Men in Uncertain Times*. Oxford. Berghahn Books, pp. 165–187.

Frederiksen, Martin Demant 2013. *Young Men, Time and Boredom in the Republic of Georgia*. Philadelphia. Temple University Press.

Frederiksen, Martin Demant 2015. The Last Honest Bandit: Transparency and Spectres of Illegality in the Republic of Georgia. In Ida Harboe Knudsen and Martin Demant Frederiksen (eds.) *Ethnographies of Grey Zones in Eastern Europe*. London: Anthem Press, pp. 157–173.

Frederiksen, Martin Demant 2017. Joyful Pessimism: Marginality, Disengagement and the Doing of Nothing. *Focaal* 78: 9–22.

Frederiksen, Martin Demant 2018. *An Anthropology of Nothing in Particular*. Washington and Winchester: Zero Books.

Frederiksen, Martin Demant and Katrine Bendtsen Gotfredsen 2017. *Georgian Portraits – Essays on the Afterlives of a Revolution*. Winchester: Zero Books.

Frederiksen, Martin Demant and Ida Harboe Knudsen 2015. What is a Grey Zone and Why is Eastern Europe One? In Ida Harboe Knudsen and Martin Demant Frederiksen (eds.) *Ethnographies of Grey Zones in Eastern Europe*. London: Anthem Press, pp. 1–25.

Geertz, Clifford 1980. Blurred Genres: The Reconfiguration of Social Thought. *American Scholar* 80: 165–179.

Goffman, Erving 1959. *The Presentation of Self in Everyday Life*. New York: Anchor Books.

Harrison, Paul 2009. In the Absence of Practice. *Environment and Planning D: Society and Space* 27: 987–1009.

Hastrup, Kirsten 2004. *Action: Anthropology in the Company of Shakespeare*. Copenhagen: Museum Tusculanum Press.

Ingold, Tim and Elizabeth Hallam 2007. Creativity and Cultural Improvisation: An Introduction. In Elizabeth Hallam and Tim Ingold (eds.) *Creativity and Cultural Improvisation*. Oxford: Berg.

Jorgensen, Dan 1980. What's in a Name: The Meaning of Meaninglessness in Telefolmin. *Ethos* 8 (4): 349–366.

Jorgensen, Dan 2002. The Invention of Culture, Magalim, and the Holy Spirit. *Social Analysis* 46 (1): 69–79.

Manning, Paul 2007. Rose-Colored Glasses? Color Revolutions and Cartoon Chaos in Postsocialist Georgia. *Cultural Anthropology* 22 (2): 171–213.

Manning, Paul 2015. *Language, Private Love, and Public Romance in Georgia.* North York: Toronto University Press.

Mattingly, Cheryl 1998. *Healing Dramas and Clinical Plots – The Narrative Structure of Experience.* Cambridge: Cambridge University Press.

Muehlfried, Florian 2014. *Being a State and States of Being in Georgia.* Oxford: Berghahn Books.

Pelkmans, Mathijs 2011. Outline for an Ethnography of Doubt. In Mathijs Pelkmans (ed.) *Ethnographies of Doubt – Faith and Uncertainty in Contemporary Societies.* London: I.B. Tauris, pp. 1–43.

Pelkmans, Mathijs 2017. Doubt, Suspicion, Mistrust … Semantic Approaches. In Florian Muehlfried (ed.) *Mistrust – Ethnographic Approximations.* New York: Columbia University Press, pp. 169–178

Robbins, Joel 2006. Afterword: On Limits, Ruptures, Meaning, and Meaninglessness. In Matthew Engelke and Matt Tomlinson (eds.) *The Limits of Meaning – Case Studies in the Anthropology of Christianity.* Oxford: Berghahn Book, pp. 211–225.

Schechner, Richard 1985. *Between Theater and Anthropology.* Philadelphia: University of Pennsylvania Press.

Schwab, Gabriele 2012. *Imaginary Ethnographies – Literature, Culture, Subjectivity.* New York: Columbia University Press.

Sontag, Susan 2009 (1961). Against Interpretation. In Susan Sontag (ed.) *Against Interpretation, and Other Essays.* London: Penguin Books, pp. 3–15.

Starn, Orin 2012. Writing Culture at 25: Special Editor's Introduction. *Cultural Anthropology* 27 (3): 411–416.

Stoller, Paul 1994. 'Conscious' Ain't Consciousness: Entering the 'Museum of Sensory Absence'. In Nadia Seremetakis (ed.) *The Senses Still – Perception and Memory as Material Culture in Modernity.* Chicago: The University of Chicago Press, pp. 109–123.

Tomlinson, Matt and Matthew Engelke 2006. Meaning, Anthropology, Christianity. In Matthew Engelke and Matt Tomlinson (eds.) *The Limits of Meaning – Case Studies in the Anthropology of Christianity.* Oxford: Berghahn Books, pp. 1–37.

Turner, Edith 1990. The Literary Roots of Victor Turner's Anthropology. In Kathleen M. Ashley (ed.) *Victor Turner and the Construction of Cultural Criticism – Between Literature and Anthropology.* Bloomington: Indiana University Press, pp. 163–169.

Turner, Victor 1975. *Dramas, Fields, and Metaphors.* Ithaca: Cornell University Press.

Turner, Victor 1982. *From Ritual to Theater – The Human Seriousness of Play.* New York: PAJ Publications.

Turner, Victor 1985. Introduction. In *Between Theater and Anthropology.* Philadelphia: University of Pennsylvania Press.

Vohnsen, Nina 2017. *The Absurdity of Bureaucracy – How Implementation Works.* Manchester: Manchester University Press.

Watson, Ian 2002. *Negotiating Cultures – Eugenio Barbas and the Intercultural Debate.* Manchester: Manchester University Press.

Zakharova, Evgeniya 2010. Street Life in Tbilisi as a Factor of Male Socialization. *Laboratorium. Russian Review of Social Research* 2 (1): 350–352.

3 'This parenting lark'

Idiomatic ways of knowing and an
epistemology of paying adequate attention

Sevasti-Melissa Nolas and Christos Varvantakis

Introduction

In this chapter, we engage with the curious signifier of the 'idiom' and raise questions about its relationship to (not) knowing and to peripheral methodologies. Traditionally, the term idiom has been used in anthropological writing to suggest a honing of the researchers' attention to the vernacular practices being employed by interlocutors to live and make sense of their everyday lives (Nolas, Aruldoss and Varvantakis 2018). Nevertheless, and as with a lot of linguistic metaphors that find their way into anthropological texts, it is notable that the term has been often used unreflexively, indicating a shared, tacit way of attending to the world. We suggest, however, that this tacit way of attending to the world that is expressed by the term 'idiom', encapsulates a particular epistemology of paying attention. We elaborate these arguments further by engaging with the question of how one might arrive at calling something an idiom. If an idiom is a way of recognising cultural practices and forms of expression, what does that experience of recognition look and feel like – given that meaning is often sedimented in and through practice, with earlier layers not always consciously accessible to researchers, and not always easily codified into written, spoken or visual language (Behar 1996; Howes 2003)?

We draw on fieldwork experiences in Athens and in London from a five-year multimodal ethnographic study that looked at the relationship between childhood and public life as this unfolded in children's everyday lives. During the Connectors Study we worked with younger children (ages 6–9) from different backgrounds, living in different parts of three cities (Athens, Hyderabad, London) and asked questions about how these children encountered, experienced and engaged with public life.[1] The study took a broadly phenomenological approach and used multimodal ethnography to explore the *relationship* between childhood and public life (Nolas 2015). Public life was understood in terms of 'associated living' and 'communicable experience' (Dewey 2009; Laplantine 2015), with publics being constituted through vital processes, *forms of connection and relationality* between people, places, objects, humans and non-humans (Fraser, Kember and Lury 2005; Latimer and Miele 2013), which both theoretically and in everyday conversation with children and parents we referred to as what 'moved' and 'mattered' to children (see Lutz 2017; Sayer 2011).

During the study we spent considerable amounts of time with children in their homes, and occasionally taking walks together in their neighbourhoods and other parts of the city. As such, the home, and its domestic rhythms, was our primary field site. In the study we took a relational and intergenerational approach to understanding childhood and, as such, also spent time with parents, mainly mothers, as well as conducting biographical interviews with mothers and some fathers. In addition, one other notable characteristic of the study was that it was focused on families with young children (henceforth, 'young families') at the same time as we, in each of our personal lives, were also parents living with toddlers in London and Athens, respectively. As such, two forms of paying attention, the maternal/paternal and the ethnographic, were unwittingly brought together through our biographies and bodies and the young family home made for a curiously familiar field site despite us being strangers to each family.

Our fieldwork across the 26 children in London and Athens, and their families that we got to meet, reflected many of these vicissitudes of young family life we were becoming more and more familiar with as our own children grew closer to the age of the children in the study. And we often responded to these undulations in similar ways in which we might in our own everyday lives: by sometimes not paying attention to what was going on, by being 'elsewhere'. As ethnographers, trained to pay attention in the 'here-and-now', this posed something of a situation to begin with. How did we come to know what we did without seemingly 'paying attention' or being 'there'? We pick up on these experiences of translocation, being disconnected from our physical contexts of co-presence on the one hand, making links with other spatiotemporal contexts and people on the other (Callon and Law 2004), as they took place in two separate afternoons we spent with families in their homes. As such, our chapter also reflects on how we attend to or miss meaning in the field, and what the implications of doing so might be. But before we go there, we provide some background on young families and practices of paying attention in parenting and fieldwork in late modernity.

Paying attention in parenting and fieldwork in late modernity

In the post-industrialised, high-income economies in which the research took place, bringing up young families unfolded to a backdrop of a 'crisis of childhood' (Kehily 2010). On the one hand, children's well-being was endlessly debated and scrutinised in policy and the public sphere. This made everyday, sensual relations (Howes 2003), ways of being together as a family (e.g. eating, playing, talking, sleeping, outings), also and often focused events of 'children's development' where particular modes of attention were called for. As such, childhood, and raising children, especially in middle-class families, was often described by sociologists at the time as intensive or 'concerted' (Gillies 2011; Lareau 2003) meaning that childhood required considerable adult investment of time, concern and thought (Castañeda 2002). Mothering, and increasingly fathering, continued to overlap considerably with the politics of the state, a case of raising 'good' (cf. disciplined) citizens (Fraser 1990; King 2016; Kjørholt 2013) to the backdrop of idealised notions of mothering behaviour (Singh 2004). This meant that parenting cultures of scrutiny and blame proliferated (Lee et al. 2014). This crisis of childhood took many forms, including the proliferation of endless manuals for consultation (for sleep, for feeding, for relationship management) as well as the emergence of competing ideologies of child-rearing (e.g. 'helicopter' vs 'free-range' parenting). Across all these domains, being there, being present as a parent, becomes of utmost importance as exemplified, for instance, in debates about parental mobile phone usage and its relationship to 'responsible' and 'sensitive' parenting (Kildare and Middlemiss 2017).

Young family life, as such, in late modernity is an intensive process of paying close attention to every aspect of the growing child and to becoming attuned to their every need and desire to a backdrop of constant barrage of advice. As parents to young children this was a familiar world. Our own experiences of bringing up infants and small children in an era of intensive parenting was similarly anxiety provoking. For example, for one of us her then-infant, toddler and young-child woke several times a night. Her initial response in the early months was to consult and consume sleep manuals, and to obsessively document her child's sleep 'patterns' in the hope of finding a 'solution'. When such was not forthcoming, the latest sleep book she had been given by a well-meaning acquaintance, who had described the book's 'method' as a panacea, was angrily flung across her living room, the words 'don't ever let me read any of this crap again' directed at her partner.

Methodologies, scales, devices, tricks and the social relations for paying close attention are also of much concern to many contemporary anthropologists (Back 2012; Cook 2018; Stewart 2007; Tsing 2015). The 'ethnographic eye' and 'ear' have always played a central role in the practice of paying attention in the field, a legacy of the mid-19th-century disciplining of the senses. As noted by David Howes (2003), this disciplining involved, amongst other things, the erasure of the body as a source of knowledge, the bodies of those the anthropologist spent time with as well as the anthropologist's own body. The textual turn, and the 'reading culture' metaphor it espoused, which followed later in the 1970s, imparted 'a visual and a verbal bias to any analysis' (ibid: 19). The practices of observation and notation were centralised in ethnography, while bodily ways of knowing in the field became marginalised.

Such privileging of sight and sound, of seeing and hearing, 'bears the imprint of a certain way of imagining the human subject – namely, as a seat of awareness, bounded by the skin, and set over against the world – that is deeply sedimented in the Western tradition of thought' (Ingold 2000: 243). It is also a strange mode of attention in that it asks us to disembody ourselves, to take leave of our senses (Howes 2003), meaning that we are more often preoccupied with our research questions and methodologies instead of perhaps the children's play we are being recruited into (Nolas and Varvantakis 2019). Yet, as we realised in our own research, to pay attention to our research questions/methodologies, would mean to loosen our attention on the games that were happening in front of us. Being a 'disciplined' researcher, focused, observant and attentive, would mean 'sucking' at the games that children had recruited us into, and which for them, at that moment, were commanding their full attention. At the same time, these games were not always comprehensible to us, children would often make up their own rules, and sometimes they were also repetitive and boring.

So, what does attention mean in this light: a 'disciplined' researcher is attentive, but attentive to what? To not be attentive to the game you are playing and instead be preoccupied with research questions? Or perhaps you find your mind wandering elsewhere? Would this be disrespectful for the person you have in front of you and the activity she's drawn into (with you)? What is the periphery and the centre of what is going on? And also, what about joy and pleasure – what about if you actually find it more pleasant to *be elsewhere,* somewhere other than the field and in company of your interlocutor? Indeed, does being 'absent' even matter? Do we know our interlocutors or our children any less if we let ourselves drift off and be elsewhere?

In the next section, we present the spaces and rhythms of the young family home, drawing on data from one family in London. We then hone in on experiences of translocation and use data from one family in Athens to further develop our argument. These were experiences of fumbling and not knowing, of being 'idiotic', as well as of being 'present/absent' in the field (bodies there, minds elsewhere). Unlike the purposive action of tuning into a Walkman (or any other device/ playlist combination), which Callon and Law describe (2004) as one practice that produces translocation, these experiences 'jarred' us; they caught us unawares. As such, these experiences challenged the sort of attentiveness and presence that is at the heart of contemporary young family life as well as of the ethnographic method; and which left us with the feeling of a transgression having been committed. There were times when we found ourselves disengaged and absent, adrift and peripheral to our field sites and interlocutors; and we were often taken by surprise by our momentary absences. We wanted to think about what these experiences might mean for attending to or missing idiomatic meaning in the field and with what, if any, implications. But now, let's turn towards the vicissitudes of young family life, and of making connections, in all its messiness, its joys, drudgery, and stink.

The spaces and rhythms of young family life

Recently, there has been a systematic attempt to re-engage with bodily knowledge (in post-colonial ways, see Howes 2003) and to, once again, suggest that ethnographers might 'come to their senses' by playing attention to a full range of bodily modes of perception including taste and touch (Classen 2005; Csordas 1993; Pink 2009; Seremetakis 1994; Stoller 1997), and, in particular, the complementarity of different sensory perceptions as modes of knowing. In this section, following a sensory approach, we explore the vicissitudes of 'young family life' through one family in London which Melissa visited over a three-year period. The fieldwork account that follows pays attention to rhythms of the day, and the ways in which various bodies make their ways through time and space on that day.

Eleanor and her family lived in an affluent area of North London. A middle-class family, with both parents employed, when I (Melissa) first meet Eleanor she has just become an older sibling. Her brother Tom is only a few months old when I visit the family home for the first time, and Eleanor's mother, Dawn, is on her year of maternity leave.

Visits to children and their families in London were typically carried out in the afternoons and over the weekends. My first visit to Eleanor's takes place on a Sunday morning. I arrive at the house just before our agreed time of 10 a.m. I hesitate and hover at the threshold, before knocking, knowing that 9–10 a.m. can typically be 'nap time' for small babies (if you follow some sleep manuals), and I really don't want to be that person who wakes the (finally) sleeping baby.

Of course, when I do knock and I am let in I discover the equally typical situation of the baby having other plans: baby Ben hasn't slept and the first time I meet his and Eleanor's dad, Ben is in his pyjamas, looking tired, and in the process of passing the baby to Dawn so that he can take a shower. I find the encounter awkward.

The rest of my three-hour stay happens at a languid pace: getting to know each other, doing some research activities, taking a walk to the local bakery, and having lunch together. At some point Eleanor runs out of steam and our time together starts to feel protracted; it's also time for Eleanor to do her homework. So, I thank her for all her help, we hug, I say goodbye and let myself out.

During the three years we also organised a full-day visit to each family, which gave us the experience of the spaces of young family lives as these criss-crossed the home, the street, the school, playgrounds, and, often, centres of commerce or entertainment. During the same time, we also became more accustomed to the often-disrupted rhythms of young family lives. For example, my day visit to Eleanor's, which took place in mid-June 2015, was one that had to be rescheduled twice: once on account of Eleanor being unwell and once on account of my own child being ill. The visit took place at a time when Eleanor's dad was travelling, as such, Dawn had been at home on her own with the two children for a few days.

On the day, the rhythms of these visits were fairly similar across the London sample, itself diverse in terms of family compositions, cultural, racial, religious, and economic backgrounds. Mornings typically involved a 'scramble' out the door at the same time as making sure that teeth had been brushed, school bags had been packed, children had eaten enough or something, the temporalities of adulthood clashing with the more languid pace of childhood ambling out the home.

Getting out of Eleanor's house that morning is hectic: Eleanor discovers a hole in her shoe and her water bottle empty at the same time as Dawn discovers that one of her favourite items of clothing has been refashioned with a pair of scissors; it is a tense atmosphere which magically dissipates the moment we all cross the threshold and find ourselves on the street and on our way to the school.

For my part, I find spending the whole day at school with Eleanor exhausting and largely boring. I am not carrying out a study of schools. The classroom feels cramped for an adult body and I resent having to stay in one place, any movements, including going to the toilet or eating, determined by an external schedule over which I have no control.

After school, Eleanor and I are picked up by Dawn and baby Tom. We go to the art store, where I take the opportunity to pick up a cardboard dinosaur to take home for my son to paint, before heading home via the supermarket. Eleanor and I play in the kitchen, Tom, who is now six months old, tries to join in. Eventually it is dinner time and we sit down to a meal of ragu and fried courgettes.

Tom is helping himself in a feeding practice I recognise from my own experimentation in that never-ending battleground of child versus parent versus food, as the latest in middle-class feeding fads, 'baby-led weaning', a feeding practice that encourages parents to allow the baby/child to take control of their eating and is supposed to encourage healthy food choices and less of a taste for sugary foods. 'I didn't know you could do baby-led and they would be okay', Dawn reflects, comparing this to the drudgery of mincing baby food which is what she did with Eleanor. I reflect on the pleasure of watching children eat with relish, something I didn't, at the time, experience at home.

Dawn and I share a glass of wine over dinner, and I find myself wondering if that's allowed in that book of fieldwork methodologies that I know doesn't exist. But it feels okay. It's been a long day, I struggled through most of it on account of my own disrupted sleep and the challenges of concentrating all day in the Year 2 primary school classroom. In the past, Dawn and I have often exchanged stories of sleep deprivation and on more than one occasion she has said to me: 'It's trying, isn't it?' Today Dawn says: 'It's nice to have dinner with a grown up now that Ben is away this week.'

Over dinner and dessert Eleanor, Dawn and I talk about second babies (real and imagined), about summer plans, and about having ice-lollies after dinner, Tom happily gobbling up ragu and courgette in his high-chair and interjecting every-so-often with gesticulations for more food.

After dinner Eleanor and I make a bracelet together and play a make-shift pretend game of lacrosse in the backyard, where she plunges me back into some of my own (English, romantic) childhood reading: the Enid Blyton series of Malory Towers. For a moment I am back in my own childhood home, a 9-year-old, in her bedroom, the door shut, her back against the balcony window, amassing the rays of winter sunshine, book in hand, devouring a story about absent parents, sisterhood, troublemaking and the forging of an ethical life. I don't stay there long, however, pulled back into the here-and-now by a tennis ball coming my way.

It's now 7 p.m., and time for me to leave. I would love to stay longer but my own young family home is beckoning.

I go up to the bathroom to find Dawn, who is bathing Tom; he is in the bath propped up in a bath seat. Dawn is sitting on the floor washing him. He is chuckling with abandon, water splashing everywhere. I thank Dawn for her hospitality.

In the meantime, Tom has spat up in the bath and spittle mixed with food is floating in the bath water. Dawn mixes the water around to dissolve the spittle in the same way that I've rubbed off dirt on my son's clothes, when they are not dirty enough for a full wash, and thought 'That will do, clean enough'.

Dawn says to me, as if we've been reading each other's minds, that she won't mention the spittle to Eleanor, who will soon be jumping in the bath with Tom. I say 'In that case there is a chunk there you may want to make disappear' and she scoops it up with one of the bath toys. We laugh about this and, as I'm leaving the bathroom, she says all of the following things, which I find myself too exhausted and brain-dead to reconstruct into full sentences later in my fieldnotes:

> 'It's funny this parenting lark … you can't lose our sense of humour … and we don't have to do it perfectly!'" 'No, just good enough, right?', I say invoking my much-beloved mantra which I never quite manage to adhere to myself, and we smile at each other.

I leave the bathroom and head downstairs to say goodbye to Eleanor, who has no interest in participating in this conventional parting ritual. She is now elsewhere, deep in that childhood practice of building herself a den: the couch, the cushion, and a bunch of sheets for her props.

I have to work hard to get her attention. 'Do I get a hug?', I ask. I really didn't want to leave without saying anything. She leaves her den-building momentarily and gives me a massive all-embracing hug, hanging herself off my body.

We squeeze each other tightly. I thank her for hosting me for the day and wish her a great summer. I'll see her in the autumn when she is in Year 3. She doesn't say anything. She untangles herself from me and goes back to ignoring me and building her den.

I let myself out and head for the tube.

Unpacking the idioms of young family life: 'this parenting lark'

According to the Longman English Dictionary, in colloquial British English, doing something 'for a lark' is to do something to amuse oneself, for a joke. The phrase can also be 'used to describe an activity that someone thinks is either silly or difficult', or maybe both. As such, Dawn's description of parenting as a 'lark' may well be an appropriate idiom for describing relational practices in young family lives. It is delivered with awareness of what often feels like a relentless call for perfection against an ever-changing standard, and for doing things the right way, at the same time as being acutely aware that such standards are socially constructed and that there is no one or right way.

As such, 'this parenting lark', as an idiom, encapsulates something of an oxymoron: the serious and silly business of bringing up a child. Accordingly, 'knowing how' often comes after 'doing that', and everyday young family life could be described as proceeding in many 'idiotic' ways (Horst and Michael 2011; Michael 2012): children 'misbehave', illness 'disrupts', stains 'persist', solids and liquids 'overspill' their containers, toys 'get in the way'. In Isabelle Stengers' terms, idiotic figures make us critically reflect on 'what we are busy doing'; indeed, they 'suspend the habits that make us believe that we know what we know and who we are, that we hold the meaning of what makes us exist' (2005: 10003). The colouring pens everywhere, mushed-up food on the floor, the spew in the bath turn spaces upside-down. Mothers colluding without words in those little meaningless deceits (clean water, clean clothes) that make everyday life more livable. Tentative exchanges about the challenges of doing young family life pass between parents, the fear of being judged for having done it 'wrong' never far off. 'It's funny this parenting lark' posed as a question, a hedging of bets in case our interlocutor finds it neither funny nor a lark.

Experiences that suspend our habits of knowing and identification may well send us 'elsewhere', as a way of anchoring ourselves anew, as a way of finding pleasure when the larking about tips more to the side of the difficult instead of the funny. It may also be the case that young family life 'can entail a range of happenings which, in one way or another, "overspill" the empirical, analytic, or political framings of those [...] events' (Michael 2012: 529). The previous section touched on the issue of 'translocation' of absence/presence (Callon and Law 2004: 7) as one example of 'overspill'. Eleanor's invocation of Enid Blyton's boarding school classic sends Melissa back in time to her childhood bedroom, alone, enjoying a book about escapism, away from her family. The drudgery of domesticity and the pleasure of being in a room of one's own, apparently felt by children too, the desire to connect with an 'elsewhere', and an ever-present 'other'.

To understand these experiences of translocation, and how they might inform our recognition of idioms, we have found it helpful to think with phenomenological and sensory anthropology and to consider somatic modes of attention and sensory ways of relating (Howes 2003). The body as 'the existential ground of culture' (Csordas 1993: 135) becomes a vehicle through which idioms might originally be created and later (re)produced (Clarke, 1989). As well as responding to the spaces and rhythms of contemporary domesticity, young family homes, and bodies that dwell in them, are also sites of affect and memory with children often positioned as the stirrers of those long forgotten 'ghosts in the nursery' (Fraiberg, Adelson and Shapiro 1975). Bodies are nurtured and formed through cooking and eating, stories of generations gone by passed down in the process (Giard 1998; Seremetakis 1994). Love and devotion are communicated through touch and consumption (Miller 2001); agency made visible through housework and home creativity (Pink 2004), themselves an ambivalent affective mixture of autonomy and dissatisfaction, accomplishment and boredom, routine and monotony, fragmentation and repetition, connection and loneliness (Beer 1983; Oakley 1974). Social movements and social change leaving their mark on the domestic, and especially on women's bodies (Fraser 1990; Hochschild 1989). In the next section, sticking with food, we further elaborate on the theme of absence/presence before concluding with implications.

When 'Makaronia me kima' is much more than just a plate of spaghetti with mince meat

Food is a way of forging and maintaining relationships and has long been considered central to the rhythms of the young family home and those who dwell within it: to 'good mothering', to children's demonstrations of agency, to our sense of self and belonging (cf. Thomson, Hadfield, Kehily and Sharpe 2012). In the context of Greece, food and food sharing is considered to be a culturally significant practice. David Sutton (2006) has written about connections between food and memory, and Nadia Seremetakis (1994) has written on sharing practices of food as shared substance and in relation to the memory of the senses and modernity, while Vassiliki Yiakoumaki (2006) has written on food and cultural diversity in the context of Greece's Europeanization.

Food also had an immense significance in our research, across the three countries and in very many different ways. First of all, the discussions that we had with children about food, about foods they like and foods they hate, as well as about eating constraints they faced and their ways of negotiating those. The sweets and snacks we brought along when visiting the families – which in time became very personalized, as we learnt about our interlocutors' preferences and their parents' constraints (often realizing that our visits were 'special' occasions, and as such would loosen some constraints) – were also a way of forming relationships, as were, significantly, the meals and snacks we shared with the families and the children interlocutors.

In retrospect, it seems absolutely moving how the families shared their dinners and meals with us (among all other things they shared with us). Such instances were invaluable ethnographic research moments, providing occasions for 'kitchen table conversations', sometimes passionate and sometimes mundane, which allowed us glimpses into the families' everyday lives. They also demonstrate the trust and safety that developed in our relationships with the families that enabled talk and gestures to emerge in the first place.[2]

As far as my experience (Christos) of fieldwork in Athens was concerned, food and food sharing were indeed an important way in which families in the study communicated relatedness, and opened up those relations to me. I often found myself feeling grateful for the invitation and opportunity to share such moments with families, some of which were really enjoyable – in fact, enjoyable to the extent of being distracting. I share below such an instance, of an anthropology of not paying attention.

Food preparation often takes place with a considerable amount of 'larking about' in young families. In Athens, Alexandros (9) and Yannis (7) provide us with an example of this. Their parents, Ioulia and Nikos, are professionals in their forties. Ioulia worked occasionally and mostly from home. She was the one who does all the cooking and undertakes most of the domestic work. She liked cooking but she disliked having to cook different things for the two boys – and this is often the case.

Take, for instance, a meal with pasta, which the family eat frequently. Yannis can't stand spaghetti, and prefers rather to eat fusilli or other sorts of smaller pasta, while Alexandros only eats spaghetti. Similarly, Alexandros can't stand (even the smell of) white cheese, and wants to have yellow, dry cheese (such as graviera) with his pasta, while Yannis will only eat his pasta with grated feta cheese. At least, both boys share a dislike of herbs and hot spices in sauces – which in fact she and her husband love. Ioulia told me that she will often prepare only the one sauce, without herbs and hot spices, for all of them, in doing so sacrificing her own desires since she is too tired to care for all other details of the meal. At other times, however, she may be more tenacious and despite her tiredness she will also prepare a second sauce for her and her husband. On other occasions, albeit rarely, sometimes she will just prepare the pasta sauce the way she likes it and tell the kids, well that's it, take it or leave it (although, they will usually then just leave it).

During one of my visits, Ioulia had just prepared lunch. Dishing out the food at the kitchen table, she called for us to come and eat. I got there first, asking her if she needed help with anything, and giving her a hand with plates, napkins and so on. The food smelled amazing. Not just a tasteful smell, rather a smell that felt very familiar, maybe even too familiar, to me. I asked, and she told me that we were having *makaronia me kima* (spaghetti with minced meat) for lunch. This is a pretty typical dish and an all-time favourite of many children in Greece (almost all children in the research, at least, were fans!) The smell, however, rang a different bell for me.

It wasn't a usual smell or the smell that *makaronia me kima* have when we cook it at home or when I get it elsewhere. It took some time before the boys made it to the kitchen and we sat and started eating. It was only then, with the first bite, that I realized: it was cooked just the way my paternal grandmother used to cook it! I haven't had this dish made in this way for over two decades (my grandmother having long passed away), and yet I remembered it exactly – that was exactly it! My favourite version of my favourite childhood dish, and it was there in front of me, a full plate of memory. Around this plate a number of things, mostly long forgotten, started to materialise in my head: my grandmother's kitchen, her smell, her flowery patterned dresses, the shape of the glasses on the table, the tangerines in the bowl in the center of her table, the patterns of her tablecloths.

Ioulia asked me if I would like a glass of wine, as she was serving herself one. I said no – I guess I would have normally accepted, but the taste experience I was having felt incompatible with wine in that moment – never having had this dish with wine before. On some level, I realized that there were exciting things happening around me, things I probably ought to be paying attention to: Alexandros was talking about how he hates cheese, Yannis wanted a different kind of pasta, both discussing and re-negotiating their preferences with Ioulia, Nikos trying to sneak/negotiate his way out of the kitchen and into the living room to watch cartoons plate in hand, which he eventually managed. But I couldn't really pay attention to those fine ethnographic details, immersed as I was in my own dish.

Naturally, I had a second serving.

Of ghosts and other sprites

Idioms are particular and sometimes peculiar ways of communicating complex life-worlds. Linguistically, they represent phrases the meaning of which is not reducible to individual words (for some fun examples in both English and Greek see the footnotes[3]). Idioms, as such, are assemblages of meanings and practices, the significance of which is found in their particular configurations. Anthropologically, the challenge with 'idioms' at an analytical level is that once recognised they solidify: domesticity (Fraser 1990), playfulness (Varvantakis and Nolas 2019), witchcraft (Evans-Pritchard 1937), and, as we argue here, 'this parenting lark', the phenomenologies that constituted them become erased. Once identified, the experiences that led to recognition fall out of this assemblage, and in so falling something of the richness and vitality of the idiom is lost; a vitality that might also involve banal experiences of absence as we have shown here, of being elsewhere, but which still, we would argue, constitute learning and still contribute to the formation of knowledge. It is a little bit of this experience of coming to learn, unlearn and re-learn the idioms of 'parenting lark' that we have tried to convey in this chapter.

In particular, we focused on moments of translocation (Callon and Law 2004) experienced by both of us, to think about what might be unlearned and relearned in the oxymoron 'absent present'. Here we might venture to say a few things based on the preceding analysis: that parenting and fieldwork, alike, can be as stimulating as they can be boring, as rewarding as they can be depleting, and as overwhelming as they can be insignificant, both central to our lives as well as peripheral. Both require attention as well as roaming in the fields of memory; both can be 'haunted' by human and non-human actors central to our own relational worlds (Roseneil 2009).

Some of the ghosts that haunted us are apparent in the lines of text: Enid Blyton and Christos's paternal grandmother, for instance. Other ghosts make their presence felt between the lines: second wave feminist interpretations of domesticity, on the one hand, and love, on the other. Second wave feminist approaches to domesticity focus on women's oppression and unremunerated labour – physical, practical and mental – in the running of households. The feelings of anger and disappointment that inequalities in the home create are well documented, especially as these relate to women's lives (Hochschild 1989; Oakley 1974). But, as Sarah Pink (2004) notes, and without diminishing the impact of these continued structural inequalities, such feelings are only one part of the affective circuits of home cultures. It took a few drafts of this chapter to loosen the hold that the second wave feminist narrative had on at least the first author's imagination, in order to allow the possibility of (an) other interpretation of the domestic and of young family lives to emerge.[4]

What, we might ask, emerges from the here-and-now from this processual interplay of opposites and the momentary glimpse of the secret worlds of thoughts (Ehn and Löfgren 2010)? Paying attention to inattention, we would argue, is important because it reminds us how we do not attend to our field sites as blank canvases, we attend with a history and a biography, and so do our interlocutors. It allows us to move out of the 'flat world of most sociological accounts of relationships and families to incorporate the kinds of emotional and relational dimensions that are meaningful in everyday life' (Smart 2007: 3), and which, as Sasha Roseneil (2009) observes, are too easy to gloss over in long-disenchanted societies currently in the grip of late modernity's individualization. What comes to matter to us, as this is shaped historically, culturally and politically, becomes visible through these oxymorons, and paying attention to these oxymorons, opens the path to a human psychology that can be reimagined as less individual and more social, relational and political (Lutz 2017: 181). The vital processes we describe become ways of understanding 'shared global predicaments', a kind of analytical solidarity, an identification of what lies between and connects one and one another and, as such, also present aspects of political and ethical life. They offer, as Catherine Lutz concludes, 'ways of talking about personhood as genuinely relational or transpersonal, beyond even what psychoanalytic theory offered' (ibid: 189).

Being inattentive, therefore, is itself an important part of fieldwork and everyday life. It is in these times of inattentiveness that we make our relatedness as persons visible to our interlocutors (whoever they may be), because we reveal ourselves to be human with an inner life. This in turn makes it possible to see interlocutors as having their own inner lives and allows us to forge relationships and shared understandings with them. It is arguably in moments of loss of focus that we might also learn anew, when gaze replaces learnt vision (Grasseni 2004), or tone replaces sounds, sensation replaces taste, and movement replaces gesture, that we are human otherwise. These are spaces and times which can connect us to some other, to more peripherally aware experiences and modes of knowledge. As such, these moments of translocation are perhaps less about absence, or of being elsewhere, and invoke instead a full engagement with the textures, tastes and sounds of the sensorium we were presented with: a book, a story, a plate of food. Being fully in the moment, we abandoned ourselves to those moments, letting ourselves be enraptured by flavours and recollections. By abandoning ourselves to those moments we found ourselves in touch with our field, the field of childhood and childhood experiences. This different plane of attention prompted recollections of our own experiences of childhood publics ('reading publics'), as well as foregrounding missing public discourses on 'parenting', namely those of love. In our text, love, hovers playfully, a sprite, between the lines.[5]

In writing about our experiences, we bracketed out the 'love' that we experienced both in the presence of the children and their families, as well as in the memories that these encounters evoked. The comforts of the home, of family members with each other, and with the ethnographer-stranger. The pleasures of eating, of drinking and of conversation, opportunities for connection and a momentary relief from drudgery and also, possibly, loneliness, and a reprieve from spending a whole day with children alone. A child's body, dangling off an adult frame, in an unambiguous and silent gesture of goodbye; and a suggestion that meaningful connections are not just the preserve of family life. Melissa's own reflections upon leaving Eleanor's home after that first visit, were that the family 'gave the impression of a close-knit, *loving* family. Dawn used a lot of *affectionate* nicknames when talking to both her daughter and husband' (Melissa's fieldnotes, 25 January 2015; emphasis added). Our own recollections are no less seeped in love.

So why is this sprite only presenting itself now, coaxed out of us by one of the editors, disrupting any possible conclusion to interpretation? Is it because, in its often idealised form, it clashes so spectacularly with its much messier lived experience? Or perhaps it is because, in terms of 'oxymorons', we would also need to talk about the 'hate' and 'cruelty', or, at the very least, 'ambivalence' (Parker 2005; Rose 2018; Robb 2020), and preferred instead to focus on an idiom, 'this parenting lark', which, like other idioms (Clarke 1989; Foss 2002), makes it possible to express darker, less socially acceptable emotions, in a palatable way? Could it be that anthropological fixation with reciprocity leaves no room for love (Venkatesan et al. 2011)? Conversely, might it be that the joy and pleasure that love (in its different guises) can bring about, appear suspicious in research and we are unsure what sort of knowledge they create? Or were we simply not paying attention in the analysis and writing of this chapter? Maybe love was another idiotic figure vying for our attention when we had simply had enough of suspending our habits of knowing and identification, too undone already to be undone any further?

We end this chapter with a recipe, as both an idiom of relatedness as well as that elusive epistemology for paying (in)attention. As argued in the text above, idioms, once recognised, become solidified, they become a recipe, a plate of food – a characteristic mode of expression, originally peripheral. Yet at the same time, and as our analysis of our ethnographic data suggest, these recipes and foods, solidified as they are in the present, on a page and on a plate, emerge from practising relatedness, infused with affect and loaded with memories. Somewhere there between the lines, if you look hard enough, and with a little bit of stirring, peripheral wisdom might start to emerge before your senses. Maybe even love.

—

A recipe for the minced meat sauce – as best as Christos could reconstruct it:
    Ingredients:
    Half a kilo thickly minced meat from beef rump (with fat).
    100ml olive oil.
    100ml tomato paste (highly condensed).
    One-two garlic cloves
    A large onion
    A glass of rosé wine (an old wine preferably)
    Five-six dried clove flowers
    One-two bay leaves
    A cinnamon stick
    Method:
    In a pot on high heat we put the oil and the garlic for two minutes, until the oil heats. We season the meat with black pepper. We add the minced meat, cloves and cinnamon in the olive oil and mix until the meat becomes pink-brown. We add the onion, mix gently and pour the wine. We let it boil for five minutes and add the bay leave and tomato paste and lower the heat significantly (keep it very low). We let it cook for about two hours.

Acknowledgements

Research for this paper was funded by European Research Council, ERC-StG-335514 to Dr. Sevasti-Melissa Nolas. We would like to thank Dr Rebecca Reynolds for her insightful and valuable feedback on an earlier draft of the paper, as well as the editors Francisco Martínez and Lili Di Puppo.

Notes

1 In this chapter we focus on Athens and London.
2 See also Nolas, Varvantakis and Aruldoss (2017) for kitchen table conversations and political talk.
3 Idioms of joy: 'over the moon'/'is someone peeling eggs for you?'('αυγά σου καθαρίζουν;'; idioms of falling in love: 'head over heels'/'s/he bit the sheet metal' ('δάγκωσε την λαμαρίνα'); idioms of weather: 'it's raining cats and dogs'/'it's raining chair legs'('βρέχει καρεκλοπόδαρα').
4 Callon and Law (2004) caution us not to treat our 'oxymorons' as fixed coordinates proposing instead that the oxymoron of 'absent/present' or 'present/absent' might be more productively engaged with as a permanent existential question in the understanding of the here-and-now.
5 Such is the 'crisis of childhood' that love rarely makes into public debates of young family life (for exceptions see Gerhardt (2003) and Gopnik (2017) psychoanalyst and developmental psychologist respectively). Earlier versions of this text wrestled with a number of technical terms (attachment, cultures of relatedness) in what we eventually settled to call relationships.

References

Back, L. 2012. Live sociology: Social research and its futures. *The Sociological Review* 60: 18–39.

Beer, W. 1983. *Househusbands: Men and Housework in American Families*. London: J.F. Bergin.

Behar, R. 1996. *The Vulnerable Observer: Anthropology That Breaks Your Heart*. Boston: Beacon Press.

Callon, M. and Law, J. 2004. Introduction: absence-presence, circulation, and encountering in complex space. *Environment and Planning D: Society and Space*, 22(3): 3–11.

Castañeda, C. 2002. *Figurations: Child, Bodies, Worlds*. Durham: Duke University Press.

Clarke, M.H. 1989. Nevra in a Greek village: Idiom, metaphor, symptom, or disorder? *Health Care for Women International* 10(2–3): 195–218.

Classen, C. 2005. *The Book of Touch*. London: Bloomsbury.

Cook, J. 2018. Paying attention to attention. *Anthropology of this Century* 22 (available at: http://aotcpress.com/articles/paying-attention-attention/)

Csordas, T. 1993. Somatic modes of attention. *Cultural Anthropology* 8 (2): 135–156.

Dewey, J. 2009. *Democracy and Education*. Lexington: Feather Trail Press.

Ehn, B. and E. Löfgren 2010. *The Secret World of Doing Nothing*. Berkeley: University of California Press.

Evans-Pritchard, E.E. 1937. *Witchcraft, Oracles, and Magic Among the Azande*. London: Clarendon.

Foss, N. 2002. Nerves in Northern Norway: The communication of emotions, illness experiences, and health-seeking behaviours. *Qualitative Health Research* 12 (2): 194–207.

Fraiberg, S., E. Adelson and V. Shapiro 1975. Ghosts in the nursery: A psychoanalytic approach to the problems of impaired infant-mother relationships. *Journal of American Academy of Child Psychiatry* 14 (3): 387–421.

Fraser, M., S. Kember and C. Lury 2005. Inventive life: Approaches to the new vitalism. *Theory, Culture & Society* 22 (1): 1–14.

Fraser, N. 1990. Rethinking the public sphere: A contribution to the critique of actually existing democracy'. *Social Text* 25/26: 56–80.

Gerhardt, S. 2003. *Why Love Matters*. East Sussex: Brunner-Routledge.

Giard, L. 1998. Doing-Cooking. In *The Practice of Everyday Life Volume 2: Living and Cooking*. M. de Certeau, L. Giard and P. Mayol (Eds.). Minneapolis: University of Minnesota Press.

Gillies, V. 2011. From function to competence: Engaging with the new politics of family. *Sociological Research Online* 16 (4): 1–11.

Gopnik, A. 2017. *The Gardener and the Carpenter: What the New Science of Child Development Tells Us About the Relationship Between Parents and Children*. London: Penguin.

Grasseni, C. 2004. Skilled vision. An apprenticeship in breeding aesthetics. *Social Anthropology* 12 (1): 41–55.

Hochschild, A.R. 1989. *The Second Shift: Working Parents and the Revolution at Home*. London: Penguin.

Horst, M. and Michael, M. 2011. On the shoulder of idiots: Re-thinking science communication as 'event'. *Science as Culture* 20(3): pp. 283–306.

Howes, D. 2003. *Sensual Relations: Engaging the Senses in Culture and Social Theory*. Ann Arbor: University of Michigan.

Ingold, T. 2000. *The Perception of the Environment:* London: Routledge.

Kehily, M. J. 2010. Childhood in crisis? Tracing the contours of 'crisis' and its impact upon contemporary parenting practices. *Media, Culture & Society* 32(2): 171–185.

Kildare, C.A. and W. Middlemiss 2017. Impact of parents' mobile device use on parent-child interaction: A literature review. *Computers in Human Behaviour* 75: 579–593.

King, L. 2016. Future citizens: Cultural and political conceptions of children in Britain, 1930s–1950s. *Twentieth Century British History* 27 (3): 389–411.

Kjørholt, A.T. 2013. Childhood as social investment, rights and the valuing of education. *Children & Society* 27 (4): 245–257.

Laplantine, F. 2015. *The Life of the Senses*. London: Bloomsbury.

Lareau, A. 2003. *Unequal Childhoods: Race, Class and Family Life*. Berkeley: University of California Press.

Latimer, J. and M. Miele 2013. Naturecultures? Science, affect and the non-human. *Theory, Culture & Society* 30 (7–8): 5–31.

Lee, E., J. Bristow, C. Faircloth and J. Macvarish 2014. *Parenting Culture Studies*. London: Palgrave Macmillan.

Lutz, C. 2017. What matters. *Cultural Anthropology* 32 (2): 181–191.

Michael, M. 2012. De-signing the object of sociology: toward an 'idiotic' methodology. *The Sociological Review* 60(S1): 166–183.

Miller, D. 2001. *The Dialectics of Shopping*. Chicago: University of Chicago Press.

Nolas, S.M. 2015. Chidren's participation, childhood publics and social change: A review. *Children & Society*, 29(2): 157–167.

Nolas, S-M., V. Aruldoss and C. Varvantakis 2018. Learning to listen: Exploring the idioms of childhood. *Sociological Research Online* 24 (3): 394–413.

Nolas, S.M. and C. Varvantakis 2019. Fieldnotes for amateurs. *Social Analysis* 63 (3): 130–148.

Nolas, S.-M., C. Varvantakis and V. Aruldoss 2017. Talking politics in everyday family life. *Contemporary Social Science* 12 (1): 68–83.

Oakley, A. 1974. *The Sociology of Housework*. Bristol: Policy Press.

Parker, R. 2005. *Torn in Two: The Experience of Maternal Ambivalence*. London: Virago.

Pink, S. 2004. *Home Truths: Gender, Domestic Objects and Everyday Life*. Oxford: Berg.

Pink, S. 2009. *Doing Sensory Ethnography*. London: Sage.

Robb, M. 2020. *Men, Masculinities and the Care of Children*. Palgrave Macmillan.

Rose, J. 2018. *Mothers: An Essay in Love and Cruelty*. London: Faber.

Roseneil, S. 2009. Haunting in an age of individualization. *European Societies* 11 (3): 411–430.

Sayer, A. 2011. *Why Things Matter to People*. Cambridge: Cambridge University Press.

Seremetakis, C.N. 1994. *The Senses Still: Perception and Memory as Material Culture in Modernity*. Chicago: University of Chicago Press.

Singh, I. 2004. Doing their jobs: Mothering with Ritalin in a culture of mother-blame. *Social Science and Medicine* 59 (6): 1193–1205.

Smart, C. 2007. *Personal Life*. Cambridge: Polity Press.

Stewart, K. 2007. *Ordinary Affects*. Durham: Duke University Press.

Stoller, P. 1997. *Sensuous Scholarship*. Philadelphia: University of Pennsylvania Press.

Sutton, D.E. 2006. *Remembrance of Repasts: An Anthropology of Food and Memory*. Oxford: Berg.

Thomson, R., L. Hadfield, M.J. Kehily and S. Sharpe 2012. Acting up and acting out: Encountering children in a longitudinal study of mothering. *Qualitative Research* 12 (2): 186–201.

Tsing, A.L. 2015. *The Mushroom at the End of the World: On the Possibility of Life in Capitalist Ruins*. Princeton: Princeton University Press.

Varvantakis, C. and S.-M. Nolas 2019. Metaphors we experiment with in multimodal ethnography. *International Journal of Social Research Methodologies* 22 (4): 365–378.

Venkatesan, S., J. Edwards, R. Willerslev, E. Povinelli and P. Mody 2011. The anthropological fixation with reciprocity leaves no room for love: 2009 meeting of the Group for Debates in Anthropological Theory. *Critique of Anthropology* 31 (3): 210–250.

Yiakoumaki, V. 2006. 'Local,' 'Ethnic,' and 'Rural' food: On the emergence of 'Cultural diversity' in *Greece since its integration in the European Union. Journal of Modern Greek Studies* 24 (2): 415–445.

Part II
Unlearning

4 Desiring the absence of knowledge

On knitting ethnography and navigating diaries

Lydia Maria Arantes

Ethnography usually means acquiring knowledge about a phenomenon with which you are not familiar. The ethnographer uses her status as a novice in the respective field in order to learn about the field through the eyes of the people who live (in) this field. To varying degrees, ethnographers are always novices in the fields they study. What happens if you are not? What happens if you are already native? Which questions can you ask, which conclusions can you draw? What kind of knowledge can you produce? What happens if you research knitting when you know how to knit yourself? What if the gap between what the ethnographer knows and what she can expect to learn in the field seems small, when the possible knowledge gain appears rather marginal and predictable? Questions like these silently accompanied me throughout my research on knitting in Austria. They are now setting the frame for this chapter in which I deal with this 'dilemma' in which I found myself. I also (re)consider different notions and facets of peripherality in the context of my research field as well as two methodological approaches which are themselves intertwined with each other.

Researching knitting

When thinking of a discipline that nowadays characterizes itself as scrutinising the everyday, the (seemingly) banal and the marginal – like European Ethnology (former *Volkskunde*) contemporarily does – it comes as a surprise that something everyday-like and seemingly banal such as knitting is not addressed. This was one of my starting points when I started my research on contemporary knitting (practices) in two Austrian regions in 2011. Soon I realized, however, that the discipline was not open at all for a field of research such as this one. It appeared too traditional and therefore reminded many of times when the discipline and its body of knowledge was instrumentalized (under the Nazi regime).[1] In some way, the latent fear was that 'returning to' traditions or traditional techniques meant providing a platform for neo-traditionalisms and hence enable a renewed instrumentalisation of the knowledge produced.

My knitters, however, were far away from knitting in order to keep 'traditions' in a *Volkskundian* sense alive. Their knitting had nothing to do with what these latent fears imagined. My question at the time was: 'Why should I not do research with contemporary knitters when they have nothing at all to do with the discipline's struggle with its own past?'[2] It had already taken me a long time to realise where the problem of legitimising this research field had come from, so when I finally became aware of it, I was not going to give in easily. This fight for legitimisation, however, left its traces throughout my research and the epistemological process itself. Just imagine being a young female researcher, trying to find her place in academia, researching a practice associated with femininity which on top of everything is seen as neither economically[3] nor academically valuable; a form of work which is not visible, a form of knowledge which is not recognised. In this regard, this research, its chosen field, the researcher and two of the methodological approaches used were located at different kinds of peripheries. It is, hence, from the margins of the discipline, of the methodological canon, of the everyday, of the economic sphere, etc. that this in itself peripheral – in the sense that it happens mostly invisibly behind closed doors – form of practical and bodily knowledge was studied. The only thing that – as one might argue – was located at some imagined centre, was the researcher's body as it was a body that appeared to know too much and therefore seemed unsuitable to play this epistemologically important role. I had to find ways of peripheralising it or at least being able to look at it from some kind of imagined periphery.

Other aspects which can and should be framed in terms of peripherality are my narrative writing style where the theoretical, the empirical and the methodological are intermingled and cannot always be told apart and my making the researcher's subject(ivity) – myself – visible throughout the texts I produce. Time and again, this approach tests the limits of what are legitimate writing styles and forms of representation within the Germanophone (European) Ethnological context.[4] While I would argue that the making visible of the researcher should ideally have epistemological benefits, this should not be the only motivation. To me, the question is not only what the epistemological surplus value of making the researcher visible is but which dimensions are hidden and unarticulated if we do not write ourselves into our texts. It is a question of transparency (I am aware that this concept is also politically charged nowadays but opt to use it nevertheless) as it is the researcher who brings various dimensions of the field together, who in essence 'constructs' the field and creates representations of it for academic purposes.

One might ask the question if it is these manifold peripheralities of the knitting research field which compelled me to use (perceived) 'peripheral' styles of representation. Do fields which are perceived to be on some sort of margin reproduce marginal(ised) ways of knowing and representing? Turning the question around: can the marginal only maintain its specific nature if we de-centralise our approaches instead of framing it with 'conventional' means? While I longed for acceptance within the discipline, I never felt the need to adopt 'conventional' representational styles, producing theory-overloaded and complexified texts hiding insecurities and intricacies which are bound to be part of any kind of research project. Sticking with the tensions, constantly challenging perceived boundaries, cultivating a feeling of lingering between various poles, enduring this (inner) turmoil which usually also pointed to inner logics within field and discipline and trying to make it academically productive – these forms of grappling with 'doing research' not only characterise my research (process) the best but also get very close to the notion of peripherality subscribed to in this volume: the peripheral as a(n important) stage on the path to knowing (more) and understanding, the peripheral as a snapshot of research-in-the-making and its various 'imperfections'.

For the reasons mentioned above, it comes as no surprise that my being native in my research field turned into a dilemma well beyond the search of analytical distance.[5] While I was aware that I probably only came across knitting as a valuable research field because I was myself part of the 'scene', this fact was not only a blessing but, to a much greater extent, a curse. Therefore, my difficulty was to 'distort reality' to some degree in order to create a fertile ground for insights to appear, for awareness to strike, for knowledge to happen.

Different from Jochen Bonz (2014), who, during the first phase of his research on Acid House, became a member of the subculture he studied and hence could reflect on the practices employed in order to become a knowing member of the club, so to speak, I cannot recall the time I was not a part of the 'needleworking subculture'. I was too young. Consequently, in a similar way that *going native* is seen as a danger to ethnographic research because the analytic distance has been lost, *being native* is equally problematic because the counterpoint that one could try to return to cannot even be fathomed. At various points during my research I therefore asked myself the same – classical – questions in different ways over and over again which all boil down to: how can I make the familiar strange?[6] How can I discern aspects immanent and specific to the field I am part of and to the technique I am capable of practising myself? And how can I perceive and reflect on the seemingly self-evident and communicate its specificities in, for my discipline in particular and the scientific community altogether, relevant terms?[7]

After I had completed an intensive and long-sought-for three-week research period (with a clear beginning and end as well as in a place a few hundred kilometres away from where I live and had done research up to then), I, however, made frustrated remarks about my approach. 'I still regret tremendously that I have not managed – either I forgot or (in hindsight the more plausible explanation) I did not find the right moment to ask – to get my research participants to get out their needles in my presence. I wish they would have explained what they do when they knit and how they go about it and what to pay attention to. To come closer to (bodily) experiential knowledge and its verbalisation would have been really interesting. However, I somehow could not get myself to ask for knitting to be explained to me.'[8] My research participants had known or quickly found out that I was an 'insider' myself and I knew that they knew. As the formulation of (socially) desired answers is undoubtedly a matter to be taken into consideration in any kind of research situation and even more so in ethnographic interviews, I was even more afraid at the time that the interview would have too obviously seemed like an exam (although – had I been brave enough to ask – it might not even have appeared as such). My knowing, my being part of the field prevented me from asking questions I would have thought to be very worthwhile.

Before I dwell on the role of my (enemy) body further below, I will briefly sketch out more details of the research and methodological context within which these questions arose and demanded reflection. In my elaborations in this chapter I mainly draw on my (research) diary, which kept me company throughout the whole research process and therefore is soaked in my subjectivity. This is also why I prefer the term *diary entry* over *fieldnote* because I view a diary to be more open to embrace feelings, irritations and aspects not yet seen as relevant to a particular research. It creates an intimate and private space, thus allowing for the subjectivity of the researcher to unfold completely and beyond control. In line with Devereux (1967), I see subjectivity 'in all observation as the royal road to an authentic, rather than fictitious, objectivity (…). When ignored, or warded off by means of countertransference resistances masquerading as methodology, these 'disturbances' become sources of uncontrolled and uncontrollable error, although (…) [w]hen treated as basic and characteristic data of behavioral science they are more valid and more productive of insight than any other type of datum' (Devereux 1967: XVII).

In order for subjectivity to unfold, it is therefore most fruitful to document *emergent processes and stages* of research instead of reconstructing and writing them up at a later point. Like Emerson, Fretz and Shaw, I see *doing* (fieldwork) and *writing* (diaries/ethnography) not as separate activities but rather 'as dialectically related, interdependent, and mutually constituitive [sic!] activities' (2011 [1995]: 19). Writing – even if it is 'only' a diary entry – is always already a form of interpretation, a form of rendering something meaningful in a specific cultural context. Ethnographic research and writing thus provokes interpretation and sense-making already in the time and place of the research process itself, even more so when inscribing it into the diary. My diary and its reflection hence posed one of the central research materials in the process of gathering, analysing and interpreting research experiences, which will also be illustrated thoroughly within the scope of this chapter.

My 'on and off research' was carried out in the region around Graz (southeast Austria) and the province of Vorarlberg (western Austria) during the years 2011–2013. Methodologically, I subscribed to an auto-ethnographic complementation of informal and ethnographic interviews as well as field observations. With varying degrees of intensity, I myself engaged in the practice studied (for a similar approach see contributions in Marchand 2010 or Ehn 2011) – and, from a contemporary standpoint, hence dived deeper into my 'nativeness'. At the time, the idea was to refine my skills of self-observation and self-questioning by reflectively immersing myself in the technique and developing an improved perceptual awareness and *kinesthetic empathy* (Sklar 1994). To a lesser degree I also analysed media discourses, historic (ego) documents and internet platforms/discourses. This was supposed to help establish a distance to my particular knitting field and hence also decentralize my (knitting knowing) body and self.

As has become clear, the body as research instrument and epistemological tool came to play a central role throughout this research. My body did not play solely a mediator's role; it did not only connect myself with my field. Much to the contrast, it also came to be perceived as a problem for my research.

More and more I realize that my body is turning into my own (research) enemy. I wish for another body at times. A body that cannot draw on previous experiences in needleworking or knitting, in order to be able to learn a sensory-bodily technique from scratch like Cristina Grasseni (2004) who learnt to develop a skilled vision of cows among Italian cattle breeders or Greg Downey (2007) who learnt to play capoeira among Brazilian capoeiristas or Erin O'Connor (2006) who learnt to become a proficient glassblower in a New York glass studio. Like them, I want to acquire new forms of bodily perception, I want to develop a novel understanding for materials and procedures. (…) I want to learn knitting from the beginning, I want to be able to reminisce about the time when I was a young schoolgirl learning the technique in school, with the help of my mother when continuing at home.

I do see it as a problem that my field is nothing special like capoeira, glassblowing or cattle-breeding. (…) I would like to learn in order to un-learn. I would like to attend knitting courses in order to be at least part of a learning setting, but I have trouble finding any. I can find quite a few sewing courses but no knitting courses. And the knitting groups I know of usually are for people 'in the know' and not for newcomers. This is probably very much related to knitting being part of the school curriculum (…). Also, knitting is not (anymore) organized in guilds; knitting knowledge is not privileged any more. One does not need a trade certificate in order to be eligible to sell knitted products. In a similar sense, there are also no knitting studios (at least none that I know of now) where I could observe master-apprentice-relationships and in doing so substitute my knowing body with the apprentice's not-knowing body.

The question prevails: How can I distance myself from embodied experience and knowledge?[9]

At this point it is worth mentioning that the question of knowing and unknowing knitting was not my central research question, even if for some time I did wish it was. As the diary entry above illustrates, I (painfully) realised that in the particular research constellation of me as a researcher, my pre-existing knitting knowledge and the (specific) Austrian context, where knitting is part of the curriculum, it was simply impossible to dwell on body knowledge-related issues. One of my main research questions – in light of the one-sided media discourses on the newly (re)discovered benefits of knitting and crafting altogether – therefore was which place knitting actually holds in the (everyday) lives of knitters. Furthermore, I was interested to find out to what extent it does lend itself to negotiating social and – not to forget – economic relations(hips) and in which way it does further the creation, transformation and transmission of aesthetic (body) knowledge.[10]

Teaching the known

At the time I was lamenting about my dear enemy-body, I did not realise that I had already had an important experience which would allow me a perspective liberated from my own (knitting) body – a perspective which would epistemologically de-centralise my body. Only much later, when starting to explicitly write up in 2014, I stumbled across a lengthy diary entry in which I talk about the intricacies of teaching my Brazilian sister-in-law how to knit. In doing so, I had managed to produce a possible setting for me to observe not-knowing-ness in this field of knitting without being aware of it. I know no one else who at her age (then thirty years old) had not had any contact with knitting needles or any other textile craft (technique) at all. So, this had been a once-in-a-lifetime chance for me – and I took it without knowing what would eventually come out of it.

Janaina came to visit us in December 2012 and stayed with me, my husband and our then one-and-a-half-year-old daughter for one month. Quite at the end of her stay she mentioned that she would like to learn knitting. We pondered which kind of piece would not only be technically manageable for a novice but could also be brought to completion before she would head back to Brazil. We agreed on a pair of knit-felt slippers. At this time, we had four days left, which is why we decided that each of us would knit one slipper. Before we could go about knitting the slippers, she had to learn the basics and practice in order to get familiar with the technique.

> Sunday evening, I taught her knitting. I took a pair of needles of size 3.5 and a remaining piece of yarn corresponding with this needle size. I tried explaining to and teaching her how stitches are cast on at first but I soon realized that it did not make sense under these specific circumstances. I wanted her to start knitting straight away and cast on the stitches myself. There I sat with my sister-in-law who had never ever knitted (nor crocheted) in her life and tried to teach her knitting in Portuguese. How do you say 'stitch' in Portuguese? How should I translate 'stitch'? How should I explain the difference between a knit and a purl stitch (literally 'right' and 'left' stitches in German)? I had never taught anyone how to knit, not even in my (German) mother tongue. It was a challenge, to say the least. We started with knit stitches; they are simpler, more intuitive, almost effortless. 'Poke the needle through the stitch, fetch the yarn and pull it back through the very same stitch. Then you may drop the stitch on the left-hand needle.' I was surprised how easy it was for her. She was a bit tense and did not know how tightly she was supposed to hold the knitting. She still had to find a middle way, somewhere between too tense – which results in her standing in her own light – and too loose – which leads to the knitting almost falling from her hands. She fetched the yarn and pulled the right-hand needle towards the right side and pulled the knitted stitch from the left-hand needle. These were two separate work steps at first. The more she knitted, the more fluent became her knitting movements. She fetched the yarn and – in the same work step – in which she pulled the yarn through the stitch she already pulled the knitted stitch from the left-hand needle. It did not seem so clumsy and jerky anymore. Instead of several small steps which were executed visibly separately one from another, now the operational steps merged, they became fluent movements. It was beautiful to be allowed to witness this.

I made her knit rows of knit stitches for quite a while, for two straight hours on that first evening of our knitting lessons. On Monday morning, after I had brought my daughter to day care, we continued. I showed her how to knit purl stitches. What distinguishes them from knit stitches is that the working thread is in front of the knitting and not behind. One pokes the stitch from the right-hand side – different from knitting a knit stitch where the working thread is behind the knitting and the loop is poked from the left-hand side in order to fetch the thread. This was going to be our distinctive feature, in the absence of a correct Portuguese terminology. Also, she had not knitted before so she could not have known herself how to call these two types of stitches. 'Thread behind the knitting' or 'the easier way to knit' referred to knit stitches (which look like Vs). 'Thread in front of the knitting' or 'the more complicated way to knit' referred to purl stitches (which look like knots or 'bolinhas' in Portuguese).

While I was picking up Marianna from day care, she practiced purl stitches and eventually knitted one row of knit and one row of purl stitches alternately, which results in the typical stockinette stitch pattern. It was going really well. The only problem was that at the end she had 38 stitches on her needles while we had started with only 20. In the course of knitting she had knitted a few stitches twice without realising it. This happens. Also, some holes were discernible where she occasionally must have dropped stitches. We smirked. However, we agreed that it was time to start with knitting the slippers. We started knitting one each at the same time. (…) I made it clear to her that she would have to make sure to count the stitches in order not to increase the number of stitches without realising it. I also suggested knitting more slowly and attentively so that mistakes could not sneak in as easily. We were supposed to decrease the number of stitches at the beginning and at the end of three rows throughout the process of knitting the whole slipper. I showed her how to do it once but I resorted to making the decreases myself each time it came to it. A few times I had to unravel a few stitches because she had too many stitches on her needle. Apart from that, her slipper was almost impeccable. The one or other stitch knitted through the back loop was noticeable but that was no problem, especially when bearing in mind that the knitted pieces would end up in the washing machine and be washed at 30°C in order to shrink by approximately 30 percent.

What stunned her most was the fact that by merely moving the needle through the stitch and back she would eventually create a slipper. She could hardly believe that a knitted piece merely consists of those tiny units, the stitches, and that something 'real' would eventually emerge from these petite actions. Not having been familiar with the technique, knitted things had seemed to point back to a technically complex origination process for her. Immersing herself into this field revealed the technique to be far less sophisticated than imagined. Knitting seemed so easy to her that we could hardly believe that she only had learnt how to hold and guide the needles a day before.[11]

Janaina's experience nicely illustrates Tim Ingold's idea of 'making as a way of weaving' which for him entails seeing *movement* (and not the idea) 'as truly generative of the object' (2000: 345); to be more precise: *rhythmical* movements. And '[f]or there to be rhythm, movement must be *felt*. Feeling lies in the coupling of movement and perception that, as we have seen, is the key to skilled practice.

(...) An operation like sawing a plank, for example, comprises not one movement but an ensemble of concurrent movements, both within and without the body' (Ingold 2011: 60, original emphasis).

Teaching my sister-in-law how to knit presented me with the unique opportunity to observe how bodily routine – acquired through repetition coupled with deliberately felt movements and consciously guided perception – eventually results in sequences of separate hand-arm movements and finger grips of varying pressure blending into each other and turning into one smooth stretch of movement, tension and release. Here, I deliberately choose 'movement' over 'moving' and 'grips' over 'gripping', abandoning the processual and usually rather smooth-appearing character of knitting because Janaina literally moved from one small movement – may it be poking the needle through a stitch, getting the right grip of the needle, or adjusting the yarn length on the left-hand index finger – to the next. Like Merleau-Ponty's famous account of the blind man's stick which 'has ceased to be an object for him' (1962: 143), the knitting needles gradually became a natural part of Janaina's body.[12] Observing the novice that she was not only made me aware of what it means to incorporate knitting needles into newly acquired bodily routines, it also allowed for seeing knitting happening through a spatiotemporal magnifying glass. It offered a view into something which in the case of more experienced knitters is usually concealed in and by the smoothness of the process. The movements were not only carried out more slowly and with tiny breaks in-between; they were also larger, her moving arms requiring more space than more experienced knitters' arms usually do.

Teaching knitting to a novice ultimately allowed for a shift in perspective; it allowed me to see the struggle (see also Arantes 2020b), the difficulty of dosing one's bodily forces in order to channel them into creating something and simultaneously learning to blend one movement into the other.[13] I am still amazed that we managed to knit and shrink the slippers, that they fit her feet and that she could ultimately take them home with her. I don't think she ever knitted again in Brazil. In this sense, she acquired (temporal) efficacy but no 'tradition', in a Maussian (1972 [1935]) sense. The quickly learnt automatic movements (not yet specifiable as 'technique') did not have enough time to sediment and become part of her body's movement repertoire, and ultimately transform into embodied knowledge.

Undoubtedly, the language barrier brought an extra level of complexity to this learning setting. It does, however, not diminish the theoretical conclusions drawn which I mentioned above. Unable to resort to technical terminology, we made up our own jargon. As it was soon clear that the knit stitch happened to come more intuitively to the novice knitter's body and the purl stitch came to be experienced as less natural, we framed the stitches by putting this body-movement and intuition-grounded perspective at the heart. Having to find a terminology in order to be able to talk about what we were doing allowed me to see more of the parameters involved in this ever-growing and transforming meshwork of yarn, needles and hands. Ultimately, it helped me see the complexity of the technique itself (anew) and made me also aware of the intricacies of transferring embodied knowledge in a specific learning setting.

Contrasting the known

While the fact that I was familiar with knitting supposedly prevented me from asking certain questions to 'my' knitters (see above), the following research situation is an example of the exact opposite. During the course of my research an informant suggested I also talk to a machine knitter because she thought it would bring an interesting perspective to my research. And right she was! One of my strongest memories of the encounter with the machine knitter, whom I will call Stefanie in this chapter, is the fact that I felt comfortable enough to ask her to dwell on all kinds of (technical) details regarding the use of the machine. No question remained unasked.

> She shows me what kinds of things she makes, how the (punch card) knitting machine works and which kind of yarn she uses. 100% merino wool (monofilament) whose wholesale price is quite inexpensive. The price amounts to roughly one Euro per 50g of wool [which is the referential unit among hand knitters, LMA]. The cones bear around 500g wool each and cost around 12–15 Euros. This makes machine knitting fairly profitable. She charges between ten and fifteen Euros per work hour including material. She needs roughly one and a half hours for the front part of a sweater, times four [a sleeve usually demands equally much yarn and time, LMA], results in 40–60 Euros per pullover.
>
> In the end, it is clear for me that the knitting machine ties the knitter spatially – even more as the sewing machine does, as the former is very heavy and fixed and therefore it would not make sense to transport it from one place to another just for fun. This is very different from knitting needles which do not require a spatial boundedness from the knitter. Machine knitting is, however, not easier at all than hand knitting with needles. Knowledge and skill are also of the essence. The machine does not knit on its own. It only does what one 'tells' it to do. Stefanie needs to move the carriage back and forth herself, row after row, and increase or decrease the number of stitches manually, if applicable. She needs to know how to transform a (new) pattern into a punch card in order to make the machine knit accordingly. The only difference from hand knitting is that it saves a lot of time. Using the machine, the knitter is much faster and can process much finer yarns, produce more delicate pieces without going crazy using needles of size number 2 or less. The machine still requires the knitter to have crafting/needleworking knowledge and an understanding of materials as well as the workings of the knit technique/procedure per se. But maybe on a different, more abstract level than when hand knitting?[14]

Up to that moment, I had not been able to talk about knowledge and skill because I could not or did not want to ask about it. In this sense, hand knitting knowledge as a concept to be considered had been absent while all of a sudden, out of all possible things, it was the machine – in many cultural-pessimistic settings framed as enemy of skill, as deliverer of and (therefore) metaphor for automatisation and deskilling – that brought aspects of knowledge and skill into my research. My desired absence of (hand knitting) knowledge had, in fact, made hand knitting knowledge among my informants invisible and hence prevented me from framing knitting as a knowledge practice. While aspects of knitting knowledge were abundant in the interviews and in my diary entries (in the emic perspective, we might say), I was unable to see it and to recognise it as viable aspects of (research on) knitting. In a sense, from an etic perspective, knitting 'knowledge' as a category had not existed[15] and therefore I also was unable to frame and analyse it as such.

In 2013, an ethno-psychoanalytical supervision group[16] was founded whom I have been a member of from the beginning. Working with the unconscious enables reflections of emotions and irritations which emerge during fieldwork and are subsequently articulated in the research diary, since it is emotions – before the mind may even be able to formulate certain questions – which point our attention to ruptures and hence are vital in the continuous reflection of the research field and process (Eisch-Angus 2019). Unravelling the emotions articulated within the research diary and thus making use of subjectivity 'as the royal road to an authentic, rather than fictitious, objectivity' (Devereux 1967: XVII), this methodological approach renders visible latent field and cultural logics. It is furthermore based on the premise that *Erkenntnis* (insight, awareness, knowledge) may only be possible via relations, via engaging with one another respectively (e.g. Bonz 2016), and leans on the theorem of transference and countertransference from the therapeutic setting, here transferred into a group setting.

In the Graz group, we freely associate research diary entries and help uncover hidden (symbolical) logics. This means that rather than interpreting the manifest content we look for what lies below the surface or between the lines of the respective texts. We try to identify relations(hips) among the actors and the scenes in which cultural meanings articulate themselves. In this sense, ethno-psychoanalytical group work draws on atmospherically present, diffusely articulating complexes of meaning distributed in scenic associative imageries. The group acts out emotions that were oppressed or rejected by researchers and/or researched and in doing so is capable of concretising dimensions that were formerly unconscious. This makes possible the thematisation of that which was repelled and ultimately might help dissolve associated perturbations and troubles (Arantes 2017: 67–69).

In this setting, it is not the field experience per se which is freely associated but *the experience of reading the diary text* framing and articulating a particular fieldwork scene. At the heart are, thus, elements which play an important role in the text, elements of field experiences which the researcher unconsciously identified as essential and therefore were given space in the diary entry. Ultimately, this methodological approach not only accounts for the long-demanded reflection of the researcher's positionality and subjectivity (Becker et al. 2013); it also helps refine and amplify epistemological means, as urged by Bourdieu (1999) in his warning of reflexivity turning into an end in itself. And, as when doing ethnography – unlike in any other kind of academic and scientific discipline – the epistemological process is part of the living process and, in this sense, partial subjectivity does not exist because ethnographic work demands the researcher and her body as a whole (Erdheim 1989), the consequence follows that these 'subjective' elements be made visible and ideally fruitful.

One day I brought with me an extended version of the diary entry above. In the group associations, the machine came to play a central role. It was perceived as an embodiment of visible/visualised work. Contrary to popular belief, the machine also demands knowledge and skill because machines do not knit by themselves either. The group discerned that my appreciation of the machine was quite strong. What is more, the necessary machine handling knowledge did not only seem to be described as on par with hand knitting knowledge. I appeared to have a much greater appreciation of machine handling knowledge than hand knitting knowledge. For the group it became clear that whoever is handling a machine would clearly be working, even more so because the machine would demand concentration and focus. In the case of hand knitting, one might be knitting and simultaneously be around and chat with other people (and hence not be 'working'). Hand knitters might knit at the dining table or on the sofa where I would usually (probably not coincidentally at all!) talk with my knitter informants. The machine (like Stefanie's machine), in contrast, would typically be found in some kind of workshop or studio, was the group's stance based on my diary entry. My argument developed from the group associations was that by way of the machine and its specific spatial boundedness – as it is not easily transportable – aspects of 'real' work are made visible and appreciable as such. 'Work' acquires its place and its value through the machine. In this sense, the machinal guarantees to render work visible and nameable as such. On a side note, this might be one reason why needlework is not perceived as 'work', neither by the knitters nor by the general public. The bourgeois separation of private and public spheres, of the cosy home taken care of by women and the (machinal) work or, say, (industrial) economic environment dominated by men at least reinforced if not implemented the association of the machine with 'real' work and the home with non-work.

The fact that the machine was so fascinating to me also points to my inexperience with handling knitting machines and, in a sense, also to a kind of insecurity linked with this inexperience. It was the first time, since I had started my research on knitting, that I had no idea about how what we were talking about works in a technical sense. I had longed for this kind of experience of difference for a long time. I had wanted to reach a place from where I could slowly develop a technical understanding. It was exactly this momentum which seemed to unsettle me to some extent, so that I resorted to citing and clutching to *numbers* of cones, prices, yarn lengths, etc. (which I did not emphasise much at all in my conversations with hand knitters), 'hard facts', in other words, and technical details in order to gain back a feeling of security, stability and control over the situation. Another aspect emerging from the group associations was that, in a similar vein, I overrated and even glorified that which seemed a bit mysterious to me, that which was unfamiliar to me. I overhyped the machine and its meaning and felt compelled to show respect to its handler. No other interview situation had made me describe it in such terms.

Upon reflection of my idealisation of the machine, I learned to recognise the hand knitting technique in a more nuanced light. Something that commonly – neither by the women, nor by the general public, and lastly nor by 'my' academic discipline – is framed as (expert) knowledge, all of a sudden could be recognized as such. I learned to look for and perceive the manifold forms of (knitting) knowledge and skills which had been part of my material all along.

Ethnography along the way

At the outset of this chapter stood my dilemma of doing research in a field I had been part of in many ways and the resulting desire to not know, to undo acquired knowledge. The two examples of teaching and contrasting the known illustrate two different ways of circumventing my own body (knowledge), thus amplifying my own ethnographic learning journey and the possibilities for more powerful ethnographic insights to strike. They also illustrate that a kind of identity split might occur throughout ethnographic research. The crafter wants to know more, she wants to refine her knitting skills and improve her technique. The researcher wishes she could put her (craft-body) knowledge on pause, she wants to (temporarily) undo her knowledge in order to develop an understanding anew. In doing so, my elaborations show the difficulties of the crafter-researcher simultaneously wanting to inhabit two different worlds, two different knowledge cultures or systems and ultimately also expose the central predicament of virtually all kinds of ethnographic research: that of establishing proximity while maintaining distance at the same time.

In the subtitle of this chapter I refer to Knitting Ethnography and Navigating Diaries. It might as well be ordered the other way around: Knitting Diaries and Navigating Ethnography. They are interchangeable because they both are equally valid forms to describe the research process I found myself in, as they point towards the way I navigated ethnographic research on knitting by way of keeping my diary. It might come as a surprise that the way I navigated research and diary-keeping has very much to do with me being a mother. Besides being a woman in a field associated with femininity, it was motherhood which strongly framed my research (practice) and established a common ground for shared experiences – in essence, for establishing personal and emotional proximity – with my knitter research participants who themselves were mostly mothers and even grandmothers.

I particularly remember two women approaching me and my research because they read about it in an article in a local newspaper. As they had been knitters for decades, they offered to share their experiences and knowledge with me and came to my place (on separate occasions). Angelika, a young-at-heart granny with then 50 years of knitting experience, had even brought a pair of knitted baby socks (as in the emails leading up to our encounter she had found out I had a baby daughter). We talked with each other sitting on the sofa while my (at that time) eight-month-old daughter was walking along the very same. Both women continuously tried to include the baby into our respective conversations by way of baby-appropriate comments. They did not only get to know me as a young researcher and crafter, they saw me as a mother.

In the same way that knitting works *along the way*, our speaking about knitting happened *along the way* and ultimately my ethnographic research and especially diary-writing happened *along the way* (Arantes 2017: 41–42), in the beginning mostly while breastfeeding. The intimate character of writing a diary was doubled (or much rather exponentiated) by the corporeal and emotional intimacy with my daughter whom I was nursing and cuddling. As I could not go anywhere, my thoughts were going places. While having had rejected smartphones for some time, I quickly came to integrate one and its useful swipe function into my (research) everyday life as a means of recording and essentially *holding on* to my thoughts, experiences, imaginations, feelings and memories. Most of the serendipitous thoughts happened to find their way into my mind when I was either breastfeeding, playing with my daughter in the sandbox, walking (home) with her (in the stroller) or when lying in bed with her. 'They come in moments of transitions (…) when my attention is far away from being directed towards my research. They don't come looking for me when I am in my office in the morning, neither when I am at home in the afternoon. They don't come when I sit still on my (office) chair. They overwhelm me when I am in movement.'[17] I learnt to be ready for (embracing) them.

The fact that insights appeared in spaces and times of transition also points us back to the subjectivity of (the) research(er). Subjectivity cannot be partialised; therefore, I am always a researcher, a crafter and a mother (and a wife – but this aspect did not have so much bearing in the context of what I am talking about in this particular chapter), and I am all of those things at the same time, wherever I am, whether I am in the field, at home or at my desk. As is visible in other diary entries and supervision group sessions,[18] motherhood not only forced me into carrying out research along the way but also to reflect on this very aspect. These reflections in turn made me realise the extent to which knitting (and ethnography!) is itself characterised by happening along the way and is itself linked with motherhood and the establishing and maintaining of (close) relationships, of proximity, of intimacy.

My writing about swiping while pushing the stroller or breastfeeding, in a couple of diary entries, instead of dwelling on the actual knitting research field, irritated a few members of the supervision group. Unravelling their reactions ultimately led us to conclude that my emphasising the swiping instead of knitting revealed parallels between these two phenomena. In essence, swiping came to be seen as a placeholder for knitting in these entries. One of the most striking insights linked to this conclusion was that the need to be constantly productive while at the same time not being 'really' working can be historically traced to the emergence of the bourgeois class and the separation into the economic world 'out there' and the private home 'inside', as referred to above.[19] In the same way that many (elderly) women still cannot be idle and thus keep needleworking along the way, I felt the need to use 'my time' when breastfeeding productively while I at the same time did not feel I was actually working (although I surely was).

Ethnographic fieldwork is something that is usually done along the way, while going about one's everyday life (albeit in a new setting maybe). The same goes for diary-keeping which in many cases happens at the backstage of ethnographic research and fieldwork. In my particular case, dwelling on issues in my diary that did not seem relevant at all at first and discussing this material in the supervision group eventually allowed me to carve out aspects about my particular research field which interestingly also point towards the many parallels of knitting and (my) ethnographic research (process). The same way that knitting happens along the way, swiping[20] happened literally on the way. The same way that knitting happens automatically most of the times, pushing the stroller happened automatically, allowing me to focus my attention on swiping down my thoughts. The same way that knitting does not interfere with other kinds of tasks (like looking after children or having a conversation), I integrated my research into my daily (family) life. The same way I was never proficient enough in knitting in order to anticipate how the knitting would exactly come out when finished (with respect to size, shape and texture), my diary-keeping intuitively froze aspects in time of which I had not yet known what (and if something academically worthwhile) would come out of them eventually. I was not only entangled in my knitting research, I was basically knitting my research, bit by bit, stitch after stitch.

Summing up the whole chapter, the diary accounts and my research trajectory altogether show that ethnographic research means enduring long phases of being in a state of limbo until eventually serendipitous happenings – e.g. my Brazilian visitor and her wish to learn knitting and a research participant's idea of me talking to a machine knitter – open up perspectives we could not have imagined in our wildest dreams. These accounts also make clear that even when serendipity does strike we are not always aware of it. We need time to ponder, time to digest, time to disentangle ourselves and put the puzzle together for it all to make sense in the end. This time is, however, not an empty time. Analyzing ethnographic data does not mean to wait for time to pass passively – until we suddenly know and understand. An active processing of the data 'in the workshop of our mind' (Bonz 2019: 172) is necessary. The task is to give contours to something that appears to be shapeless at first. All of this ultimately exemplifies that ethnographic research itself is a form of peripheral knowing if one allows it to.

Tying my chapter back to the overall theme of this volume, my accounts of tricky stages throughout my research on knitting include aspects of peripherality and peripheral methodologies on various levels and in many ways. I have specifically mentioned various loci of peripherality and my dilemma in navigating them, such as the rejection of the research field per se, the visualisation of the researcher's subjectivity in my writing, etc. While the ethno-psychoanalytical approach can be labelled as a form of peripheral methodology, as a form of making visible that which is latently there but (at first) resists articulation, research diary entries themselves might also be seen as a peripheral form of knowing.

Diaries include stages of knowledge acquisition, they illustrate the path from field experiences to academic knowledge and its legitimisation. The format of the diary – experienced as something private, proximate and intimate, not yet open for public inspection and therefore not yet forced to contain fully polished, analytically framed ideas and academic statements – allows for the thinking and articulating of intuitions, of hunches, of knowledge that does not seem like knowledge at all yet – or infra-knowledge, as the editors of this volume suggest. By way of the not-yet-fully-formulated, unfinished thoughts and the inclusion of dilemmas and inner conflicts, diaries are not only rich in atmosphere and tension. They eventually represent snapshots of a research's processuality and particularly upon inclusion in so-called polished texts make the epistemological journey retraceable (for the reader). They hold together snippets of knowledge which are present and which ultimately call for densification and analysis. In my case, the diary serves as a mediator between field and researcher, between researcher and academia, between theoretical concepts and research experiences, between the researcher's mind and her body. It holds a place for that which is present in traces, that is always already in the process, in the making, on the way to...

Acknowledgements

I would like to thank Jochen Bonz for guiding the supervision group with great empathy and passion over the last years. I have not only learned so much about my research field but also about myself as a researcher. I am also very grateful to the editors Francisco Martínez and Lili di Puppo for their insightful and valuable comments on earlier versions of this chapter.

Notes

1 I could find a couple of rather recent perspectives on knitting from a European-Ethnological perspective, like Greiner (2002, from a socio-historical perspective) or Bredereck (2014, focusing on group knitting). Much more literature was to be found in sociology (e.g. Turney 2009), design history (e.g. Hackney 2006), feminist studies (e.g. Myzelev 2009), to name a few. However, these disciplines do not have a problematic past like *Volkskunde* does in this regard.

2 Diary entry from 20.11.2014. All translations are made by the author.

3 Most of the knitters do not see knitting as labour in an economic sense, but rather as a hobby. Knitting, thus, mostly circulates in gift economies and can be framed as 'relational practice', knitted things as 'relational things' (Arantes 2020a), which means that the (imagined) preferences of recipients-to-be are usually present in the making process from the beginning, influencing the maker's choices regarding form, texture, colour etc. However, even in settings where knitting and textile crafts are sold, the (still mostly) women do not view it as work, a notion retraceable to the bourgeois idea of *Liebesarbeit* (labour of love), see Arantes (2017).

4 In many reviews of my book (Arantes 2017), which stems from my research on knitting, the issue is addressed whether or not the visibility of the researcher is appropriate. At least ever since the Writing Culture debate this matter does not seem to have to be dealt with very much in the Anglophone context. In the Germanophone setting, however, these issues still need addressing and demand constant justification.

5 I still remember how desperate I was to 'be able to get out of this actor-centred frog perspective. I am totally enchanted by things textile, things knitted more specifically. Analytic meta-perspective – where art thou?' I longed for being an (idealised) Social Anthropology PhD student who would head to her research field somewhere remote. I even thought it might be helpful to imagine being an extraterrestrial being or someone coming back from the future. I was hoping that 'thinking from these times and places' would help me frame worthwhile questions. What would researchers like these be interested in? Where would their curiosity be attracted to? (see diary entry from 14.11.2012)

6 This is no new issue in the field of anthropology and ethnography. However, I think there is a great difference between being 'only' part of a specific cultural context (e.g. when doing 'anthropology at home' like Daniel Miller in an English village [e.g. 2016] or in the context of European Ethnology, former *Volkskunde* altogether)

and on top of this also being part of the specific subculture, knowledge culture, etc. researched as it was in my case.

7 See diary entry from 21.04.2012, 23.04.2012.

8 Diary entry from 28.02.2013.

9 Based on diary entries from 06./07.04.2013, 11.04.2013, 13.10.2013. At the time I was also astonished that even not having practiced knitting for years, basic knitting knowledge was still there, readily available, like riding a bike. It was incapsulated in my body. The dilemma with my own still knowing body made me realise that certain types of knowledge sediment in the body. Certain residues of technical knowledge and skill persist over times of abstinence. And, after a short time of re-carrying out a long-paused technique, initial struggles and scepticism suddenly give way to a rather surprisingly routinised execution of the craft-body technique. (The hyphen ought to highlight that I am speaking of knitting as a craft and as a body technique. There is no craft technique without a body [technique]. It also ought to emphasize that craft is a specific form of body technique.) This whole issue surrounding the embodiedness of (certain types of) knowledge, however, opens up entirely different dimensions which I cannot dwell on in this chapter.

10 In the resulting book (Arantes 2017), I thus carve out sensory, material, mathematical, social, historical, economic and gender dimensions of a practice hitherto rather ignored in anthropological and, more specifically, European Ethnological research.

11 Diary entry from 08.01.2013.

12 'To get used to a hat, a car or a stick [or knitting needles, LMA] is to be transplanted into them, or conversely, to incorporate them into the bulk of our own body' (Merleau-Ponty 1962: 143).

13 Similarly, Gary Urton, who did research among Andean weavers, observed: 'Working with young girls proved to be a very good approach to studying weaving. Older women – the master weavers – have routinized and incorporated the rhythms of weaving so deeply into their bodily movements that it is difficult for them to articulate clearly the step-by-step movements, especially the regimes of counting, that are required to weave a particular design' (1997: 115).

14 Diary entry from 22.02.2013.

15 This also might have to do with the rejection of this research field in my home discipline.

16 Ethno-psychoanalytical methods can be seen as a form of peripheral methodology or a 'third space where experiences "from the margins" may be verbalized' (Sturm, Nadig and Moro 2011: 205). For an extensive overview of the particular ethno-psychoanalytical *supervision group* setting as methodological approach, see the recent comprehensive volume on *Ethnography and Interpretation* edited by Bonz et al. (2016, in German). For a recent overview of the ethno-psychoanalytic approach in general (in English), see Andersen (2018).

17 Diary entry from 17.07.2013.

18 E.g. supervision group session minutes from 11.12.2013 and diary entries from 17.07.2013 and 12.12.2013.

19 Particularly in the bourgeoisie, knitting was intended to happen within the context of the private home and was not allowed to bear any monetary value. It was relegated from a craft organised in guilds and carried out by men (as well) to the 'worthless' context of female, feminine, monotonous, continuous, demonstrative and unpaid labour of love. Though it is technically a mode of production, dominant collective cultural memories link knitting with the reproductive, emotionally stable and intimate sphere of the private home (see Arantes 2017).

20 On a side note concerning swiping and digitality in general, it is remarkable that knitting does not actually form an anti-pole to a time and world which has come to be characterised by the digital. On the contrary, the parallels go far beyond the ones connecting knitting and ethnography via the smartphone. The digital world more and more happens *along the way*; it can be integrated into the flows of the everyday life

without difficulties. Like knitting it is portable. We can carry the virtual world – stored in small gadgets – around with us. Like knitting, it provides a means of connecting people. Like knitting, it opens up spaces of communication and is itself a means of communication (Arantes 2017: 324–325).

References

Andersen, Linda Lundgaard (2018). Psychoanalytic Ethnography, in: Stamenova, Kalina; Hinshelwood, Robert D. (eds.): *Methods of Research into the Unconscious. Applying Psychoanalytic Ideas to Social Science*. Abingdon: Routledge, 241–255.

Arantes, Lydia Maria (2017). *Verstrickungen. Kulturanthropologische Perspektiven auf Stricken und Handarbeit*. Berlin: Panama.

Arantes, Lydia Maria (2020a). On knitted surfaces-in-the-making, in: Anusas, Mike; Simonetti, Cristián (eds.): *Surfaces. Transformations of Body, Materials and Earth*. London: Routledge, 152–166.

Arantes, Lydia Maria (2020b). Unraveling knitting. Form creation, relationality and the temporality of materials, in: *Journal of American Folklore* 133 (528): 193–204 (Special Issue *Dwelling in Craft*, edited by Anneli Palmsköld and Viveka Torell).

Becker, Brigitte et al. (2013). Die reflexive Couch, in: *Zeitschrift für Volkskunde* 109 (2): 181–203.

Bonz, Jochen (2014). Acid House als Grenze des praxeologischen Kulturverständnisses, in: Arantes, Lydia Maria; Rieger, Elisa (eds.): *Ethnographien der Sinne. Wahrnehmung und Methode in empirisch-kulturwissenschaftlichen Forschungen*. Bielefeld: transcript, 233–249.

Bonz, Jochen (2016). Subjektivität als intersubjektives Datum im ethnografischen Feldforschungsprozess, in: *Zeitschrift für Volkskunde* 112 (1): 19–36.

Bonz, Jochen (2019). Ethnografisches Feldforschen als Einbindung anderer und eigener Wahrnehmungen und Wahrnehmungsweisen in den Diskurs, in: *bricolage. Innsbrucker Zeitschrift für Europäische Ethnologie* 10: 163–184 (Theme *POP*, edited by Sandra Mauler, Elisabeth Waldhart and Jochen Bonz).

Bonz, Jochen, Marion Hamm, Katharina Eisch-Angus, Almut Sülzle (eds.) (2016). *Ethnografie und Deutung. Gruppensupervision als Methode reflexiven Forschens*. Wiesbaden: Springer VS, 241–258.

Bourdieu, Pierre (1999). Narzisstische Reflexivität und wissenschaftliche Reflexivität, in: Berg, Eberhard; Fuchs, Martin (eds.): *Kultur, soziale Praxis, Text. Die Krise der ethnographischen Repräsentation*. Frankfurt am Main: Suhrkamp, 365–374.

Bredereck, Maren (2014). *Warum treffen sich Menschen zum gemeinschaftlichen Handarbeiten? Stricken zwischen Individualisierung und Social Support*. Hamburg: Diplomica.

Devereux, Georges (1967). *From Anxiety to Method in the Behavioral Sciences*. The Hague; Paris: Mouton & Co.

Downey, Greg (2007). Seeing with a 'Sideways Glance'. Visuomotor 'Knowing' and the Plasticity of Perception, in: Harris, Mark (eds.): *Ways of Knowing. New Approaches in the Anthropology of Knowledge and Learning*. New York; Oxford: Berghahn, 222–241.

Eisch-Angus, Katharina (2019). *Absurde Angst. Narrationen der Sicherheitsgesellschaft*. Wiesbaden: Springer VS.

Emerson, Robert M., Rachel Fretz, Linda Shaw (2011 [1995]). *Writing Ethnographic Fieldnotes*. 2nd ed. Chicago: University of Chicago Press.

Ehn, Billy (2011). Doing-it-yourself. Autoethnography of manual work, in: *Ethnologia Europaea* 41 (1): 53–63.

Erdheim, Mario (1989). Subjektivität als Erkenntnismedium und ihre Krisen im Forschungsprozeß, in: Breyvogel, Wilfried (ed.): *Pädagogische Jugendforschung. Erkenntnisse und Perspektiven.* Opladen: Leske + Budrich, 81–93.

Grasseni, Cristina (2004). Skilled vision. An apprenticeship in breeding aesthetics, in: *Social Anthropology* 12 (1): 41–55.

Greiner, Sylvia (2002). *Kulturphänomen Stricken. Das Handstricken im sozialgeschichtlichen Kontext.* Weinstadt: Greiner.

Hackney, Fiona (2006). 'Use your hands for happiness'. Home craft and make-do-and-mend in British women's magazines in the 1920s and 1930s, in: *Journal of Design History* 19 (1): 23–38.

Ingold, Tim (2000). *The Perception of the Environment. Essays in Livelihood, Dwelling and Skill.* London: Routledge.

Ingold, Tim (2011). *Being Alive. Essays on Movement, Knowledge and Description.* London: Routledge.

Marchand, Trevor H.J. (2010). Making knowledge. Explorations of the indissoluble relation between mind, body and environment, in: *Journal of the Royal Anthropological Institute* 16 (s1): 1–21.

Mauss, Marcel (1972 [1935]). Die Techniken des Körpers [Les techniques du corps], in: König, René; Schmalfuß, Axel (eds.): *Kulturanthropologie.* Düsseldorf; Wien: Econ, 91–108.

Merleau-Ponty, Maurice (1962). *The Phenomenology of Perception.* London: Routledge.

Miller, Daniel (2016). *Social Media in an English Village.* London: UCL Press.

Myzelev, Alla (2009). Whip Your Hobby into Shape. Knitting, Feminism and Construction of Gender, in: *Textile. The Journal of Cloth and Culture* 7 (2): 148–163.

O'Connor, Erin (2006). Glassblowing tools. Extending the body towards practical knowledge and informing a social world, in: *Qualitative Sociology* 29: 177–193.

Sklar, Deirdre (1994). Can bodylore be brought to its senses? in: *Journal of American Folklore* 107 (423): 9–22.

Sturm, Gesine, Maya Nadig, Marie Rose Moro (2011). Current developments in French ethnopsychoanalysis, in: *Transcultural Psychiatry* 48 (3): 205–227.

Turney, Joanne (2009). *The Culture of Knitting.* Oxford: Berg.

Urton, Gary (1997). *The Social Life of Numbers. A Quechua Ontology of Numbers and Philosophy of Arithmetic.* Austin: University of Texas Press.

5 Acquiring mētis in ceramic production

Patterned changes and peripheral participation

Ewa Klekot

Eccentric knowledge

Centring a lump of clay on the wheel is a necessary foundation for all the throwing that is to come. It is also one of the most difficult tasks a pottery learner has to master: in pottery, the toughest technique to learn comes at the very beginning.[1] This technique involves positioning the centre of the lump on the rotation axis of the wheel and fixing the clay to the disc at the same time, as otherwise it will break off in throwing. Or, as described by American avant-garde artist and potter Mary Caroline Richards, the act which precedes all others on the potter's wheel entails 'bringing […] the clay into a spinning, unwobbling pivot, which will then be free to take innumerable shapes as potter and clay press against each other' (Richards 1989: 9). A clay lump is an irregular solid; for a pot to be thrown evenly, it should be made into a regular solid, usually a low cylinder, or a conical frustum, with its axis corresponding to the axis of revolution of the wheel. The potter should arrive at this shape by pressing with both hands the clay placed on a quickly revolving wheel. The pressure applied must be modified at all times according to the feeling she has of the moving solid's centre. This can be accomplished in a sequence of throwing a high cylinder, flattening it to the form of a thick disc, and then repeating the whole process while feeling the centre of the solid, its rotational axis, and trying to move it to the axis of the wheel. The stability and balance of the potter's body matched with the regular revolutions of the wheel are transmitted to the clay by pressure of her hands, constantly adjusted in time and strength according to the feedback received from the rotating wheel-cum-lump of clay aggregate. The potter detects the tendencies of clay as she works it up and down. With her hands wet and covered with silky, liquid slip, she fine-tunes her body position and hand pressure in time, following the propensities of the material. In the process, the co-dependent movements of the clay, the wheel and the potter's body produce what potentially can become a pot: a well-centred piece of clay. Mastering the skill of centring can take a long time: Richards herself[2] needed seven years before she knew how to centre any given piece of clay (ibid.: 11).

A snippet of an ethnography of centring in the opening of a contribution to a volume on the topic of peripheral wisdom (see the introduction) may have resulted in unintended irony. However, the knowledge gained by the ethnographer-potter is peripheral, or rather eccentric in the context of scientific discourse based on the Cartesian dichotomy between body and mind, where the notion of *skill* might produce a categorial monster: 'the term *skill* is a hybrid that refers both to concrete behaviour and to theories of action' (Toom 2012: 672). Even in somewhat scientific contexts the notion of skill has proved to be ambiguous and problematic, its definitions ranging from 'the human equivalent to a jig in wood-working or a mould in ceramics' or 'the ability to reduce error' (Adamson 2007: 73), to the readiness for active exploration of material contingencies and 'a way of being within society' (ibid.: 100). To be sure, in different understandings of the notion of skill questions that arise from knowledge used in centring accrue, but some of them seem unarticulated or absent. The relationality of this knowledge is one of its salient features, sometimes making it difficult for the potter to realise where it exactly resides: it seems to be distributed among the potter's body, the clay, and the wheel. 'The potter by being a potter, possesses a different body', says Lambros Malafouris in his theoretical study of material engagement, adding that 'the being of the potter is co-dependent and interweaved with the becoming of the pot'" (Malafouris 2013: 221, 210). Apparently, this wisdom can also be seen as not situated in a place, but contained in the engagement of the potter's body with the world here and now, distributed among the parties of the process. The knowledge of centring is eccentric.

In this chapter, I propose to associate this eccentric knowledge with the Greek term *mētis* which, according to Marcel Detienne and Jean-Pierre Vernant, signified 'a type of intelligence and of thought, a way of knowing ... applied to situations which are transient, shifting, disconcerting and ambiguous, situations which do not lend themselves to precise measurement, exact calculation or rigorous logic' (Detienne and Vernant 1991: 3–4). *Mētis* reads both symptoms and traces; it is the intelligence of a diagnostician as well as of a detective (cf. Ginzburg 1983). The knowledge and skills of craftspeople was one of the instances of *mētis*. Hence, in the first part of this chapter I will discuss *mētis* as a peripheral wisdom *par excellence*, not only because of its position within classical Greek thought (which served as a foundation of Western philosophy), but also because of the social peripherality of its bearers, as well as the peripherality of its methods, mostly due to its ineptitude for abstraction and its non-verbal character. Next I will focus on the acquiring of *mētis*, pointing to the fact that its development is mostly related to what Jean Lave and Etienne Wenger call 'legitimate peripheral participation' in communities of practice (1991). In the final part, I will contextualize *mētis* within the idea of the propensity of things as expressed by the Chinese notion of *Shi* [勢] (cf. Jullien 1995; Law and Lin 2017) and the conception of streams of materials, as proposed by Deleuze and Guattari (2011: 404–415) and brought to anthropology by Tim Ingold (2007, 2010).

My involvement in ceramic production itself could be seen as 'legitimately peripheral' when I practiced pottery as an amateur at a friend's ceramic design studio, as well as during research, which I carried out on industrial fine porcelain production in the factory in Ćmielów, Poland (Klekot 2017, 2018, 2020). Both in the studio and in the factory, I collaborated closely with ceramic designers, with whom I also co-taught courses for undergraduate students of design. In these circumstances, focused on the knowledge residing in the body, I was conducting research 'not only *of* the body in the sense of object, but also *from* the body, that is deploying the body as tool of inquiry and vector of knowledge' (Wacquant, after Samudra 2008: 666). My position of an anthropology teacher at a design school, of which peripheral participation in the school ceramic workshop has been part and parcel, provided yet another encouragement for developing tools for the discursive rendering of the processes in which I partake. These different pragmatics – ethnography and education – of the *discursification* of knowledge involved in ceramic production are behind the reflections and observations presented below.

Peripherality of mētis

French classicists Marcel Detienne and Jean-Pierre Vernant called *mētis* 'a cunning intelligence of the Greeks' and observed that it was the kind of knowledge neglected by Plato and Aristotle, and therefore for a long time absent from the Western philosophical reflection on cognition. In their opinion, neglecting *mētis* resulted from the radical dichotomy that informs Greek philosophy, namely the one between *being* and *becoming,* and the stress on *being* as a source of metaphysics and logic of identity. This dichotomy translated into a 'complete system of antinomies defining two mutually exclusive spheres of reality. On the one hand there is the sphere of being, of the one, of the unchanging, of the limited, of true and definite knowledge; on the other, the sphere of becoming, of the multiple, the unstable and the unlimited, of oblique and changeable opinion' (Detienne and Vernant 1991: 5). In Aristotle, the dichotomy of being and becoming is expressed as two parts of the rational soul when it comes to knowledge: the first (*to epistêmonikon*) is used for understanding things which do not admit to change, whereas the second (*to logistikon*) is used for considering things which are prone to change. Knowledge applied to things that admit change and which could either exist or not, brought to existence precisely with the use of this knowledge, called *technê,* can itself be expressed in irreversible and precise rules, regulations and statements. According to Aristotle, *technê* determines the true and the false in doing. In its most strict sense, it is based on logical deduction from basic rules and the person who has *technê* goes beyond experience to universal judgement (Parry 2014). Those knowledgeable in *technê* were, in Aristotle's opinion, wiser than the 'mere artisans', because they knew 'the cause, the reasons that things are to be done' (also in Parry 2014: 23); and to name the *mētis* bearers – 'mere artisans' – he abandoned the word *demioergos,* traditionally used for the craftsman, and used *cheirotechnês* (hand-worker) instead (Sennett 2008: 23).

By contrast, *mētis* is characterised precisely by the way it operates in continuous oscillation between the two opposite poles of *being* and *becoming.* Because 'when the individual who is endowed with *mētis,* be he a god or a man, is confronted with multiple, changing reality whose limitless polymorphic powers render it almost impossible to size, he can only dominate it – that is to say enclose it within the limits of a single, unchangeable form within his control – if he proves himself to be even more multiple, more mobile, more polyvalent than his adversary' (Detienne and Vernant 1991: 5). According to Detienne and Vernat, *mētis* was the ability of coping with any surprising situation, 'intelligence which, instead of contemplating unchanging essences, is directly involved with difficulties of practical life with all its risks, confronted with a world of hostile forces which are disturbing because they are always changing and ambiguous' (ibid. 1991: 44).

In classical Greek language *mētis* meant not only a particular kind of knowledge but also the ability to advise based on this knowledge: *meteita* – a sagacious advisor – is what Zeus is called by Homer. Hesiod speaks of an Oceanid of the name Mētis who was the first wife of Zeus, married when his Olympian sister and further spouse Hera was still imprisoned in the entrails of their father Cronus. As a matter of fact, it was Mētis who gave Cronus the vomit-provoking remedy that made him release all his previously eaten children back into the world. Subsequently, Zeus and his siblings overthrew their cruel father and seized power. However, fearing that his own son by Mētis would in turn overthrow him and the Olympians, Zeus asked Mētis to change into a fly (like other marine deities, she was endowed with the power of metamorphosis) and swallowed her. Mētis was pregnant, so Zeus himself had to give birth to Athena – from his head. Mētis therefore ceased to exist separately from Zeus, being reduced to the role of his (literally) embodied knowledge. That is why *mētis* always resides in the body: immediate and changeable. Mētis, a daughter of Okeanos and a cunning goddess who made the devoured children of Cronus flow back to the world in the liquids of his stomach, was also a patron of fortune-telling from water (ibid: 11, 20, esp. 57–129).

Zeus, therefore, won his Olympian power not by force, but by a cunning trick of Mētis, only to get hold of *mētis* by another cunning trick played on her – or rather, from her perspective, by a perfidious trap. Certain aspects of *mētis* can be seen as cheating, treachery, or a trap by which the weaker party, against every expectation, finds the resources for putting the stronger at their mercy and changing power relations. Shifting loyalties, cheating and treachery are 'the despised weapons of women and cowards' (ibid. 1991: 13). Plato in the *Laws* condemns hunting with nets and traps (yet another form of *mētis* (ibid. 1991: 27–54), 'because all these techniques foster the qualities of cunning and duplicity which are diametrically opposed to the virtues that the city of the *Laws* demanded from its citizens' (ibid. 1991: 33). However, it was not the virtues of the polis that granted Zeus his sovereign power but *mētis,* for 'whatever the strength of a man or a god, there always comes a time when he confronts one stronger than himself' (ibid. 1991: 13). As Homer says in the Iliad, 'It is through *mētis* rather than through strength that the wood-cutter shows his worth. It is through *mētis* that the helmsman guides the speeding vessel over the wine-dark sea despite the wind' (also quoted in Detienne and Vernant 1991: 12). There is an opposition between using one's strength and depending on *mētis*: *mētis* is the intelligence of those who know that they are too weak and vulnerable to confront their adversary head-on. The condition of being vulnerable to others is what *mētis* is built upon.

Master potter Benedict Fludd, a protagonist in *The Children's Book* by A.S. Byatt, observes that failure with clay, when it happens, is particularly spectacular and almost complete. 'You are subject to the elements. ... Any one of the old four – earth, air, fire, water – can betray you and melt, or burst, or shatter

– months of work into dust and ashes and spitting steam. ... You need to know how to play with what chance will do to your lovingly constructed surfaces in the heat of the kiln' (Byatt 2010: 131). For the ancient Greeks there were many activities in which one had to learn to engage powerful, antagonistic forces, and make use of them despite themselves 'to implement the plan in mind by some unexpected, devious means: they include ... the sleights of hand and trade secrets which give craftsmen their control over material which is more or less intractable to their design' (Detienne and Vernant 1991: 47). It is therefore not through their strength that potters show their worth, but through *mētis,* the crafty intelligence.[3] *Mētis* has also been interpreted as a female type of knowledge: kitchen ways, grandmothers' wisdom, midwives' experience, as well as all the invisible from the outside but indispensable home methods, which ascertain that the world keeps going. These skills manifest themselves in the most mundane levels of the every-day, always variable, temporary, logically inconsistent, and located in the body (Dolmage 2014: 193–296). Women are at the margin of the polis; as are craftspeople, in their majority *metics,* freedmen or slaves, who occupy peripheral positions and are not expected to take part in the civic activities of the polis. They know too well that in the struggle with materials, what counts is not heroic resistance but crafty cunning and persistence which allow for evading open battle. The lower positioning of *mētis* in the social hierarchy of knowledges has also been expressed in Frederick Taylor's theory of scientific management, where the workers were represented as the body of the factory submitted to its mind, or the management (cf. Klekot 2020). In *Seeing like a state* by James C. Scott (1998), *mētis,* understood as knowledge insusceptible to normalisations, represents traditional local wisdom and embodied knowledge practiced for generations in particular places by particular communities, as opposed to the knowledge promoted and enforced by the modern and modernising bureaucracy of a nation-state, or colonial empire. It is the knowledge of the subalterns/peasants.[4]

'Intelligence which operates in the world of becoming, in circumstances of conflict' and shifting, transient situations, requiring 'to foresee the unforeseeable' (Detienne and Vernant 1991: 44), has to be a situated knowledge. *Mētis* is both acquired and applied in direct contact with the concrete and diverse fragments of material reality accessible to its practitioner here and now. It is these encounters that define its methods. To know when the clay is ready and the kneading should be finished, or what it means that the glaze is mixed 'well enough' to be poured over a piece of ceramic, the potter attends to the changes (which she can recognise from her previous experiences of kneading and glazing) already transformed by the current encounter. Any new batch of substance works slightly differently and *mētis* means to understand that changeability is an intrinsic part of identity. Therefore, *mētis* means 'thinking less about finding definite causes, tracing networks, or finding theoretical and predictive models; and instead feeling, detecting and following the local and immanent tendencies of things as these pulse and flow' (Law and Lin 2017: 15), or as they become.

Mētis is embedded in the complexity of the direct bodily experience of the concrete encounter, which makes it change all the time, because 'we are contaminated by our encounters' (Tsing 2015: 27). The encounter engages all the senses, including the proprioception (or *kinesthesia*), and other ways that the living body is engaged in the process of world-making, of which world-knowing is a part. While 'centering the clay, and then ... opening it and pulling up the walls of the cylinder [Robert Turner] was not looking at the clay. He had his ear to it. He was listening. "It is breathing," he said; and then he filled it with air' (Richards 1989: 13). This complex concreteness is both the power of *mētis* and its limitation, for it results in the 'inability of using the powerful and terrible tool of abstraction' (Ginzburg 1983: 85). To abstract from the concreteness of the encounter is to betray this complexity. To abstract does not mean just to put Cartesian *res cogitans* in the centre and to get rid of *res extensa*, this untrustworthy, watery, contingent substance that, at the end of the day, results peripheral to the knowledge of truth; 'to abstract means to tear the body in pieces rather than merely to leave it behind' (Serres 2016: 26).

The *mētis'* resistance to abstraction encompasses even the most 'natural' human way of abstracting – language. Researching *mētis* therefore poses an ethnographic problem of translating direct experiential data into language, the medium of academia (cf. Samudra 2008). Thus, the intention of understanding the potter's actions aims at rendering into discourse exactly those practices she would consider verbally inexpressible. The logocentric concept of knowledge and inherently discursive character of modern scholarship has led to conflating bodily, non-verbal knowledge with the unconscious, as Jaida Kim Samudra rightly observed, while 'one can be a fully conscious actor in the body without necessarily encoding the meaning of one's actions in words' (ibid.: 666). To be consciously in the body does not mean, as Richard Sennett suggests in his acclaimed book *The Craftsman*, that one has to *think about* what the body is doing[5] – on the contrary, one has to *think with* the body. This is *mētis:* knowledge which is fully conscious but predominantly non-verbal, communicated and understood *from* the body.

Through situated learning it is possible to build up somatic awareness which 'enables us to consciously hone the accuracy and coordination of our practices', as well as to 'derive embodied understandings of the know-how displayed by others' (Marchand 2008: 261).[6] Watching the complicated choreography of glazing in the porcelain factory (cf. Klekot 2020), I always used to marvel at the same point: when a piece was being submerged in the creamy glaze. I knew that inside the depths of the basin containing glaze the hand of the glazer loosens its grip and for a fraction of a second lets the dish freely plunge so that the glaze can cover its whole surface. I always felt her movements in my body, and was almost able to feel the thickness of the glaze on my skin, although I would never dream of executing the whole glazing choreography with similar dexterity. On some occasions, I could not help putting my hand into the basin to have the real feel of the glaze. The situated character of *mētis* prevents also its further abstractions, including into mathematics, the universalising language of modern science. This makes it also non-scalable, in contrast to fully scalable *technê*. Non-scalability automatically puts it on the peripheries of the modern concept of knowledge: it has no applicability for expansion (cf. Scott 1998). 'Scalability requires that project elements be oblivious to the indeterminacies of encounter ... [it] banishes meaningful diversity, that is diversity that might change things' (Tsing 2015: 38); and it is exactly this diversity that is at the core of *mētis*.

Crafty intelligence of mētis

First year undergraduate students of design do not learn throwing: they attend only a six-week crash course in ceramics and what they make is porcelain casts. The task consists of preparing a design, making a model (bearing in mind the shrinkage of porcelain in firing), then executing a plaster mould according to the model. Next then the casts are normally fired twice and glazed, and optionally decorated. The students learn hands-on at all the stages of porcelain production, with the instructor and two assistants, in a workshop where their senior colleagues also work on their different projects. The workshop is open from 8a.m. to 8 p.m. on weekdays. One of the first things students realise is the temporality of making ceramics, which to many of them comes as a surprise. When during my anthropology class on the social construction of time they are asked what cannot be sped up, quite a few immediately answer that drying a slip-cast pot will always take as long as it takes.

Casting porcelain means pouring in the slip, filling the mould up to the rim, adding some more after a while, once the porcelain is settled. Then you wait again and pour it out, leaving the mould upside down for all the slip to flow out, except for the thin layer of porcelain "skin" that sticks to the walls of the mould because of the hygroscopic properties of plaster. Then you wait again, much longer, for the cast to harden enough to be taken out of the mould. Once it has been removed from its plaster shell and cleaned (and not crushed in cleaning), it has to dry before it is put to the first firing. When they arrive at the stage of cast making, the students come to the workshop every now and then, check their casts, take them out, leave, come back, re-shelf them from the 'drying stuff' to the 'ready for the first firing stuff', and come back later, to do something else. Only at the beginning do they ask the instructor 'when': 'When should I pour it out? When will it dry?' They quickly learn, however, that the only question that makes sense is: 'Is it now? or should I wait?'

Mētis means waiting, attentively and for as long as the waiting needs to take, in 'continuous concentration on activity that is in progress'. It also means knowing the proper moment to act, 'as prompt as the opportunity that it must seize on the wing, not allowing it to pass'. However, in spite of its swift response, 'the operation of *mētis* is diametrically opposed to that of impulsiveness. … the man of *mētis* … displays at the same time a greater grip of the present where nothing escapes him, more awareness of the future, several aspects of which he has already manipulated, and richer experience accumulated from the past' (Detienne and Vernant 1991: 14–15). When the forms come out of the kiln, they are glazed and dried, which means more waiting, before they can be fired for a second time. Some of them will collapse in the kiln, while others will come out deformed. In the majority of cases, this will happen because porcelain remembers the way a cast was handled all the way from the mould until it dries. Any pressure on its soft, humid and flexible body, any bending or flopping of a wall – still too wet to keep the shape outside of the mould – which was hastily put back into place for the form to look as if nothing had happened: all this gets stored in the material's memory. When the temperature reaches over 1200°C in the second firing, the heat forces the porcelain ware to remind its maker of all the careless touch it had suffered.

Situated knowledge is mostly acquired under conditions of 'legitimate peripheral participation', by which the authors of the term, Jean Lave and Eugen Wenger, mean engagement in social practice that entails learning as an integral constituent, but is itself 'far more than just a process of learning on the part of the newcomers. It is a reciprocal relation between persons and practice' (Lave and Wenger 1991: 116). 'Peripheral' refers to the intensity of the engagement, and not to the position in space versus a supposed centre of the community of practice: 'peripherality suggests an opening, a way of gaining access to sources for understanding through growing involvement' (ibid.: 37), and is coupled with 'full'. Moving out of peripherality towards full participation is related to taking responsibility and risk. Such conditions are usually associated with apprentice-style learning, both in traditional apprenticeship structures of workshops lead by a master craftsman, and in vocational courses and schooling.

Trevor Marchand, writing on acquiring craft skills and competences, touched upon the question of communication between the instructor and the learner. Marchand suggests that 'practice communicates', while skilled actions could be 'parsed' like sentences in language, and in consequence 'acquired' as 'motor-based mental representations'. Such representations 'may be re-combined either to mimic or to generate improvised expressions of practice-based knowledge. ... Parsing a movement generally relies on watching and observing it' (Marchand 2008: 263). Using language as a structural model for non-verbal communication taking place in the process of the transmission of craft skills, as Marchand does, can be misleading, especially if one is to agree with the observation made by Thorsten Gieser that 'we usually perceive not just movements, but actions, that is movements with intentions' (Gieser 2008: 313). Fortunately, Marchand is aware of possible misinterpretations of the language model in the context of bodily practices by those conflating somatic knowledge with the unconscious. 'The content of kinaesthetic interpretation", he writes, "is not a semantic depiction of what that practice *means* but a motor-based one describing the *sense* and *feeling* of doing it' (Marchand 2008: 264). Within the community of practice speech is used both for instructions and corrections, as well as in narrating, but knowledge is communicated, understood and transmitted largely without words, through showing and observing, mimesis and repeated practice. Gieser (2008) points at the importance of empathy in this process, proposing to see it as something that connects the movement of two people involved in the transmission of embodied skills.

When I started learning the technique of throwing on the wheel, nobody told me that centring consisted of placing the centre of the lump on the axis of rotation of the disc. I was told, however, that centring was difficult; so difficult that in crash courses in ceramics or during classes with children, it is the potter who does the centring for everybody. I started learning by preparing 'proper lumps': I had been told to make balls that would more or less fit between my two hands. I observed the teacher, as I did not really grasp what the balls were for or how I was to make them 'proper'. She would toss around a ball of clay and pat it with both hands each time that it would land in one of her palms. Mimicking her, I tried to make the surface of my lumps as smooth and even as possible. This was most likely because I thought that they would become more 'proper' if I made them closer to regular spheres. But trying to smooth out the little bumps and bulges with fingers is not a good strategy, because some air usually gets sealed under the clay's surface. Even if these trapped air bubbles do not produce an immediate effect during centring or throwing, they can bring about imbalance and weaken the form until it gets torn off, ultimately making the piece crack during firing in the kiln. The lump should acquire its roundness as it is tossed and rolled between the potter's hands. I was sure to imitate the teacher, but (precisely according to the pattern pointed at by Gieser [2008: 313]), I focused my attention on her actions, or movement-cum-intention units, not on the exact sequence of her movements. In the meantime, my knowledge of her intentions was limited to what she had explicitly stated at the beginning of the task: we were to make 'proper' lumps for our first throwing class. I had to understand on my own that a ball does not mean a smooth, regular, round surface, as of an inflatable ball, or a globe, but a solid. It was not about the sight, but about weight, balance, gravity centre. It was less about the visual cognition, and much more about somatic awareness, or, as Trevor Marchand has it, 'motor-based understanding' (Marchand 2008).

During the entire process of throwing the potter constantly reaches into a bowl with water to dunk her hand and moisten the clay. As she does so, the clay becomes more susceptible to the workings of her hands and more silky to the touch. To me, the silky touch of wet clay used in the first stages of throwing makes for so enjoyable a sensation that I could just easily keep adding more and more water. But in doing so, I would only be inviting the ultimate failure, because if the clay in throwing becomes too wet, the walls already formed can easily collapse. When the pleasure of touch for pleasure's sake replaces the attentiveness, the potter, disconnecting from her *mētis*, loses touch with the potentiality of the pot revolving on the wheel. Having centred the clay, the potter starts throwing by opening it, which means pressing in the rotating lump at its centre with one or two fingers. Under pressure, the clay recedes to the sides and a cavity forms in the middle. Then with only two fingers – one working from the inside and the other from outside – the potter starts pulling the walls up. 'When we are working on the potter's wheel, we are touching the clay at only one point; and yet, as the pot turns through our fingers, the whole is being affected, and we have an experience of this wholeness', Richards observes (1989: 24). The entire form develops between the potter's fingers following the material.

Mētis: *The propensities of ten thousand things*

It is to the concept of 'following the material' that Tim Ingold (2007) resorts when he builds up his arguments against the hylomorphic concept of making and the idea of 'materiality' as undifferentiated, inert matter of which 'material things' are made. He proposes 'an ontology that assigns primacy to the processes of formation as against their final products, and to the flows and transformations of materials as against states of matter' (Ingold 2010: 92). With its focus on closely following changes in the immediate environment and reacting for change with a change *mētis* is *par excellence* the knowledge of non-hylomorphic making – again, in contrast with Aristotle's ideas. 'To create anything, Aristotle reasoned, you have to bring together an agent with a particular design in mind, while matter, thus rendered passive and inert, became that which was imposed upon' (ibid.). Thus, instead of resonating with classical Greek ontology founded on the concept of being as an ideal which does not admit to change, *mētis* seems closer to the classical Chinese ontology of being as ebbs and flows of the *Dao* 'which never becomes immobilized in any one disposition' and 'remains forever inexhaustible' (Jullien 1995: 34), making the world a 'constantly changing but non-dualist *tides-cape* ... a patterned but never exactly repeating movement of flows and counter-flow' (Law and Lin 2017: 9).

Mētis, the crafty intelligence, presents itself on the one hand as bodily, sit-uated, alien to any abstraction, normalisation, scalability, or universalisation. On the other hand, it appears distributed, relational and dynamic because it is always responding to a change of some sort: be it a change in conditions, mate-rial, or the performer's body. The processual character of *mētis* resonates both with Ingold's concept of the streams of materials and with the concept of ebbs and flows because of the inherent movement inscribed in them: the movement that produces variations to which *mētis* is a knowledgeable response. 'It would be useless to say that metallurgy is a science because it discovers constant laws', Deleuze and Guattari write in their *Treatise on Nomadology*, 'for example, the melting point of a metal at all times and all places. For metallurgy is insepara-ble from several lines of variation: variation between meteorites and indige-nous metals; variation between ores and proportions of metal; variation between alloys, natural and artificial; variation between the qualities that make a given operation possible, or that result from a given operation ...' (Deleuze and Guat-tari 2011: 405). Ebbs and flows produce variations because the movements are continuous, but the circumstances never repeat themselves. In the world of var-iation, change and diversity become inscribed in identity, so the divide between homogeneity and heterogeneity ceases to make sense, and things are neither pure nor impure (cf. Law and Lin 2017: 6).

Flow, or flux in relation to the question of homogeneity/heterogeneity division, come out also in Ingold's thinking. The knowledge of working wood along the grain is one of the instants of human movement with the streams of materials that Ingold (2010) quotes. In another place (Ingold 2007), however, he extends the metaphor outside of the sphere of craft into the human condition in general, stating that human beings, like all other creatures, 'swim in an ocean of materials. Once we acknowledge our immersion, what this ocean reveals to us is not the bland homogeneity of different shades of matter but a flux in which materials of the most diverse kinds – through processes of admixture and distillation, of coag-ulation and dispersal, and of evaporation and precipitation – undergo continual generation and transformation' (ibid.: 7).

Mētis operates in a world conceived as continual generation and trans-formation by following its rules, as 'victory over a shifting reality whose continuous metamorphoses make it almost impossible to grasp, can only be won through an even greater degree of mobility, an even greater power of transformation' (Detienne and Vernant 1991: 20). However, in their vision of the constantly transforming world, both Ingold and the Greeks (at least as presented by Detienne and Vernant) focus more on accommodating surprise, than on admitting the existence of any patterns of change, which are part and parcel of the world of ebbs and flows. As social scientists John Law and Wen-yuan Lin write, 'sensibility to patterned change' of ebb and flow is crucial to understanding the Chinese concept of *shi,* or propensity, which means '(local) disposition, direction of movement or change, predilection, inclination, all within non-dualist immanent and non-repeating ebb and flow changes that tend to fill and empty, grow and contract, or expand and withdraw' (Law and Lin 2017: 9).

The knowledge built on this concept of patterned change resembles *mētis* in its preference of manipulation over brute force and ploys over heroic battle. The situated character of *mētis* seems to correspond with the fact that '*shi* is traced *locally* by examining and sensing circumstances without being pinned to claims about larger causal schemes' (ibid.: 10). The non-dualist idea of ebbs and flows, where the opposites are rooted in one another, together with a *shi*-based ontology where 'a thing does not exist in itself but in the propensities of ten thousand things' (Law, Lin 2017: 6, n. 17); the streams of materials which we can follow, and the ocean of materials in which we are immersed; the 'deterritorialized matter in variation' (Deleuze and Guattari 2011: 407), and, finally, the Greek *mētis* itself add to a framework, or rather network of concepts, metaphors, aphorisms and paradoxes, aiming at *discursification* of a knowledge that refuses to be abstracted from the body, where it resides.

Notes

1 See, for instance, Robert Turner's insights (Richards 1989: 11)
2 M. C. Richards's *Centering: In Pottery, Poetry, and the Person*, arguably one of the most acclaimed books on pottery, places the process of centring in the context of personal and spiritual development, and possibly owes its title to a compilation of Zen koans published in 1957.
3 I would like to thank Regina Bendix for the idea of the 'craftiness' rather than the 'cunningness' of the potter's *mētis*.
4 Scott also provides many helpful examples of *mētis* in the context of contemporary life and professional practices (cf. Scott 1998: 309–341).
5 In describing the process of making a Barolo goblet by Erin O'Connor, he writes: 'she was no longer *conscious* of her hands, she no longer *thought about* what they were doing: her consciousness focused on what she saw' (Sennett 2008: 176; my emphasis), and he comes up with the analogy of a musician observing the conductor during performance, as if they were unconsciously moving their hands on a keyboard, or supporting the sound with the diaphragm (as professional jargon describes the crucial part of vocalist's *mētis*). Samudra in her text refers to the same conflation made by Pierre Bourdieu.
6 Writing about a mode of knowing that is directly related to experiences of inhabiting the Arctic, Kirsten Hastrup (2018) also refers to this somatic knowledge, in following Gaston Bachelard's 'muscular consciousness' (1964: 11).

References

Adamson, Glenn 2007. *Thinking Through Craft*. Oxford: Berg.

Bachelard, Gaston 1964. *The Poetics of Space*. Translated by Maria Jolas. New York: Orion Press

Byatt, Antonia S. 2010. *The Children's Book*. London: Vintage Books.

Deleuze, Gilles and Félix Guattari 2011. *A Thousand Plateaus: Capitalism and Schizophrenia*. Translated by Brian Massumi, Minneapolis: University of Minnesota Press.

Detienne, Marcel and Jean-Pierre Vernant 1991. *Cunning Intelligence in Greek Culture and Society*. Translated by Janet Lloyd, Chicago: University of Chicago Press.

Dolmage, Jay Timothy 2014. *Disability Rhetorics*. Syracuse: Syracuse University Press.

Gieser, Thorsten 2008. Embodiment, Emotion and Empathy: A Phenomenological Approach to Apprenticeship Learning. *Anthropological Theory* 8 (3): 299–318.

Ginzburg, Carlo 1983. Señales: Raíces de un paradigma indiciario. In Aldo Gargani (ed.) *Crisis de la razón: Nuevos modelos en la relación entre saber y actividad humana*. México: Siglo XXI Editores, 55–99.

Hastrup, Kirsten 2018. Muscular Consciousness: Knowledge Making in an Arctic Environment. In Tomasz Rakowski and Helena Patzer (eds.) *Pre-Textual Ethnographies: Challenging the Phenomenological Level of Anthropological Knowledge-Making*. Canon Pyon: Sean Kingston Publishing, 116–137.

Ingold, Tim 2007. Materials Against Materiality. *Archaeological Dialogues* 14 (1): 1–16.

Ingold, Tim 2010. The Textility of Making. *Cambridge Journal of Economics* 34: 91–102.

Jullien, François 1995. *The Propensity of Things: Towards A History of Efficacy in China*. Translated by Janet Lloyd. New York: Zone Books.

Klekot, Ewa 2017. Sprawczość w fabryce porcelany. *Kultura Popularna* 52: 92–107.

Klekot, Ewa 2018. Ceramic Production as Intangible Cultural Heritage and Its Visualization. In Nadja Valentinčič-Furlan (ed.) *Visualising Intangible Heritage*. Ljubljana: SEM, 111–130.

Klekot, Ewa 2020. The Craft of Factory Labor. *Journal of American Folklore* 133 (528) (Spring 2020): 205–227.

Lave, Jean and Etienne Wenger 1991. *Situated Learning: Legitimate Peripheral Participation*. Cambridge and Melbourne: Cambridge University Press.

Law, John and Wen-yuan Lin 2017. Tidescapes: notes on a *Shi* [勢]-inflected social science. Available at: http://heterogeneities.net/publications/LawLin2017TidescapesNotesOnAShiInflectedSocialScience.pdf. Accessed 22.12.2019.

Malafouris, Lambros 2013. *How Things Shape the Mind: A Theory of Material Engagement*. Cambridge, MA: MIT Press.

Marchand, Trevor H.J. 2008. Muscles, Morals and Mind: Craft Apprenticeship and the Formation of Person. *British Journal of Educational Studies* 56 (3): 245–271.

Parry, Richard 2014. Episteme and Techne. In *The Stanford Encyclopedia of Philosophy*, ed. Edward N. Zalta et al., http://plato.stanford.edu/archives/fall2014/entries/episteme-techne/. Accessed 28.12.2019.

Richards, Mary Caroline 1989. *Centering: In Pottery, Poetry, and the Person*, 2nd ed. Middletown: Wesleyan University Press.

Samudra, Jaida Kim 2008. Memory in Our Body: Thick Participation and the Translation of Kinesthetic Experience. *American Ethnologist* 35 (4): 665–681.

Scott, James C. 1998. *Seeing Like A State*. New Haven: Yale University Press.

Sennett, Richard 2008. *The Craftsman*. London: Allen Lane.

Serres, Michel 2016. *The Five Senses. A Philosophy of Mingled Bodies*. Translated by Margaret Sankey and Peter Cowley. London: Bloomsbury.

Toom, Auli 2012. Considering the Artistry and Epistemology of Tacit Knowledge and Knowing. *Educational Theory* 62 (6): 621–640.

Tsing Lowenhaupt, Anna 2015. *The Mushroom at the End of the World: On the Possibility of Life in Capitalist Ruins*. Princeton: Princeton University Press.

6   Hammering on the edges

Thresholds of un-knowing in Santa Clara del Cobre, Mexico

Michele Avis Feder-Nadoff

Lessons in skilled practice: An introduction

This chapter proposes un-knowing as a methodology for understanding the skilled practices of artisans. It also discusses how ways of knowing through un-knowing can be relevant for ethnographers. The arguments and narrative presented are based in the author's long-term apprenticeship with master artisans in Santa Clara del Cobre, Mexico.[1] This essay draws from this research in Santa Clara studying the soma-onto-epistemic processes of makers, most particularly, looking at how un-knowing in bodily practice can be experienced as a paradoxical methodology of knowing in shared sociality.[2] For the mestizo coppersmiths of Santa Clara, un-knowing constitutes an existential practice, in which failure, rupture and alterity shape artisanal skill, performance and agency. My principal teachers, Maestro Pérez Ornelas (1926–2014) and his sons, understood explicitly that my objectives were to study how to be(come) an artisan, rather than merely learn how to make things.[3] Maestro Pérez warned that it took a lifetime to become an artisan and that he himself would never stop learning until the day he died. Here, I focus, however, on the instabilities of the peripheral as expressed in the artisan's affective, sensorial and social geographies. We will thus examine un-knowing as an edgy methodological approach to access 'peripheral wisdom' (see the introduction and conclusion to the volume) through apprenticeship research ethnography. Peripheral wisdom will also be seen here as a form of edgewalking, since to be on the peripheries of knowing means to be on an edge, as observed by art historian Linda Schele:

> There are people who are centralists and there are people who walk on the edge. I think it is the edgewalkers that continually push the box and push the shape at the edge. I think they are the people who make fields change. I have always deliberately chosen to be an edgewalker, knowing that my work is going to be wrong, because I am putting out new ideas; But I also change the nature of the field or change its directions and get other people to take on different kinds of questions that I would never be able to do if I was a centralist and beyond that, I am not a trained academic. I am a trained painter… The only place that we have a chance to exist as leaders is on the edge. [4]

As an anthropologist who is foremost an artist, my work begins by making things, rather than merely text. I am more comfortable on the margins of the verbal, in the in-between and unsaid, at home when using the language of making and of gestures. Craft apprenticeship allowed me to examine these non-linguistic processes to see how they benefit anthropological research. Through observation and experience I came to identify these processes as knowing through un-knowing. Un-knowing constitutes a critical practice for the coppersmiths of Santa Clara del Cobre, in which failure, rupture and alterity reshape artisanal skill, performance and agency. This means that artisans hone their (bodies of) knowledge through relational experiences of friction (Tsing 2005), tension, and resonance[5] rather than tacit flows. Santa Clara's copper-trade responds to complex ancestral-cultural and socio-political history.[6] Through these smithing techniques and aesthetics, the artisans variously assert, resist or conform to their marginalized rural, mestizo, working-class status.

Learning by un-knowing

Artisans expand these corporeal and social geographies by constantly attuning peripheral knowledge and facility by being *'listo'*, *'abusado'* or *'bien preparado'*. These colloquial Spanish Mexican expressions mean being smart, intelligent. Yet, even more than that, they refer to being ready, alert, attentive, street-wise, able to read your surroundings, watch your own back and, at times, even be cunning.[7] Intelligence means to be observant, prepared to respond to the unexpected, the un-known. In other words, to be wise to your peripheries. These attitudes for navigating life are carried forth into the forge.

The keen master smith hones and re-hones this perceptivity and perspicacity through constant re-attunement. Counter-intuitively, this depends upon dis-attunement, and learning by un-knowing.[8] For artisans, or ethnographers, not being in tune with other people, places, materials and things can lead to knowing them better. Even more complicated, this attunement occurs through dis-harmony. When peripheries of sense, sensibilities and sensitivities are dis-aligned, tested and crossed, they become identified, as encountered through friction.

Heightened relational awareness challenges both the artisan and the ethnographer's orientation. Yet it is precisely this dis-orientation that expands peripheral wisdom through a renewed effort of re-location and re-attuning. To a great extent, it is what anthropologist Jason Throop (2010: 6) aspires to understand via an 'anthropology of ambiguity', in which 'granular' and 'coherence' theories of experience are made dialectical. As Throop (2010: 6) explains:

> Granular theories tend to take experience to be disjunctive, fragmentary, discordant, discontinuous, formless, and punctuating at its core. Coherence theories, in contrast characterize experience as conjunctive, integrated, concordant, continuous, meaningfully formed, and temporally structured.
>
> (Throop 2010: 6)

Throop's anthropology of ambiguity emerged from his studies of chronic and acute pain,[9] intense phenomena, in which sufferers move between thresholds of granular and coherent experiences. Inherently ambiguous, pain can be a 'world-destroying' (Scarry 1985) experience blending somatic and psychic intensities defying language. Although pain is a prime 'disjunctive and granular' experience, subjective retrospection (temporarily) restores its 'coherence'. The sufferer's restoration process – how they reflect upon and articulate this experience – is personally, culturally and temporally orientated (Throop 2010: 6–7).[10] For these reasons, Throop argues, pain's ambiguity and its often 'intransigent opacity and active resistance to formulation', make it an 'especially compelling site to examine how processes of meaning-making are implicated in the articulation of experience and its ensuing objectification' (ibid.: 6–8). Also, Throop stresses that 'greater attention needs to be paid to those experiences that reside on the fringes of our abilities to articulate, verbalize and interpret' (ibid.). Because, despite their ambiguity and indeterminacy, these experiences still have decipherable meanings.

Similarly, artisan practice is an especially fecund site for examining how meaning-making is articulated in processes that jostle opacity and clarity.[11] Like the sufferer passing through thresholds of intense pain, artisans defiantly stretch peripheries and limits. To make matters more complex, the artisan, as the sufferer, can experience a simultaneous distancing, or auto-body alienation while still also feeling overwhelming immersion into bodily sensation. This existential split of consciousness, however, is welcomed by the artisan-maker. Unlike the subject of pain, the artisan develops an agile receptivity (both passive and active) in order to plumb these disorientating edge-shaking experiences. This conflation is expressed in how despite that coppersmiths might 'appear' to lose themselves in work rhythms, they are always maintaining critical assessment of this material encounter.

Despite vigilance to peripheries the artisan practices a deliberate vulnerability to material indeterminacy, as we will return to below. The smith knows how to lead copper, but, even more importantly, they also know how to be led by this metal. To be keen my master teachers must be mobile and motile.[12] They know how to modify techniques, rather than just scaffold and sediment their experiences. The 'good' piece *maestro* Peréz explained was one you did not make every day and that was outside normal routine.[13] That was why he had so many different types of hammering stakes each for different pieces. He added that this unexpected variety would please clients, that they couldn't be 'crooked like the pieces you make'. A good piece does not mean it is 'beautiful'; it means it is 'well-made'.

Winnicott (1971) suggests that there is an 'intermediate area of experience' where 'inner and outer realities' are negotiated through play and imagination.[14] This zone is where artisans navigate perceptual consciousness and collective practice, integrating granular with coherent experience. This ludic zone is also where artisans practice un-knowing. The fluctuating horizons of practice are dispersive; they include moments of integrity and moments of collapse. The artisans know enough to expect certain outcomes, yet, given artistic and laboral freedom or forced by precarity, creativity is taken at a risk. And 'hunger', maestro Jesus' youngest son confessed, makes creativity a necessity.

Play with materials and processes, the interchange with other artisans, clients and designers, life experiences in the world are all inspirational (re)sources. When maestro Jesús traveled to the United States as a visiting artisan[15] he collected leaves from trees he was unfamiliar with, saving them pressed into a gifted book of botany. He had only a vague idea of how exactly their silhouetted patterns would later become incorporated into his future work. Things, and what artisans make with them, often lead to something unexpected. 'I will see how it comes out!' they often say, even when working on an often-repeated design. In these ways habitual forms of making are dislodged in the artisan's ongoing enskillment and aesthetic attunement to changing marketplace demands and socio-political-economic circumstances. For example, a designer who is an important client might insist upon a roughly hammered decorative surface that runs contrary to an artisan's training and sense of a well-executed finish.

Peripheral wisdom as body politics

Despite the resurgent interest in making[16] that has brought makers and their ways of learning, knowing and being – their bodies of knowledge, to the forefront; it is often forgotten that this corporeality and materiality is (also) political. Bifurcations that separate ontology from epistemology and mind from body are hierarchical. These divisions inform and have roots in the politics and policies of labour, race, ethnicity, class, status and power, all feeding into the contingencies faced by Santa Clara coppersmiths.[17] But this does not mean that the coppersmiths have a very limited agency. On the contrary. But it does acknowledge the peripherality of their bodies of knowledge in politically pragmatic terms (Feder-Nadoff 2017).

Peripheries refer to bodily and social limits and extensions, the place between people, places and things where they might meet or exchange or even torque. I negotiated and analysed these shifting peripheries and zones of in-between through my training with *maestro* Pérez, my primary mentor-master and his sons. In the family forge and household this practice of un-knowing by crossing borders accidentally was key to learning the vernacular coppersmithing methods and aesthetics, and also community ethics, as a sort of threshold experience (Fornäs 2002). As an artist-maker, the forge is a space of commonality and difference. To become an artisan in Santa Clara I must set aside aesthetic principles, skills and goals instilled in me as a young art student and subsequently practiced throughout my decades-long career, such as following subjective instinct and direction more than the collective. That said, using the body as a testing laboratory is supported by my kinesthetic experience that trains an artist to re-skill him/herself. My apprenticeship requires 'somatic attention': I must attend 'to my body' (and to the bodies of my teachers) while also attending 'with my body'. But as a woman, this ability is also used to adopt new gestures, movements, muscles and attitudes, to enter a primarily male-gendered space, to form camaraderie, and examine the doing and learning-the-doing from-inside.[18] This does not mean there aren't mistakes. On the contrary, this is precisely where and how you find them.

Peripheries: Mistakes and shame

Making mistakes, errors and failing are central to the artisan and to the apprentice in ethnographic practice. To mistake is to misstep, to take a wrong step, unintentionally. According to the Merriam-Webster dictionary, a mistake is 'an action or decision that is wrong or produces a result that is not correct or not intended'. It is 'to be wrong about or fail to recognize something or someone'. Recognising a mistake can be provoked internally or externally, especially in unfamiliar situations. There are mistakes that we make with internal subjective awareness of a goal, that, despite our best intentions, we fail to realize. This first instance is what the artisans call, '*lo que duele*', what bothers you subjectively about a (copper) piece you are working on. On the other hand, there are mistakes that we become aware of only by the reaction and judgement of others, recognized externally, via el *regaño*, harsh criticism. This is what '*lo que duele al maestro*!', what bothers the *maestro*!

How I (learn to) perform in *maestro* Jesus's studio is not the same as in my own. I am not free, nor am I working alone. There is an audience that constantly judges me in a collective environment. Creation in a social context has aesthetic parameters, resistances, tensions and constraints. I obey my master-teacher when he asks me to create anthropomorphic vessels in his style with 'feet' and 'heads' (see Figures 6.1, 6.2 and 6.3). The results pronounced my failure to imitate the style and techniques of his work adequately. More importantly, these errors articulated by contrast and mis-takes, the master's aesthetics of smoothness, symmetry and balance. The surface play of hammered texture, reflective light and shadows of my failed pieces might have interested Giacometti but not *maestro* Jesus, who said these pieces were *feas* (ugly) and 'should be thrown into the street'. His shouting voice, so strong all could hear it, forced me to be doubly-whipped by shame.

Figure 6.1 Maestro Jesús Pérez Ornelas. Three doves. Hammered, engraved and forged copper. 2000. (This illustrates the Photograph M. Feder-Nadoff.)

Figure 6.2 Maestro Jesús Pérez Ornelas. "Las sirenas". Hammered, engraved and forged copper. This piece illustrates the late middle-period work. Photograph Leah Solkoff Pohl

Marcel Mauss (2006: 80) wrote that he never forgot his third-grade teacher who reprimanded him for walking with his 'arms flapping' at his side. It is very likely this shame is at the heart of his theories of techniques of the body. The teacher's harshness startled him out of his unconscious actions, perhaps generating his seminal theories so re-visited today. The *regaño* awakened his perceptive consciousness. Indeed, mistakes are unkind. Yet they indicate what needs to be un-learned. Mistakes make you pay attention. They also indicate what is un-known. After a tumult of criticism had fallen on me, *maestro* Jesus' sons would comfort me, saying that if their father didn't care about my education, I would be ignored, left unaware: ignorant, un-conscious.

The pitfalls of flow

For all these reasons, the term flow[19] as popularized by the psychologist Mihaly Csikszentmihalyi, and so often applied to making, is woefully inadequate. Flow ignores the maker's experience of complex rhythms,[20] cadences and frictions – the fluctuations of awareness, perceptual and reflexive temporalities, relational correspondences, the mistakes and insights provided by un-knowing. Csikszentmihalyi (2008: 3) describes flow as an 'optimal experience', of enjoyment, a state of determinant participation, attention, and being in control of our lives and thus obtaining happiness. 'Instead of being buffeted by anonymous forces, we… feel in control of our actions, masters of our fate. On the rare occasions that it happens, we feel a sense of exhilaration, a deep sense of enjoyment', states Csikszentmihalyi (ibid.). He explains that flow is:

> what the painter feels when the colors of the canvas begin to set up a new magnetic tension with each other, and a new thing, a living form, takes shape in front of the astonished creator [and] the best moments usually occur when a person's body or mind is stretched to its limits in a voluntary effort to accomplish something difficult or worthwhile.
>
> (ibid.: 3)

But painting is not simply happiness, as noted by Merleau-Ponty (1993) in his study entitled 'Cézanne's Doubt'. Csikszentmihalyi concept of flow ignores its ambiguous and peripheral substrates, and contrasts with the concepts of experience and consciousness outlined by the phenomenologist Edmund Husserl and the pragmatist William James. To describe the complexities of lived experience, William James (1950 [1890]) also used water metaphors, likening the structure of consciousness to a stream that ebbs and flows. In bringing attention to the 'processes and constituents that arise at the fringe of our stream of awareness' James highlights the importance of peripheries and our knowledge of them in-action.[21] Also, Husserl's (1964, 1993) use of flow metaphors focuses on the entanglements of lived experience and consciousness. By presenting lived experience as a 'unity of becoming... undergoing a continuity of alteration', Husserl (1993: 42) acknowledges the wrestling between experiences of coherence and disjunction (Throop: 2003: 231).

This philosophical discussion is less abstract when seen in its application to artisan practice where subject and object relationships are at once ambiguous and adumbrated in mutual constitution. This can be seen, for example by looking at tools and tool use. Tools, and their use, like rituals – ceremonies and festivals with a collective past – induce resonant amalgamations of both voluntary and involuntary memory, perception and apperception, coherent and granulated consciousness. These are alternately and discriminately called upon in skilled practice, as will become elaborated further below.

The dispute in anthropological theories of experience ask philosophical and methodological questions of how to hold the inchoate and felt non-linear experience within a conceptual framework of coherent narrative. In this essay I propose that these experiences interweave. Artisan practice is a practice of shifting peripheries, in which both domains remain non-exclusive and co-determinant. To address questions of experience, which, as Throop argues, are fundamental concepts for anthropological theory and method, this entails the question of what knowledge and wisdom is revealed through these experiences. It is important, then, to remember that experience is a verb, not only an object or subject. It is also important to stress that for a maker, the relationship of subject and object is similarly balanced. And that for the artisan experience is knowledge-in-action.

Metal modalities in the family forge

Metalsmithing is super-synesthetic, an acrobatic craft, demanding agility and responsive improvisation. Apprenticeship literally keeps me on my toes.

Exceptionally multimodal, sensorial and kinesthetic, the laborious work requires the training and development of large and small muscles and the intertwining of gross and fine-motor movements. To be efficient and effective, execution must be precise. Errors and sloppiness can be dangerous in the forge's collective space. This is not an industrialized forge and we work body with body. There are concrete tangible dangers: being burned, injured by a flying ingot that bounces, or cut by a chisel. Although increasingly industrially made copper discs are now used, in this studio the 'traditional' copper smelted ingot is still used to initiate the functional or decorative vessel forms (Feder-Nadoff 2004).[22]

To shape and extend this copper ingot, *plancha,* into a *tejo,* the elemental flat pancake-shaped disc requires coordinated hammering by more than one person, including a *capitán,* who holds the ingot firmly with a long pliers moving it in rhyme with the unfolding process. If the men do not observe the others around them, they will be injured. Never feeling confident enough to work in the group, I mostly carry out the first steps of forging only with the *capitán* and myself. The one time my *maestro* stepped in to hammer with me while I was extending the *tejo* thrilled me; but then regretfully, becoming so nervous, I had to stop. There are countless other ways we work together to help each other in the forge, moving the bellows to keep the fire alight, or holding steady a copper piece. Smithing requires balance, sensitive tonal hearing, touch, comprehension of aural and visceral vibration all interwoven into fine-tuned haptic perceptions and great variances in rhythms. These activities demand constant re-attunement and anticipation of the movements and intentions of the other artisans in the space. For all these reasons it is useful to return to the critique of flow.

Entangling flow

The popularized use of flow (as proposed by Csikszentmihalyi) freezes the body into idealized perfection, ignoring peripheral entanglements of a training artisan whose corporal boundaries and perceptions constantly change.[23] In apprenticeship my body becomes fragmented and confused – un-known. In the hyper-consciousness imposed by apprenticeship, my body is not mine. I am no longer an artist. I am no longer a woman, nor am I a man. And, the forge in Santa Clara is my adopted world. Just like my imperfect Spanish, I trip over my hands, arms, like my tongue. My body becomes a heavy obstruction; like an adolescent boy, whose limbs grow too fast to keep track of where they end and begin. I have to look to find where my hand is located, check the position of my fingers or shoulders, elbows and back. By observing the bodies of others – my teachers' postures, I mimetically straighten my own spine, adjust the position of my legs to cradle and secure both the equilibrium of my body and that of the copper piece.[24]

Flow also ignores the body's self-alienation provoked by injury, aging or illness.[25] *Maestro* Jesus suffered a stroke after my Fulbright year of research in 2010–2011 before my return to Santa Clara in April 2012 to begin my doctoral research. When my apprenticeship began anew, I observed the changes in my mentor's work and his difficulties moving, even walking. But I also noted how he consciously worked to retrain his body with determined discipline. Each day he woke up early before most of the household to first cut wood, which exercised and re-developed many of the same muscles, required in the coordination of coppersmithing movements. This workout also helped him regain stamina. Of course, despite this his body was never the same as before, but he still created new works accommodating the changes into a new endearing aesthetics, that perhaps less perfect was still full of heart and 'made with great passion'.[26] As he would say to me upon asking me what I thought of a piece he made, 'Don't tell me it is nice!' (see Figure 6.3)

Without the mimesis of apprenticeship, craft becomes idealized, and, as in a sophisticated level of sport, hides the fact that there is no constant easy flow, nor static sedimentation. Muscles only grow when they are torn and limberness only comes from stretching. Nor are tacit movement, know-how, or embodied knowledge sufficient terms for the athletic and physiological processes that take place in intensely physical craft. This does not mean 'making' is less mental. As *maestro* Jesús would insist, pointing his forefinger to his head when I failed in the forge.

Ecologies of perception

The liquid analogy of the flow also ignores the artisan's ways of comprehending variety, spatial extension, blockages: the different currents, movements and connections between water sources, air, wind and temperatures. Flow ignores the consequence and contingencies of these complex material 'ecologies of perception' required in smithing, that are not so much about reading surfaces, as emphasized by James Gibson (1979) but more about perceiving space, densities, emptiness, fullness, tones, light, heat, vibration and movements of objects and the self within these contours, openings and atmospheres.

Figure 6.3 Maestro Jesús Pérez Ornelas. Three owls. Hammered, engraved and forged copper. 2014. This illustrates the later works created the year of the maestro's death. Photograph M. Feder-Nadoff

The geography and (mole)ability of bodies

Crucially, flow ignores ways of sensing peripheries and their resonance. This is the multimodal knowledge gained through what Greg Downey (2007) calls the 'sideways glance'. Smithing moves the primacy of focal vision to peripheral vision. Like capoeira artists, smiths constantly interpret space. This haptic and somatic knowledge-in-movement is blind. One does not and cannot look at one's arm striking nor the copper underneath the hammer stroke. One feels these actions and performances. The sense of mistake or failure, the need to correct, reorientate, comes from inner senses of perception, feelings that rely far less on the visual – optical vision, than upon a complex of orchestrated senses of bodily placement and awareness of space and the objects in them. This blind-visuality, I call humorously: 'the mole-theory'. Yet, as we have seen earlier this unity is hard-won and temporary, disabled and disjointed easily.

This kinesthetic propio-perception[27] and the constancy of re-orientation challenges the concept of the orderly *chaîne opératoire*, the linear progression of technical steps. Generally applied to studying skilled making by anthropologists and archeologists, this term originates with the theories of 'operational sequences' proposed by André Leroi-Gourhan ([1964] 1993: 230) who explained that these take place on three levels of behaviour: automatic, mechanical and lucid.[28] It is not so much that operational sequencing is not applicable, nor helpful for analytical purposes; rather, it is that within artisan practice this attempt to logically organize provides only one view on the 'constellation' of activities in which techniques combine with affective aesthetics in the active design and assemblage of making things. As anthropologist Thomas Wynn writes:

> The array of tools and procedures that can successfully achieve a task-on-hand is, if not infinite, at least immense. When an artisan assembles a constellation of knowledge he is choosing, often quite arbitrarily. Certainly, characteristics such as economy – how much time and effort the artisan is willing to invest – come into play, but these are matters of the personal history of the artisan, not the task *per se*.
>
> (Wynn 1993: 398)

This is all applied to *maestro* Jesus who said often that if he counted how many blows he struck to create his works he would go crazy; besides, no client could afford his work. It must be remembered that these are all elements that are part of the constellation of making, and are drawn upon in the various types of perception the artisans require to carry out their activities. It is also why the notion that perceptual fields are arranged according to a hierarchical function from feet to head does not suffice. This is suggested by Leroi-Gourhan in assigning the uprightness of humans to the divided domains of tool use and the liberation of speech. Perhaps his angst and fear of the human hand being turned into a mere lever for turning on and off machines is resolved by his own emphasis upon gesture and its relationship to speech as expression. Because it cannot be forgotten that expression can be made by gestures into objects, made things. Language and symbols are material and sensorial, sensible and social.

It is not only that cognition does not reside in an isolated brain. As neurological studies confirm, tool use and the brain are correlated.[29] The brain is not dis-embodied. Rather, the brain circulates inside and outside our bodies through its neurological paths, just as our muscular hearts pump oxygenated blood. In this way we might also understand that movement does not end at our fingertips. Rather it extends into the peripheries, as my master's reach with the hammer draws his outward path in(to) the universe. As the lunar tide, this dendritic path is pulled as much as cast.

Tools, peripheries and memory

This means that when artisans work with tools they extend peripheries. Artisans don't only use tools, as my teachers, they often make and so also imagine them. And, artisans perform not only with tools, but as tools, agents and instruments of agency, their own and at times of others. As such, the term 'hand-made' obscures artisan's tool use and making; artisans not only use their hands, they also use their entire body-mind gathered within a cognitive sensorial confluence moving not only between distal to proximal.[30] This refers not only to spatial and corporeal distances and peripheries, but also to the variations of memory, consciousness and perception recollected and reassembled and prompted in the making of the new piece.

Tool use is also relational and conformed to use and disuse, abuse or care across their lifetimes. Like artisans, tools age and respond. In this sense, tools and their use are always imminently and immanently modifiable, as is the body, and in this sense un-knowable. That said, however, tool use as a peripheral process, functions effectively and affectively without being named.

Shaping actions and words

In my apprenticeship, how I was taught to use a tool and even to create tools – specific stakes and hammers, and chisels – is based upon what is considered by most scholars to be peripheral wisdom because it cannot be articulated into words. How can one describe in words all the bends and turns, depressions and rises, textures at the end of the chisel or stake required to create a specific copper piece? Let alone, how can we name and describe all the aspects of the body in movement and adjustment to create this piece, to wield and manoeuvre the tools including the most complex tool, the body itself with its component limbs, nervous system, ligaments and other myriad parts? How can this all come together in words? This composition relies upon a coherence produced in movement within fields of forces, equally motile and mobile as the artisan.

Within the master–apprentice relationship, speech is peripheral to action. I was supposed to understand by carrying out the command with little explanation. Understanding comes through carrying out and meaning is only acquired over time with reflection interwoven into action. Expressions such as 'You are not listening!' from my teacher as he enters the forge hearing my hammering from afar and commenting upon entry is an instruction that expands over time. Through practice one realizes what is meant and inferred as one builds capacity and awareness. At times, just a simple glance or the action of my teacher standing near me watching signaled beware. But it could come out in anger and frustration: 'How long have you worked here? Long enough to already know how to do this after so many years!?'

The analysis of a central emphatic criticism of *maestro* Pérez given repeatedly during my apprenticeship illustrates (his) intuitive understanding of the critical biomechanics of the optimal hammering stroke and also highlights the synergetic acuity of the metalsmith's performance. Scientific analysis affirms why *maestro* Pérez's repeated criticism was crucial to smithing in the forge. This instruction highlighted fundamental dynamics of hammering and also demonstrates how peripheral knowledge-in-praxis and knowledge-in-theory are contiguous, coexistent. Each does not cancel the other. Rather, they are different types of knowledge; the former attained inside experience, and the latter obtained from the-outside. They are both auxiliary to understanding and rather than be seen as divided, can coalesce. What is seen as peripheral knowledge just depends upon what side of the border you are on: language or action.

In frustration, *maestro* Jesús repeatedly declared that my hammer stroke was tense, too rigid, and that my arm and efforts were not accomplishing anything. In comparison, when he demonstrated the correct way to hammer, his gestures appeared fluid, dancelike and powerful. The unity of these movements seems simple to an unknowing observer. Yet they are complexly coordinated. The *maestro* would demonstrate my inefficiency clearly by imitating my movements: he would hammer, lifting his arm angled and stiff, striking without changing the bend of his elbow at the copper disc with his body, inclining and rocking at the waist, his torso as rigid and stiff as his arm. Indeed, I had felt my force restrained and impacted in my effort to strike correctly in the right spot on the metal. He indicated through performances how a looseness of the elbow-joint is needed as the forearm is led by the conjunction with the hammer handle that extends the arm, hand, trunk and entire body. An accumulation of force and speed finally brings down the hammer head, propelled by the swing of the stroke and the generated velocity slowed down with precision into the striking zone. The gravity of the hammer is put into action, by a velocity that to some extent feels guided by the hammer itself, propelled and released by the loose swing of the hand upwards led by the forearm, leaving the elbow relatively stable in the same point in space. The inability to maintain a flowing movement of the successive units of the arm, trunk, and legs block the ability to attain this required velocity. Yet, this does not mean that hammering occurs in unregulated flows.[31]

The dance of agency[32]

As doctor of biological sciences and sports expert Galina Ivanova explains, a tennis player requires 10–13 years to learn to achieve the velocity in the coordination of their bodily joints required for an effective stroke. Achieving this velocity hinges upon responding to all the stroke's peripheral disturbances and irregularities; then she notes that a long period of motor learning is necessary 'to acquire the sensory corrections allowing one to take into account these dynamic disturbances and still produce the desired final velocity […] After a long period of training, this biomechanical system, characterized by flexibility in coping with such reactive forces, becomes highly integrated and effective' (Ivanova 2005: 119). This orchestration is not just mechanical; the segments of the body must work in 'specific muscular synergies' in conjunction with 'waveform' of 'impulse transmission' that moves from proximal, near the body trunk, to the hands and fingers, to distal segments of the body. Many complications occur within, and to the body. As it acts, it also reacts to the force and movement. A type of constant adjustment takes place in reaction to the intentional movement of force and volition. This was all magnified and multiplied for a novice like myself, when focusing on the multiple simultaneous aspects involved in the task. This included not only the striking left arm, but also the right arm, that gripped and rotated the copper ingot disc with the large, and for the novice unwieldy, pliers. *Maestro* Pérez accomplished all of these tasks with smooth, graceful, unified movements and an effective and forceful stroke.

The entire corporeal posture – its stability and agility – is involved in the execution of an efficient stroke. In the accompanying photo, one can see how 'velocity generation originates in the feet and legs' (ibid.: 121). This photo (see Figure 6.4) was taken when *maestro* Jesus was extending the copper *tejo*, and yet even in the work solo, the hammer stroke also originates and involves the lower body. Velocity is generated and accumulated from one part of the body to the next, from feet to pelvis to trunk and shoulders, through arms to striking hammer. When *maestro* Pérez and the other artisans are working, their entire body is attentively implicated; even in the sitting position, the entire body is at work, the feet, spine, back and shoulders stabilizing both tools and copper piece.

Figure 6.4 "The dance of agency". Maestro Jesús Pérez Ornelas (center) forging the round tejo, copper ingot with his sons, José Sagrario Pérez Pamatz (left) and Napoleón Pérez Pamatz, in the family forge, Santa Clara del Cobre, 2011. Photograph M. Feder-Nadoff

This confirms what the coppersmiths have always stressed, that a lifetime of training goes into learning to being a smith. It demands navigating complex material and bodily 'structures of feeling' (Williams 1954). This subsidiary awareness, or what Karl Polanyi calls the tacit dimension, is not 'unconscious or preconscious awareness'. Rather, 'what makes an awareness subsidiary is the function it fulfills […] as a clue to the object of our focal attention' (Polanyi 1966: 95–96). Not being aware of all the stimuli that is drawn upon in behaviour and activities does not diminish the complexity of its 'ground'[33] and the depth of its 'field'.[34] As Polanyi asserts, the tacit dimension is certainly not mindless, although its epistemic processes are not always clear.

Against concluding

The focus on un-knowing and the peripheral in this chapter highlights that artisanal 'making' does not conclude in finished objects. Like culture, making craft 'is not an end, or a blueprint for thinking and acting, but a constant beginning again – a search, an argument, an unfinished longing' (Stewart 1996: 6). It is from this perspective that we must acknowledge peripheral wisdom as a methodology of placing the self in constant re-position in tandem with un-knowing. Wisdom, like skills, cannot be *had*. Nor is it fixed, bounded and contained. Making is carried forth as a momentum into proceeding creations through social and material encounters with error and desire. The latter of which *maestro* Jesús would call 'ambition' and 'vision'. As the *maestro* would insist, failures led him along to the next piece, bringing him forth in his perpetual becoming as an artisan. Artisans, like ethnographers, follow by learning-in-doing, by being led by their subjects. Works of making are not things, rather they are progresses. Just like the people we meet in the field, their lives and our own do not begin nor end where our paths meet and intersect for a time. Horizons have short durations, even if their upsweep is gathered from a long way behind. But it doesn't finish there.

To extend peripheries means that the artisan, or ethnographer, must feel their way blindly along shifting horizons composed of multiple perspectives and paths that extend behind and beyond. Invisible to sight, but not to feelings, those horizons do not end. This requires being open to the unexpected, hidden, unseen and peripheral. In this promise of invisibility, they reveal the future, an un-known, whose clues, and our choice to follow them, can create countless new imaginaries. This also means that the wisdom of an artisan is more about reach than grasp, more about extending than holding fast. Un-knowing as a methodology of apprenticeship, in the field or forge, requires us to let go without always knowing where we will end up but trusting somehow that we will find the way.[35]

Notes

1 Located above the Lake Patzcuaro basin of the northwestern Mexican state of Michoacán, a region of craft communities, Santa Clara is specially renown for its ever-evolving copper craft production.

2 This essay builds in partnership with another unpublished essay entitled, 'Learning by (Un-)knowing: Copper Craft Apprenticeship in Santa Clara del Cobre, Michoacán, Mexico' that analyzes the interface of bodily ways of knowing and sociality by reflecting upon long-term artisan apprenticeship.

3 Research in Santa Clara was initiated in 1997. I had been studying with these teachers prior to the doctorate and entered the period of doctoral research with acquired facilities that were expanded upon and became more focused on these existential and phenomenological dynamics and aspects.

4 Documentary: Edgewalker: a conversation with Linda Schele, 2010. Directed by Andrew Weeks, Simon Martin, Lori Conley.

5 Although resonance is employed here as the distinct intertwining of artisan's antennal emotional, corporeal and social capacities, it is of value to look at Whyte (2014) and Curtis and Elliot (2014) on empathy, emotional resonance and the history of 'Einfühlung'. See also Wikan (1992) and Owen (2015) on the ability to communicate without words through resonance and the importance of emotions and emotional intelligence in ethnographic research and analysis.

6 For more information on the history of Santa Clara del Cobre and ancient metallurgy in West Mexico, see Feder-Nadoff, (2004, 2017); Horcasitas de Barros ([1968] 2001, 1974); Hosler (1994).

7 González (2017) also writes about cunning and power among capoeira masters.

8 In this chapter, I use of the term 'un-knowing' and knowing and similar seemingly opposite states, such as attunement and dis-attunement. The intention is not to bifurcate terms, but rather to understand how they support each other. We can be both absolutely engaged and also outside of the experience. In ethnographic situations, this is why it is possible to be simultaneously immersed, lost inside experience, and also outside of it, able to reflect. It also allows for the mimetic efficacy of apprenticeship and its slippages.

9 Throop's (2010) study of pain with the people of island of Yap (Waqab), Federated States of Micronesia, is based in the broader objective of clarifying what is experience as conceived and employed in anthropological terms. He stresses that anthropological theories of experience although core concepts within anthropological theory and method have not been adequately addressed and that this aporia influences empirical research results and our ability to work and think cross-culturally.

10 It of course must be remembered that for the ethnographer, perceptive positionality is also always subjective. See also Csordas (1993: 137) explaining that for Merleau-Ponty 'perception was always embedded in the cultural world'.

11 See Grimshaw and Ravetz (2015: 271) who similarly look at drawing and filmmaking as part 'of a broader concern about how to bring into focus certain knowledge processes that remain unarticulated and resistant to description – states of consciousness that can be more effectively evoked than represented since they are by their very nature *processual*, emergent rather than extant'.

12 Herzfeld (2004) based upon his research stresses the 'cunningness' of artisans. Indeed, there is an interesting relationship between the word 'crafty' and its relationship to craft.

13 This was one of my few discussions with my teacher based upon a direct question, 'What is a good piece?' and occurred days before his death in June 2014.

14 See Winnicott (1971) on the transitional object, transference and play; the context in which he proposed this intermediary state of experience.

15 *Maestro* Peréz travelled to the USA through a transnational artistic exchange programme the author designed and carried out under the auspices of the Cuentos Foundation.

16 This resurgence of craft as skilled practice has also stimulated long-needed, revised approaches to studying material culture, once considered essential to anthropological research, as originally modeled by Franz Boas.

17 All these factors played a persistent role in my study with *Maestro* Jesús and formed the context and impetus for my apprenticeship whose objectives were philosophical and ontological, as well as epistemological and political.

18 See Butler (1993) for gender-based actions that are performed to not only reproduce social gender norms but to 'subvert' them, drawing from the phenomenology of Merleau-Ponty and feminists such as Simone De Beauvoir.

19 Flow especially is an almost romantic, exoticizing view of bodily practice that ignores the skill and training demanded to reach rare moments of unity that may be described as a flow. These are not so easily accessible without extreme preparation and are transient and interpenetrated by breaks and disruption.

20 See Dobler (2016) on the complexities and variations of rhythm in work so aptly applied also to the coppersmiths of Santa Clara.

21 The watery metaphor of the stream is central to James' (1950 [1890]) theories of the structure of consciousness and poetically echo Bergson's concept of duration and theories of memory (2014 [1911]). Throop (2003: 228) explains that for James 'a stream ebbs and flows continually forward while retaining the undercurrents and residues of past experience'. Yet, despite these watery similes, unlike "flow theory" this 'stream of consciousness is neither a completely unified and coherent field nor a disjointed, fragmented conglomeration of mental contents' (ibid). For James, the 'content of consciousness is surrounded by a "fringe" or "halo" of anticipatory and residual movements [that] frame and give definition to the focus of our present moment of awareness as it arises in the context of the "here and now" (James, 1950 [1890]: 254, 255, 258, 259, 606)' (ibid).

22 This process harkens back to the precolonial period when copper was smelted in shallow pits as noted by Barrett (1987).

23 According to Merleau-Ponty, the world, the body, the person are 'intact', defined and enclosed. It is certainly true that one does not and cannot look at one's arm striking nor the copper underneath the hammer stroke. One feels these actions and performances. Haptic and somatic movement as described above is blind yet they also include disruption and halts.

24 I defer here from Merleau-Ponty, who explains, that: 'when the word 'here' is applied to my body […] it indicates […] that the anchor of my active body is in the object and the situation of the body facing its work to do'. When the coppersmith is in front of their task-scape, their tools, they do not need to look for their hands and their hammer because they are moved based on the artisan's perception through their 'intentional threads' that tie them to their work and tasks. Merleau-Ponty explains that this forms a dynamic triangle consisting of 'poles of actions' that define each specific situation that when left open demands resolution. 'The body is only one element in the system of subject and their world' (2012 [1945]: 108–109).

25 See also Marchand on injury and aging (2014).

26 Garrido and María (2015: 140, 421–422, 424, 484–485, 491) emphasized the major criteria of *ambákiti,* the local indigenous purépecha word that denotes a well-made piece is according to the definition by Gilberti ([1559] 1901), a piece made with passion.

27 See Paterson (2007) on propio-perception.

28 This echoes his doctoral-director, Mauss' ([1934] 2006: 82–83) concept of 'tradition' as bodily techniques that continue because of their effectiveness. This approach to bodily techniques also echoes Bourdieu's concept of habitus, also expanding upon Mauss to further theorize how techniques of the body and society are interconstituted within symbolic patterns and constraints to bodily comportment. See also Ingold on the difficulty of breaking down steps in the fluidity of metallurgy (2013: 26).

29 See for example, studies by Stout (2016, 2005) on stoneknapping.

30 This hand is often stressed in craft versus the body. Hence the expression 'handmade' rather than 'body-made'. Both are problematic terms that retain binaric and hierarchic divisions between body mind. Residues of this division can still be found in excellent writings on craft, such as Marchand 2012.

31 In 1923 and 1926, the year of *maestro* Pérez's birth, Nikolai Alexandrovich Bernstein conducted cyclogrammometry studies of the hammer stroke to describe the mechanics of generating velocity in the striking element of the hammer. Bernstein was able to identify two main principles which occurred: Firstly, the direction of the stroke is only effective if the hand velocity is aligned with the future hammer movement, and secondly, it is necessary to decelerate the upper arm, forearm, and hand to allow the stroke to be realized with the full impact and velocity. As Ivanova explains (2005: 119), the optimal hammer stroke is effective when 'the hand, foot, racket, or hammer [...] reach the desired final velocity'.

32 Feder-Nadoff (2017); See Ingold on the dance of life (2013: 99–102).

33 This also harkens to Merleau-Ponty's terms of the ground and horizons, in the focus of tasks.

34 This refers also to Bourdieu's field of practice as the milieu of the habitus, implicating the social and political.

35 This chapter was completed in the throes of the global pandemic of coronavirus, whose danger brought attention to how peripheries and extensions intwine in our shared world. We were made mindful of the necessity to attend to what may be invisible to trace, but can be felt and transmitted. It behooves us to remember that, like artisans, our bodies do not end at our fingertips and that our breath circulates, is not isolate, nor self-contained. In a mechanized and virtual world we are still vulnerable, mortal, material and connected. What was un-known now is known in its un-knowingness and unyielding ambiguity. What seemed peripheral to wisdom has, in an instant, become critical. The meshwork that connects us, can also infect us. Peripheral wisdom is social and political; it also brings new meaning to the questions of humanity's continuity and discontinuity: to our collective durée and responsibility.

References

Barrett, Elinore 1987. *The Mexican Colonial Copper Industry*. Albuquerque: University of New Mexico Press.

Bergson, Henri 2014 [1911]. *Creative Evolution*. Mineola: Dover Publications.

Butler, Judith 1993. *Bodies that Matter: On the Discursive Limits of Sex*. New York: Routledge.

Csikszentmihalyi, Mihaly 2008. *Flow: The Psychology of Optimal Experience*. New York: Harper.

Csordas, Thomas J. 1993. Somatic Modes of Attention. *Cultural Anthropology* 8 (2): 135–156.

Curtis, Robin and Richard George Elliot 2014. An Introduction to Einfühlung. *Art in Translation* 6 (4): 355–376.

Horcasitas de Barros, María Luisa 1974. *Cobre martillado: Vocabulario tradicional, utillaje y técnicas de manufactura*. Cuadernos de trabajo, Técnicas 1. Mexico: INAH.

Horcasitas de Barros, María Luisa [1968] 2001. *La artesanía con raíces prehispánicas de Santa Clara del Cobre*. México: Secretaría de Educación Pública.

Dobler, Gregor 2016. 'Work and Rhythm' Revisited: Rhythm and Experience in Northern Namibian Peasant Work. *Journal of the Royal Anthropological Institute* 22 (4): 864–883.

Downey, Greg 2007. Seeing Without Knowing, Learning with the Eyes: Visuomotor 'Knowing' and the Plasticity of Perception. In Mark Harris (ed.) *Ways of Knowing*. Oxford: Berghahn Books, 222–241.

Feder-Nadoff, Michele A. (ed.) 2004. *Ritmo del fuego: El arte y los artesanos de Santa Clara del Cobre, Michoacán, México*. Chicago: Fundación Cuentos.

Feder-Nadoff, Michele A. 2017. *Body of Knowledge – Between Praxis and Theory – The Agency of the Artisan and Their Craft: Towards an Anthropology of Making, Santa Clara del Cobre*. PhD Thesis, El Colegio de Michoacán, México.

Fornäs, Johan 2002. Passages Across Thresholds: Into the Borderlands of Mediation. *Convergence: The Journal of Research into Technologies of New Media* 8 (4): 89–106.

Garrido, Izaguirre, and Eva María 2015. *Donde el diablo mete la cola: Estética indígena en un pueblo purépecha (México)*. PhD thesis. Madrid: Universidad Complutense.

Gilberti, Maturino [1559] 1901. *Diccionario de la lengua tarasca ó de Michoacán*. Re-edited by Antonio Peñafiel. México: Palacio Nacional.

González Varela, Sergio 2017. Power in Practice. The Pragmatic Anthropology of Afro-Brazilian Capoeira. New York: Berghahn Books.

Grimshaw, Anna and Amanda Ravetz 2015. Drawing with a Camera? Ethnographic Film and Transformative Anthropology. *Journal of the Royal Anthropological Institute* 21: 255–275.

Herzfeld, Michael 2004. *The Body Impolitic: Artisans and Artifice in the Global Hierarchy of Value*. Chicago: University of Chicago Press.

Hosler, Dorothy 1994. *The Sounds and Colors of Power: The Sacred Metallurgical Technology of Ancient West Mexico*. Cambridge: MIT Press.

Husserl, Edmund 1993 [1931]. *Cartesian Meditations*. London: Kluwer Academic Press.

Husserl, Edmund 1997 [1948]. *Experience and Judgment*. Evanston, IL: Northwestern University Press.

Husserl, Edmund 1964. *The Phenomenology of Internal Time-Consciousness* (trans. James S. Churchill, ed. Martin Heidegger). Bloomington: Indiana University Press.

Ingold, Tim 2013. *Making: Anthropology, Archeology, Art, and Architecture*. New York and London: Routledge.

Ivanova, Galina 2005. The Biomechanics of the Complex Coordinated Stroke. In V. Roux and B. Bril (eds.) *Stone Knapping: The Necessary Conditions for Uniquely Hominid Behavior*. Cambridge: University of Cambridge, 119–128.

James, William 1950 [1890]. *The Principles of Psychology Volumes I & II*. New York: Henry Holt & Co.

Leroi-Gourhan, André [1964] 1993. *Gesture and Speech*. Boston: MIT Press.

Marchand, Trevor 2012. Brain, Hand and the Use of Tools. In *The Sage Handbook of Social Anthropology*. Thousand Oaks: Sage.

Marchand, Trevor 2014. Skill and Aging: Perspectives from Three Generations of English Woodworkers. In E. Hallam and T. Ingold (eds.) *Making and Growing*. Farnham: Ashgate, 183–202.

Mauss, Marcel 2006. "Techniques and Technology" [1941–1948]; "Techniques of the Body" [1935–1947]; "Technology". In N. Schlanger (ed.) *Techniques, Technology, and Civilization*. Oxford: Berghahn Books.

Merleau-Ponty, Maurice [1945] 1993. Cézanne's Doubt. In G. Johnson (ed.) *The Merleau-Ponty Aesthetics Reader: Philosophy and Painting*. Evanston: Northwestern University Press. 59–75.

Merleau-Ponty, Maurice [1945] 2012. *Phenomenology of Perception*. London: Routledge.

Owen, Joy 2015. Resonance: Beyond the Words. *Anthropology Southern Africa* 38 (1–2):158–160.

Paterson, Mark 2007. *The Senses of Touch: Haptic Affects and Technologies*. Oxford: Berg.

Polanyi, Michael 1966. *The Tacit Dimension*. New York: Doubleday.

Scarry, Elaine 1985. *The Body in Pain: The Making and Unmaking of the World*. Oxford: Oxford University Press.

Stout, Dietrich 2005. The Social and Cultural Context of Stone-Knapping Skill Acquisition. In V. Roux and B. Bril (eds.) *Stone Knapping: The Necessary Conditions for Uniquely Hominid Behavior*. Cambridge: MacDonald Institute for Archeological Research, 331–340

Stout, Dietrich 2016. Tales of a Stone Age Neuroscientist. *Scientific American* 314 (4): 28–35.

Throop, Jason 2003. Articulating Experience. *Anthropological Theory* 3 (2): 219–241, Sage Publications (London, Thousand Oaks, Ca and New Delhi).

Throop, Jason 2010. *Suffering and Sentiment: Exploring the Vicissitudes of Experience and Pain*. Berkeley: University of California Press.

Tsing, Anna L. 2005. *Friction: An Ethnography of Global Connection*. Princeton: Princeton University Press.

Whyte, Iain Boyd 2014. Editorial. In Special Issue. *Art in Translation* 6 (4): 349–352.

Wikan, Unni 1992. Beyond the Words: The Power of Resonance. *American Ethnologist* 19 (3): 460–482.

Williams, Raymond 1954. *Culture and Society*. New York: Columbia University Press.

Winnicott, Donald 1971. *Playing and Reality*. London: Tavistock.

Wynn, Thomas 1993. Layers of Thinking in tool Behavior. In Kathleen Gibson and Tim Ingold (eds.) *Tools, Language and Cognition in Human Evolution*. Cambridge: Cambridge University Press, 389–406.

Part III

Absence of knowledge

7 Isomorphic articulations

Notes from collaborative film-work in an Afghan-Danish Film Collective

Karen Waltorp and ARTlife Film Collective[1]

How to let knowledge *unfold* and embrace modes of attention that entail unlearning? And how could we grasp the in-between, grayness of living, that which lays beyond a binary thinking? This chapter takes its point of departure in the ongoing research project: ARTlife: Articulations of Life among Afghans in Denmark'[2] and its experiments with co-generating spaces of articulation beyond the verbal and that which can be grasped within conventional academic discourse. I focus specifically on the collective conceptualization and practical efforts in the ARTlife Film Collective: A group of four women of Afghan background, who grew up in Denmark, and one anthropologist of Danish background. In this 'research-through-filmmaking' we aim to produce a film that will be screened at international festivals, and hopefully on one of the channels of the Danish Broadcasting Corporation, reaching a diverse audience. The empirical material is what is generated in the process of planning, scripting, filming, and editing the film. In this chapter, I unpack the notions of 'collaboration' and 'workshop', that are pivotal in this project. I discuss how the circulation of images in social media was part of the knowledge emerging between us in the collective.

Our collaboration is situated within a media landscape – a media ecology – consisting of broadcast media, print media, social media etc. This media ecology concretely impacts on us both implicitly and explicitly. We react to it and dialogue with it – and this is an integral part of the inquiry: How we meet and interface with the actors and expectations of the media industry in a *productively peripheral* position vis-à-vis the media industry. Studying (in) this media ecology, and as part of a collective where things only become manifest as we go along and with constant input from a range of actors, implies a dialectic move between strict and loose thinking: An assemblage that only stabilizes temporarily and where the anthropologist (experimentalist) is always part of the assemblage interrogated (Waltorp 2020: 5–6). The outcome of this process is what I term isomorphic articulations.

Gregory Bateson (2000) advocated remaining systematic and rigorous in working open-ended with no narrowly predefined goal. Eduardo Kohn, inspired by Bateson, suggests an anthropological thinking that is isomorphic, i.e. corresponding or similar in form and relations.[3] Such an anthropological thinking that is isomorphic with that which is thought, radically builds from and with the aesthetic, imagistic, mimetic and the resonant emerging from the ethnography (Kohn 2018).

It is an analytics that is empirically derived. In ARTlife Film Collective, themes that are experienced as significant to the women involved are included, and take shape over time, in the form of scenes. This happens gradually during discussions, participant observation, collaborative script-writing, (planning of) filmmaking, and presentations to various audiences – but also very much in images shared courtesy of digital infrastructures, as well as in dream images in the 'Imaginal realm'.[4] This mode of attention and 'making together' opens up to knowledge existing in different registers than the strictly verbal.

The flow of images cannot be controlled or directed but is occupying the space in-between concrete techniques, practices and products (formats) on the one hand, and abstract imaginaries, ideals and images on the other (Waltorp 2020). Working multimodally (see Dattatreyan and Marrero-Guillamón 2019; Waltorp 2021) and collaboratively in the ARTlife Film Collective entails paying attention to the slow formation of issues, towards isomorphic articulations in the modalities of writing and moving images: When does a product (also an articulation) adhere more strictly to genre expectations, and when is a product allowed to be impacted more radically by 'that which is thought' by the collective (rather than the individual)? Other scholars have suggested both the inherent contingency of life and research (Irving 2016, 2018), its 'ongoingness' and openness (Dalsgaard and Frederiksen 2013), and the move towards more collective work in a culture of the 'sole anthropologist' (see Biehl and Locke 2017; Pink 2018). I describe instances of the ARTlife Film Collective's work across writing (in different register), social media and filming. These instances afford isomorphic articulations that are different *and* more than what is thought by the sum of its members.

How it all began: Methodology and the politics of inviting

The ARTlife Film Collective consists of Nilab Totakhil, Asma Mohammadzai Safi, Sama Sadat Ben Haddou, Mursal Khosrawi and myself, Karen Waltorp. I met all of the women through my personal and professional network in late 2017. I introduced my idea for a film project carried out in a radically collaborative way, where we would jointly arrive at significant themes for a film in a number of workshops. All would have expenses for travel, food, and accommodation in relation to the project reimbursed. No one would be paid for their work, except for me as I am paid out of my salary as a researcher at university. Should the film win prize money or otherwise generate a surplus it would be split equally between the five co-directors. All equipment and expenses for producing the film would be paid out of my project budget, and further funding collectively applied for, in the post-production phase.

After I had met with three of the four women individually,[5] the collective held its inaugural workshop in February 2018. It lasted 11 hours, and we said goodbye to each other, tired and excited: Heavy from all the Indian food we had consumed at Restaurant Columbo at the Vesterbro neighborhood in Copenhagen, but uplifted by the prospect that we might together create something that could obviate what seem the settled position for a young Muslim woman in Danish media representations – either celebrated as 'free' (having turned her back on Islam) on the one hand, or pitied as subdued 'unfree' (veiled) woman (having embraced Islam) on the other (Ahmad and Waltorp 2019). After our first workshop we agreed that we wanted to show different women's lived lives, and different positions, not easily reduced to any one stereotype. What scenes the film would entail, how the stories would be told and more sensitive issues evoked remained open at this point in time, as did the question of whether it would be an art-video on the web or an observational-style documentary. Mursal created a private Facebook group for us on the very same day of our first workshop. I started filming shortly after, and we followed each other on Instagram and let each person's style and aesthetic inspire how we thought about format. It could not easily be aligned into a coherent visual aesthetic, so we pondered a series format, which was abandoned again (for the time being).

The inaugural workshop was held at the home of visual anthropologist Sine Plambech and film director Janus Metz. Sine has worked with representing women, migration and everyday life. Janus has directed an award-winning film on Danish military involvement in Afghanistan, following young Danish soldiers deployed to the Helmand province. Two 'inspirational' talks were given by guests; film director Sine Skibsholt and the editor of Danish National Broadcasting's youth channel DR Ultra Sara Pagh. The two guests (re)presented different ways of communicating and evoking in a filmic language, and with the use of different 'tools', depending on what we wished to convey, how, and to whom. These spaces and people were chosen carefully, seeking to be clear about my 'politics of inviting' (Lindström and Ståhl 2016). Kristina Lindström and Åsa Ståhl note that a little-explored practice in design anthropology is the crafting of invitations and how publics are made. Specifically, they study invitations to user studies, to interviews, to ethnographic fieldwork projects, to co-design workshops, to prototyping and to public engagement events. These artists suggest paying attention to and refiguring what we invite to, how and when. They argue for the value of inviting participants to take part in co-articulations of issues that arise in the course of 'the ongoing', as the issues and potentialities that emerge in everyday life can never be fully predicted. They practice inviting as a collaborative formation that engage with issues connected to the ongoing living with technologies through 'designerly public engagements' – as devices collaboratively designed and arrived at (see Criado and Estalella 2018; Waltorp 2018).

As we met as a group for the first time, I wanted to 'perform' for Nilab, Asma, Sama and Mursal how I would contribute to our collective with a network of film and TV professionals as well as academics that could help us in our endeavours – and that they might individually connect with these people in other ways in their work life. Besides this, I brought to the table my own funding and experience – having worked with related themes and directed the award-winning film *Manenberg* (Waltorp and Vium 2010) and *Joyous are the Eyes that See You* (Waltorp 2017a). I stated as honestly as I could why I wanted to do this project, my motivation, stakes and hopes – and I wanted the other women to share their stakes, motivations and reservations. I hoped that overlapping stakes would appear between us, while also accepting that our stakes would not be entirely the same – for any of the women in the collective (see Rabinow et al. 2008 on a discussion of overlapping stakes). This is not to "imply, however, that all women suffer the same oppression simply because we are women... to distort our commonality as well as our difference. For then, beyond sisterhood, is still racism" (Lorde 1983: 95, 97). The idea that friction should not be avoided, and 'agreeing to disagree' was shared by all, and even though we in the group clearly feel that we take different positions on many topics, we have been seen as a 'performance team' (Goffman 1959), which I elaborate on below.

My invitation into this project took the above form so that the invited (non-paid) members of the collective could determine whether they wanted to invest their time and energy in it and make it theirs too. The only contract that we have is the time and energy that we each have invested, and the fear of someone losing interest and opting out has been intense on my part at times. I wanted to be as forward as possible, and I really wanted the others to want to attend the next workshop. Our second workshop was held at Elk Film, owned by Andreas Dalsgård, who holds a BA in Anthropology and who made the film *Afghan Muscles* (2006) with my partner Christian Vium, also part of the larger ARTlife research project team. From then on, workshops have been held at Sama's home in Vallensbæk west of Copenhagen, in Nilab's home in Kastrup, as well as in my apartment in Aarhus and later at my home in Copenhagen; we have met at the Danish Film Institute, META Film, and at the Moesgård Museum in the Eye and Mind Laboratory, Department of Anthropology, Aarhus University. Later meetings have been held at Monies Film with film director Lea Glob who has become part of the larger ARTlife Collective too. Those formal and informal workshops have been interspersed with visits, filming, and communication in social media. This process has also seen us present together to various audiences such as at an international conference at Aarhus University 'Exploring Dimensions of Afghan Migration to Europe' in February 2019. Sama's father, Mir Abdul Vahed Sadat, joined and babysat his daughter's four-month-old baby. He is taking part in the project, as he and Sama's mother Malalai Kargar, tell their story of the flight to Denmark in a scene in the film.

Prior to a workshop and presentation to our Advisory Board, a professional women's network of which I am a part, *Netwerket*, in March 2019, Malalai, Sama's mother, joined us in my apartment. She had come along to look after Sama's baby in the two-day event. Yet she ended up very much engaging and offering new perspectives into our discussions 'backstage' in my apartment and in our workshop-meeting with the Advisory Board the following day. We had two meetings with a scriptwriter, Mille Haynes, who provided professional feedback on the script as it developed. This is not a manuscript in the strict sense, that is, one written to be played out and filmed. It rather depicts scenes already filmed, and scenes that each of the participants imagine to include as part of their story, wherefore we have shifted between defining it as a hybrid film, an ethno-fiction (Henley 2009, Rouch 2003) and, finally, a poetic documentary.

We need to 'look beyond accepted ideas, to find out if there's something there' as visual anthropologist Jean Rouch invited for in his call for experimenting with storytelling in anthropology and film (2003: 148): 'we are still constrained to something terrible, formal... why haven't we exploded this stage system', he asks (ibid). Rouch was excited for the new digital possibilities, noting how the 'Little Pale Fox' of the Dogon's myth writes the news for tomorrow with its paws...introducing the 'digital' in our electronic systems (ibid: 160). In a digitally integrated world, other forms of representation fuse the power of the arts and the social sciences (Stoller 2017: 28) yet with these new electronic platforms, digital innovations, and evolving forms of scholarly and artistic representation, Paul Stoller (2017) invites us to remember Rouch's central question – where is the story? Will the story connect with the audiences and/or how can it be better imagined? Stoller (1997) himself tacks between the intelligible and the sensible, as he interweaves different modes of ethnographic and theoretical writing into his work in such a way that enables us to engage with different modes of knowing and understanding (Pink 2020: ix). Our manuscript consultant Mille listened to our visions and desires while keeping the role of film professional, asking about 'the conflict' and the 'clear story'. Our talks with her were crucial, and the push-back from her and other film and TV professionals in terms of our insistence on 'gray zones', the boring and the mundane in the film, helped us grasp the outline of it. Below is an excerpt from the draft manuscript, which we shared with her. Some parts are still in keyword form. It shows the montage of the women's sto-ries/storylines creating more than the sum of each story on its own:

Four Women, four segments:

Sama: The journey and background: Sama's parents, Malalai and Mir, recount their lives in Afghanistan and the move/flight to Denmark, where they built a new life for Sama and her brother and sister. Generations: When they buried Sama's grandfather at *Vestre Kirkegård* it became clear that life is here in Denmark, and the family's growing new roots. The parents still feel heartache and longing toward their native Afghanistan, though. We follow Sama in her present life with her marriage to Karim and the birth of their son Musa – the future.

Mursal: Mursal engages in the political debates taking place in Denmark around migration, integration, Islam etc., seeking to provide nuances to these debates and shed light on all the misunderstandings related to Islamophobia and everyday racism. We follow Mursal's conversations with politicians at Christiansborg, on national TV and radio, and this is juxtaposed with her con-versations with her little sister on existential questions. In her personal life she is at a crucial point - about to marry the man she will build her life with.

Nilab: Nilab is changing people's perceptions about what a young (Afghan) woman *can* do and be, step-by-step – in this case, moving into her own apartment and living a life where career, traveling and friends take cen-ter stage, instead of getting married and having children: Something that is not always fully accepted by neither the Danish nor the Afghan society – how can one not want a family and children of one's own? Is it truly enough for a woman to only want to travel and create a life for herself? This scepti-cism is something which her family is faced with by the Afghan society – and due to *her* lifestyle, *they* are challenged by other Afghan-Danish families. In her career, Nilab is helping others become an integral part of the society *and* changing society through engaging in politics and in a pedagogical pro-gram TeachFirst. We follow her on the outskirts of Copenhagen with the 7th grade students she teaches.

Asma: Asma is a graduate student living in Odense; she's a poetic hipster in jeans, t-shirt and big curly hair one day, shifting into scenes in Afghanistan with her family in Jalalabad the next. The conflicts between different sets of expectations and values might be there continuously in her life – but they are solved (mostly) without drama, ongoingly and every single day – Asma's story is one of being your amazing 'composite' self *and* insisting on being a 'normal' person first and foremost. This part is an insight into a daily life balanced between cultures, forging one's own way with the elements, that are appreciated – and those that are just part of you. This does not add up to a hyphen-identity, but is rather something else altogether with the elements fusing- and influencing each other, as they are at the same time shaped by the environment.

The four parts will be interwoven as all five women gather in the same social space (or social media space), as we transition from one woman's story, to the next. The transitions between the individual parts are to be workshops, dinners, visits, sleepovers, cinema festivals, activities – where all five, or several of the women, are doing something together. Social media graphics will also be used as transitions: Facebook posts from the group's Facebook group and chats, and Instagram posts- and stories from the individuals' accounts, respectively. (ARTlife draft manuscript).

My story is missing. We have alternated between including it and excluding it. The absence will not be complete, as 'in-between' scenes will include meta-layers of the Collective meeting and discussing scenes, planning filming, and debating various themes in the film. I prefer to remove myself, but others in the Collective feel differently, and for the time being we're keeping it open.

ARTlife Film Collective shares some general characteristics with the processes and films emerging from (fine) arts and sciences institutions discussed by An van Dienderen (2008) in that 'they are mostly state funded, and thus not engendered by commercial interest. Instead the "author" is the driving force between the project and is most often the producer. The crew consist of a small number of people, with a mixture of "professionals" and volunteers. Because of their specific audio-visual choices, be it on the elaboration of the medium, the process, the authorship of the narrative, these cases can be considered as "alternative", "experimental" or "independent" cinema' (Van Dienderen 2008: 62–63) – in other words: on the periphery in relation to both the centres of the Film and TV industry and standard ways of carrying out social science research projects in academia as well.[6]

The detailed description of the beginning of the project above serves to unpack what 'collaboration' means in this concrete example, and what kinds of spaces and dynamics, which the ARTlife 'workshop' format entails: Multiple actors, entities, technologies and infrastructures are part of the becoming of the ARTLife film (Collective). The ARTlife Film Collective's film officially has multiple authorship as all five women involved are co-directors, yet the initial driving force is me wherefore I have more of a producer/project coordinator role, and I do not wish to indicate a flat landscape of collaboration in the collective: We have different roles, some enjoy filming and editing and do that alongside me, while others do not take on that role with passion, but rather co-create the contents of the film in other ways. As mentioned above, stakes are not identical but overlapping. When we present for other audiences, though, we have been told that we become akin to a 'performance team' (see Goffman 1959). This has been remarked as both impressive in a positive sense, as well as with the obvious concern that this prevents a 'critical edge' and the (re)presentation becomes bland. None of the members of the collective are interested in taking on the role of PR persons, or representing themselves as other than what they are. As the majority ethnic Dane in the collective, I have been asked if I did not worry that I was being used to forward someone's (presumably) pro-Islam agenda. The women who are ethnic minority Danes might face other concerns, indicating that they are being used in someone else's project as 'præmie-perkere' (successful prize minority person according to the majority ethnic Danes).

I am interested in the dynamic of us as a (perceived) performance team towards various audiences, and in the worry voiced by some, that working together across differences will make our film and other representations collectively produced bland. Staying with this, the word *bland* in English means dull, flavourless, uninteresting and watered down, pointing to a valid concern in relation to our collaboration. At the same time, bland also retains the connotation of smooth, soothing, flattering and alluring from the Latin 'blandus' it is derived from. Below I stay with 'bland' to 'gray' and consider what peripheral knowledge might emerge from this in a media logic where the drive is towards the opposite pole of bland and gray.

"Where's the conflict?" Pitching the 'gray' at the Danish National Broadcasting Corporation

Example of rundown

We were accepted with our pitch (from which the below excerpt is taken) into a talent-and-concept development workshop, held every year at the Danish

in	out	dur	element	Description
00:00	00:10	00:15	intro+title	Overview shots of mountains in Afghanistan transitions into a Danish summer landscape, seen from a train window, and the reflection of Asma, sitting on the train scrolling, checking Instagram on her smartphone with Afghan music in her ear-phones – she is looking out the window.
00:1<u>5</u>	01:30	01:15	Anslag (teaser)	VO (Voice-over): 'When we hear about Afghanistan, it is often related to war, the Taliban and women in Burqa. Then there is the football player Nadia Nadim from the national Danish women's Football Team. How about other young Afghan-Danish women? Who are they? What do they do? And what do they dream about?'

(Continued)

in	out	dur	element	Description
				How do you reconcile expectation from friends, with whom you have grown up in Denmark, the family here, in Afghanistan and across the world? What happens when you want to move away from home, but do not want to get married or have children? How does it impact your dreams for the future, when politicians on TV constantly tell you, that you're not Danish and you do not really belong? How to hold on to *who* you are, when you're a young Muslim woman in your 20s with big dreams and people's eyes on you at all times?
01:30	05:30	04:00	Build-up 1	VO (Sama's voice): Our parents came to Denmark when we were so young – many don't remember much, but there are glimpses you never forget...
				Malalai and Mir, a couple in their early 60s, sit in the gray corner sofa in their daughter Sama's apartment west of Copenhagen. Their adult son is also there, and they are looking at old photographs spread out on the sofa table. SYNC: 'We came here to make a life and a future possible for you' (Malalai) Sama arrives with a tray with Flora Danica coffee cups, her son is playing on the wooden floor.

Broadcasting Corporation. This time it was with the subtitle and theme: 'New Voices'. The three-page pitch saw me reiterate some of the stereotypes, that I/ we seek to displace with our collaborative filmmaking. At least it also succeeded in getting us accepted, and we jumped at the chance of presenting our ideas and work, and get feedback from TV professionals.

We had arrived from Sønderborg, Århus, Køge and Kastrup, Sama had cancelled due to her son falling ill. The people behind the workshop programme had not revealed much – on purpose. We were thrown into the exercise, and had to improvise as best we could in the situation. We were walking down the halls of the Danish Broadcasting Corporation's head offices with huge windows opening onto Emil Holms Canal to the famous radio studio. We had just been told that we had 5 minutes to tell about our project to a radio host, the programme would be recorded but not broadcast. As we enter the room, the host turns to us and smiles warmly: 'It's amazing to hear about all these new ideas for programs today, and now there's a whole girl gang entering the studio.' We sit down in front of a microphone each and the host looks at me, asking what the story is about. I feel awkward that he asks me, but I quickly reply and fall back on the pitch mentioned above, trying to keep things a bit more nuanced, and I notice that I say 'when you are a young Danish woman... who is also a young Afghan woman'. The host turns to Mursal, and poses the next question to her:

> Host: But, is it on DR – in the cinema – where is it, that we will see the story about your lives?
>
> Mursal: Well, we're hoping that it will be with DR, a documentary of 90 minutes: Where you tell four stories, that are completely different, but that also binds us together in the sense that, we are in our 20s, late 20s, and ehm... the cool things is that it will come out and push back on some of the stereotypes in place. Because what we all share, besides being in our 20s, is kind of the fact that we do not see ourselves represented in the media. That's why we want to come out and tell our own story, to represent ourselves, but also those that look like us.
>
> Host: And Nilab, what are you hoping that this film will do for others who are like you?
>
> Nilab: I think Mursal says it quite well in the form of, I hope – or we hope (pointing also to Asma who is to the other side of her) – that we can create some alternative images around what it means to be an Afghan woman – or – a woman with an Afghan background in Denmark, or any other background – than what we see in the media. So, you don't all the time have to have two polarized – two poles, that you constantly need to situate yourself according to. There's actually something in-between, that's 'gray', there's four different versions of what's in-between (she gestures to Mursal and Asma who both smile) – that's very 'gray'.
>
> Host: You're awesome women, and I hope this goes somewhere. The men need to really get their act together, when listening to you (laughing, both host and us), wow – the tempo's high. Thanks so much for stopping by and telling us about your idea. All the luck your way.

A different exercise was 'pitching', presenting in a way that hooks your audience and makes it clear what the story is about, and why they should care. We did not completely succeed in pitching our idea. How do you pitch a wish from the women in the collective to portray the gray, the normal? I felt a bit uneasy, when we presented as our hosts kept asking us 'Where's the conflict?' The driving force in any story is the conflict, driving it forward as the protagonist seeks to resolve it. We all stood on a line facing our audience and presenting. Asma, Nilab and Mursal all reiterated that there was much *less* conflict than what we usually hear about in the media when hearing about 'women like them' – young Muslim women of other ethnic background than Danish. They pointed to the much more mundane and ongoing solving of whatever dilemmas arise, big or small, as 'no big deal'. Consequently, it seems as if there would be no big, apparent conflict to build the dramatic curve in the film on. I bit my lip. A part of me wanted to disagree, to state that from my point of view, there is no lack of conflict: There are so many expectations from family, peers, public and politicians. In the Danish society, they are the ones in the family with the linguistic and 'cultural' expertise; they feel the pressure from (loving) hopes and expectations that they make the most of all the opportunities afforded them; and expectations, on the other hand, from certain segments in the Danish society that they demonstrate continually that they are free and not subdued Muslim women who suffer social control from their families. Striking a balance where everyone is happy is quite a feat.

I wanted to suggest, then and there, that only when you have grown up with cross-pressures like this do you develop a skill set affording navigation of such 'transcontextual', or double-bind, situations (Bateson 2000). Someone differently positioned would probably see this as a conflict. But I did not say this. I have written about this transcontextual situation, and the need to be able to navigate it as a young Muslim woman in Denmark, elsewhere (Waltorp 2020). The knowledge generated with people in earlier fieldwork should not stand in the way of listening closely, listening anew – to unlearning and being perplexed. So, I fought my wish to speak about clear, straightforward conflicts, and stayed with trying to understand the insistence on gray meanings and tonalities of living, and how that could be methodologically represented and engaged with.

Chromatic, plain gray, Trinh T. Minh-ha tells us (2010: 70), is a new hue that is neither black or white. In the middle where possibility is boundless. Gray is composed of multiplicity. When the two can't be distinguished. What does it really mean when Nilab insist that there is a lot of gray, or when Asma insist that her story is about 'just the normal', 'boring'? I quote here Trinh T. Minh-ha at length:

> ...if you are focusing on everyday life, building on the gestures of a culture via ordinary activities, and composing a distinct tapestry of sense, sight and sound as you go, it doesn't seem like a subject for a number of film consumers, especially film programmers and funders, who always ask for 'a story'... So even when you make a documentary they beg you to develop an individualist, character-story with a beginning, middle and end, abiding by the normative theatrical three acts and its conflict-driven climax. For me, filmmaking is not at all about stories or messages. Those come along, but they can't define cinema. Why not approach filmically a country, a people, a culture by starting with what comes with an image (mental, material, digital)... Through the specific apparatus of film and video, how does one show, tell and receive while refusing merely to represent?
>
> (Minh-Ha in Minh-ha and Mercier 2018: 80)

We have been faced with the demand for a recognisable story, and the demand for conflict in our (productive) meetings with actors from the film and TV industry. We strive to see whether we can create a film by starting with the images – mental, material and digital – which we share, and create an isomorphic articulation, evoking also 'gray' as 'composed of multiplicity'. We can ask with Kim TallBear (2013) which articulations (of identity) come to matter and carry weight within which system? The concept of articulation, famously, has the meaning of both giving utterance to something, and denotes two discrete things that come to be connected, such as a car and an articulated lorry (see Clifford 2001; Hall 1980;

Hall et al. 1996). Stuart Hall writes that articulation is the form of the connection that can make a unity of two different elements, under certain conditions. It is a linkage which is not necessary, determined, absolute and essential for all time. And we have to ask, under what circumstances can a connection be made? (Hall 1986; Hall et al. 1996). As Paul Stoller alerts us to with reference to Jean Rouch; new digital technologies have altered the landscape of anthropological expression, yet these new digital application and technological possibilities are of limited value if there is no story to be told. It is the quality of the story that determines whether an ethnographic work will remain open to the world (Stoller 2017). It is this kind of story – one that comes along and that remains open to the world – that we strive for in the ARTlife Collective, both insisting on the more sensuous registers (Stoller 1997) as well as embracing and letting ourselves be 'inhabited' by the technologies with(in) which we work (Waltorp 2020).

In the film, Asma will be speaking in her scenes, but the voice-over will not be there to explain, but to evoke. Minh-ha writes that interviews occupy a dominant role in documentary practices in terms of authenticating information, validating the voices represented, and claiming to give voice (Minh-ha 1992). Asma's voice (over) will be less authoritative and explanatory, more stream-of-consciousness. It will be accompanied by scenes filmed by her in Afghanistan, and film shot by me in her Danish everyday environments. I have referred to the modality of images, and to images shared. Below, I describe one example of such a 'flow of images' emerging in relation to Asma's scenes. This could not be planned-for and is telling in terms of what an isomorphic articulation might be on a micro-scale – which is at the same time global and intimate, courtesy of digital technologies and infrastructures.

Transmutation as soundtrack and the flow of images

What am I, she thought: A Danish woman with Afghan roots, or an Afghan young woman, living in Denmark?
(Asma Mohammadzai Safi, ARTlife draft manuscript)

Haathoon ki lakiron pe mat ja ae Ghalib, naseeb unke bhi hote hain jinki haath nahi hote (Do not follow the lines of the hand, those who have no hands still have a destiny).
(Mirza Ghalib quoted by Asma Mohammadzai Safi, ARTlife draft manuscript)

In one of the early workshops we discussed introducing 'hybrid' elements in the form of musical elements such as the traditional Afghan instruments *rabab* (rhubarb) and *tabla*, respectively a string instrument and drums. And in our draft manuscript, the aesthetic techniques (*greb* in Danish) applied in each of the women's parts, is described:

Sama: Old vernacular photos/archival footage of Afghanistan.
Mursal: Snapchat/Facebook/Instagram (video) as a layer.

Nilab: Nilab speaking directly to the camera.

Asma: Poetic take on modern Afghanistan and Denmark in images and art, and Asma's voice-over monologue (stream-of-consciousness) with instrumental (traditional afghan in modern version) such as rabab and tabla.

(excerpt, ARTlife draft manuscript)

We shared links of images of *tabla* and *rabab* and the music played on these instruments in our Facebook group, and toyed with the idea that it should be played by only women in the film, though that is not seen in Afghanistan, where only men play these instruments. A cold November afternoon, I had visited Asma in her brother's apartment in Gellerup. We drove to my place afterward and looked at some of her material from Afghanistan. She filmed in 2017 as she visited family there, and was now editing it together. I showed her a scene, which I had filmed during the summer, with her on the train. I had edited the scene and added a piece of music played by Qais Essar, an Afghan-American *rabab*-player, whose music Asma had introduced me to as possible soundtrack for some of her scenes. Essar plays the *rabab* and fuses various elements into very sensuous musical pieces. I had chosen the track 'Transmutation'. Asma liked the feeling that the scene evoked with images and sounds together, and she asked me to play the scene again on my laptop, which I did, and she filmed it with her smartphone and posted it to her Instagram story. I was not aware in the moment as I was simultaneously preparing dinner for us and my family. Only later that evening did I realize as Qais Essar had seen Asma's story, where he was 'tagged', and he shared this with all of his followers on his Instagram profile: Asma's story of his track playing over her image, on my laptop. Asma then shared his reposting of her Instagram story of the image of herself sitting on a train with her smartphone in hand and with the 'transmutation' track playing. I took a screen shot of this beautiful Instagram matryoshka doll.

The very way I filmed Asma in the first instance was inspired by her own aesthetics, which I had come to know through following her Instagram profile and spending time with her around image-making. This time spent, and the images created together and shared in social media, is part of the isomorphic move, in that it inspires how Asma and her story is evoked. The Oxford Learners Dictionary definition of 'transmutation', the name of the track that was inspiring our scene and was shared as described above, is 'an act of changing, or of being changed, into something different' it is also the supposed alchemical process of changing base metals into gold. The editors of this volume also point to the notion that we are acted upon by peripheral wisdom and this transforms us. This notion dialogues with Kohn's discussion of the isomorphic, inspired by Bateson's 'psychedelic anthropology', with which I started this chapter. These discussions allude to what happens when we let ourselves be taken over in the field. It is a move resisting premature analytical closure; resisting the masterly and expertly at expense of attuned listening; resisting clichés (Bateson 2000) and gate-keeping concepts (Appadurai 1986).

Kohn describes the isomorphic via 'psychedelic analytics' and Bateson's 'double description' thus: 'I have become increasingly interested in thinking with psychedelics, by which I mean a series of techniques for thinking that manifest in

the minds of their thinkers in ways that dissolve those thinkers into the manifestation of the minds that think them, in what would be called psychedelic analytics.
In following this concept, I keep coming back to Bateson's (2000) development
of what he terms "double description", which is a prime example of "an empirically derived analytics"' (Kohn 2018: 64). This looking at something *and* looking
at ourselves simultaneously. An analytics that belongs neither to Bateson nor to
anthropology, as Kohn writes 'Rather, it is a kind of thought that thinks us, a kind
of thought that we can think with if we can use it in such a way that its psychedelic – that is, mind-manifesting – properties can become apparent to us' (ibid.).

Also Tymek Woodham has studied how material processes are used as inspi-
rations for experimental poetic form, and how this linkage of material process
and form contributes to anxieties surrounding individual and collective agency.[7]
In his writing on the 'material imaginations' of poets such as Langston Hughes
(known for 'jazz poetry' and a prominent figure in the 'Harlem Renaissance'),
Woodham identifies inspiring ways of working across modalities as a technique
towards relinquishing control, of suspending the moment of knowing and extending the uncomfortably-playful moment of learning peripherally:

> It is this hidden verb that helpfully conjures to mind the experience of
> peripheral vision: from the corner of one's eye, a flash appears – a spark so
> intriguing that it *carries the perceiver away* from what they were doing or
> the place to which they were going. In this sense, the agency of the periphery
> lies in its capacity to pick us up and spirit us off: it is not a static point which
> occupies the edge of a frame – rather, it is the very motor of our on-going
> self- dislocation; it is that which takes us away from our centre. This notion
> of the periphery as an active concept.
>
> (Woodham 2018: 4)

Outro

I asked in the beginning about how to let knowledge unfold and embrace modes
of attention that entail unlearning. In this chapter, I have given detailed descriptions of instances of the work in the ARTlife Film Collective, and suggested that
this kind of 'research-through-filmmaking' and 'making-together' invites for letting collective knowledge emerge. The examples illustrate how this knowledge
unfolds in-between the actors involved and is also informed by the questions pur-
sued as well as the infrastructure and media ecology which is part of the assemblage interrogated. In this take, the word 'periphery' literally means 'to carry',
'about' or 'around'. Letting ourselves be dislocated and pay attention to what
appears at the corner of the eye is 'peripheral knowledge'. I have contemplated
what 'bland' and 'gray' tells us in the empirical material generated in the collective efforts of the ARTlife Film Collective, and described the 'flow of images'
emerging in relation to Asma's scenes circulated in Instagram with Qais Essar's
track of transmutation and the sound of the *rabab*. Other isomorphic articulations
from the ARTlife Film Collective are in the making.

Notes

1 The members of the collective are Nilab Totakhil, Asma Mohammadzai Safi, Sama Sadat Ben Haddou, Mursal Khosrawi and the author of this article. The reason for adding the collective as a joint co-author is that parts of our draft manuscript and other elements have been included, and these have multiple authorship.
2 https://projekter.au.dk/artlife/ The research group consists of three researchers, one PhD and five MA-students who experiment with the methodological and conceptual affordances embedded within the technologies of photography, film, social media, theatre and material objects in an attempt to understand what recent arrived refugees and Danish-Afghans, that might have lived in the country for decades, themselves see as the challenges of everyday life in Denmark. It is funded by AUFF NOVA supporting high-risk–high-gain research that approaches known problems in the humanities and social sciences in radically new ways.
3 See 'What is it about us as thinkers, and the places from which we think, that makes us receptive (or not) to certain kinds of analytics. Because an analytics seems to require a form of anthropological thinking that is isomorphic with that which is thought, it appears that developing an analytics always involves an epistemic privileging of the iconic (i.e., of the resonant, the mimetic, the imagistic, the aesthetic, the formal), which is buttressed by some sort of ontological claim (implicit or explicit) as to why this mode of thought should be privileged' (Kohn 2018: 16).
4 I propose elsewhere that the flow of images across realms can be (studied) across dimensions or realms such as social media images in digital infrastructures as well as dream-images in the imaginal realm (Corbin 1976; Marks 2015, 2016). The dimension drawing in night dreams will not be discussed in-depth here, see Waltorp 2017b and Waltorp 2020 for a thorough discussion of the flow of images in digital infrastructures, dream images, and notions of an 'Imaginal realm' in Eastern Islamic thought.
5 I met with other women too, and had coffee meetings and more formal interviews with a number of them. For various reasons they either were not able to – or did not wish to – participate in the film part of the project, but all agreed to be interviewed. Space does not allow for the relevant discussion here relating to the story (untold) about the people who choose not to take part in our studies as we frame the projects and invite into them.
6 Van Dienderen chose this position 'alongside' the TV industry after quitting a job at VRT (The Flemish Broadcasting Corporation), where she was asked to shoot a documentary programme about a Turkish family, and obliged to follow a script that was written by colleagues without the slightest intention of – or attempt at – collaboration or research with the people concerned (2008). Luckily this is quite far from the experience that we/I have had 'at the periphery' of the Danish Film and TV industry.
7 Woodham's forthcoming PhD dissertation (UCL) is equally concerned with Charles Olson and Frank O'Hara in addition to Langston Hughes, and is focused on the politically fraught topographies of post-war US culture.

References

Ahmad, M. and K. Waltorp. (2019). Kontroversen om Exitcirklen: Racialisering af muslimske kvinder i den danske mediedebat. *Jordens Folk*, 54(1): 65–79.

Appadurai, A. (1986). Theory in Anthropology: Center and Periphery. *Comparative Studies in Society and History*, 28(2): 356–361.

Bateson, G. 2000 [1972]. *Steps to an Ecology of Mind: Collected Essays in Anthropology, Psychiatry, Evolution and Epistemology*. Chicago: The University of Chicago Press.

Biehl, J. and P. Locke. (2017). The Anthropology of Becoming. in *Unfinished: The Anthropology of Becoming*, pp. 41–89. Durham: Duke University Press.

Clifford, J. (2001). Indigenous Articulations. *The Contemporary Pacific* 13(2), Special Issue: Native Pacific Cultural Studies on the Edge: 468–490.

Corbin, H. (1976). *Mundus Imaginalis: Or, the Imaginary and the Imaginal*. Ipswich: Golgonooza Press.

Criado, T. S. and A. Estalella. (2018). Introduction: Experimental Collaborations, pp. 1–29. in A. Estalella and T. Sánchez-Criado (eds), *Experimental Collaborations: Ethnography Through Fieldwork Devices*, pp. 114–131. London: Berghahn Books.

Dalsgaard, A. L. and M. D. Frederiksen (2013). Out of Conclusion: On Recurrence and Open-endedness in Life and Analysis. *Social Analysis*, 57(1): 50–63.

Dattatreyan, E. G. and I. Marrero-Guillamón. (2019). Introduction: Multimodal Anthropology and the Politics of Invention. *American Anthropologist* 121(1): 220–228.

Goffman, E. (1959). *The Presentation of Self in Everyday Life*. New York: Doubleday.

Hall, S. (1986). Gramsci's Relevance for the Study of Race and Ethnicity. *Journal of Communication Inquiry*, 10(2): 5–27.

Hall, S. (1980). Encoding/Decoding. in S. Hall, D. Hobson, A. Lowe and P. Willis (eds), *Culture, Media, Language: Working Papers in Cultural Studies 1972–79*, pp. 128–138. London: Hutchinson.

Hall, S., D. Morley and K.-H. Chen. (1996). *Stuart Hall: Critical Dialogues in Cultural Studies*. London: Routledge.

Haraway, D. (1988). Situated Knowledges: The Science Question in Feminism and the Privilege of Partial Perspective. *Feminist Studies*, 14(3): 575–599.

Henley, P. (2009). *Adventures of the Real. Jean Rouch and the Craft of Ethnographic Cinema*. Chicago: Chicago University Press.

Irving, A. (2016). New York Stories: Narrating the Neighbourhood. *Ethnos*, 82(3): 21.

Irving, A. (2018). A Life Lived Otherwise: Contingency and Necessity in an Interconnected World. *Anthropologica*, 60(2): 390–402.

Kohn, E. (2018). Analytics and Anthropology. Forum. What Is Analysis? Between Theory, Ethnography, and Method. Holbraad, M. et al. *Social Analysis*, 62(1): 1–30.

Lindström, K. and Å. Ståhl (2016). Politics of Inviting: Co-Articulations of Issues in Designerly Public Engagement. in R. C. Smith, K. T. Vangkilde, M. G. Kjaersgaard, T. Otto, J. Halse and T. Binder (eds), *Design Anthropological Futures*, pp. 183–198. London: Bloomsbury.

Marks, L. U. (2015). *Hanan al-Cinema: Affections for the Moving Image*. London: MIT Press.

Marks, L. U. (2016). Real Images Flow: Mullâ Sadrâ Meets Film-Philosophy. *Film-Philosophy*, 20(1): 24–46.

Trinh T. Minh-ha. (1992). *Framer Framed*. London and New York: Routledge.

Trinh T. Minh-ha. (2010). *Elsewhere, Within Here: Immigration, Refugeeism and the Boundary Event*. London: Routledge.

Trinh T. Minh-ha and L. K.-C. Mercier. (2018). Interview: Forgetting Vietnam. *Radical Philosophy*, 2.03.

Pink, S. (2018). Afterword: Refiguring Collaboration and Experimentation. in A. Estalella and T. Sánchez-Criado (eds), *Experimental Collaborations: Ethnography through Fieldwork Devices*, pp. 201–212. London: Berghahn Books.

Pink, S. (2020). Foreword. in K. Waltorp (ed), *Why Muslim Women and Smartphones: Mirror Images*, pp. vii–xii. London and New York: Bloomsbury.

Rabinow, P., Marcus, G. E., Fabion, J. D. and Rees, T. (2008). *Designs for an Anthropology of the Contemporary*. Durham and London: Duke University Press.

Rouch, J. (2003). *Ciné-Ethnography*. Minnesota: University of Minnesota Press.

Stoller, P. (2017). Storytelling, Rouch and the Anthropological Future. *Journal des afri-canistes* 87(1–2): 368–378.

Stoller, P. (1997). *Sensuous Scholarship*. Philadelphia: University of Pennsylvania Press.

TallBear, K. (2013). Genomic Articulations of Indigeneity. *Social Studies of Science*, 43(4): 509–534.

Van Dienderen, A. (2008). *Film Process as a Site of Critique. Ethnographic Research into the Mediated Interactions during (Documentary) Film Productions*. Saarbrücken: VDM Verlag.

Waltorp, K. (2017a). *Joyous Are the Eyes That See You*. (film), Aarhus: WaltorpVium & Aarhus University.

Waltorp, K. (2017b). Digital Technologies, Dreams and Disconcertment in Anthropological World-Making. J. Salazar, S. Pink, A. Irving & J. Sjöberg (eds), *Anthropologies and Futures: Researching Emerging and Uncertain Worlds*, pp. 101–116. London: Bloomsbury.

Waltorp, K. (2018). Fieldwork as Interface: Digital Technologies, Moral Worlds and Zones of Encounter. in A. Estalella and T. Sánchez Criado (eds), *Experimental Collaborations: Ethnography through Fieldwork Devices*, pp. 114–131. London: Berghahn Books.

Waltorp, K. (2020). *Why Muslim Women and Smartphones: Mirror Images*. London and New York: Routledge.

Waltorp, K. (2021). Multimodal Sorting: The Flow of Images Across Social Media and Anthropological Analysis. in A. Ballestero and B. R. Winthereik (eds), *Experimenting with Ethnography: A Companion to Analysis*. Experimental Futures Series. Durham: Duke University Press.

Waltorp, K. and C. Vium. (2010). *MANENBERG: Growing Up in the Shadows of Apartheid*, (film), distributed by DR International sales/Royal Anthropological Institute.

Woodham, T. (2018). Foreword: Peripheries. *Moveable Type*, Vol. 10, 'Peripheries'.

8 Here, there and nowhere in provincial outskirts and haunted houses[1]

Kirsten Marie Raahauge

Anthropological inquiries into the periphery give rise to quite a few discon-certing, thus inspiring challenges concerning methodological and epistemolog-ical approaches, also impelling us to gauge what is the specific character of the periphery as a field of study. In this chapter, the periphery will be explored with a double gaze, towards what can be gained from the field as well as from the methodologies when (un)focusing on the peripheral.[2] Hence, the chapter will be divided into two parts:

The first part addresses the periphery through an exploration of two stud-ies: *From Province to Periphery*, dealing with the city of Tønder; and *Haunted Houses*; both are taking place in Denmark. While the Tønder study will be the major point of departure, the study of haunted houses is included because it dis-plays several key concerns that resonate in Tønder. It will be suggested to gaze at the field of Tønder in a *defocused* way, in order to gain knowledge about some of the relevant, yet somewhat obscure aspects of the field. This defocused gaze is concerned with spatial and temporal aspects of the field, and with noticing ways of conceiving of the city and its present situation that might not be obvious in the first place. The defocused gaze also allows for a concern with *loss of control*; the citizens of Tønder as well as the anthropologist are subject to a sensation of loss of control, I argue, not only in the fields that I work with, rather as a premise of life, and of anthropology. Lastly, the effort to keep a defocused gaze allows fluid notions and perspectives not to crystalize; concerned as it is with vagueness and waiting as a productive state of being.

The second part makes further inquiries into methodological and epistemo-logical issues evoked by putting *the peripheral* at the centre. Here, a broader methodological bearing is unfolded, as it surfaces when dealing with the periph-eral – addressing how this object of study conditions anthropological enquiries, yet not forgetting that some of these aspects might be evoked by but not limited to *the peripheral.*

Both of the studies that are discussed here are differently related to the periph-eral: Tønder, since the site is becoming spatially and economically peripherised; and haunting, since it is considered camp by many anthropologists as well as most Danes, relegating experiences with haunting into a residual, fringy sphere. Both studies have given rise to a series of methodological enquiries, related to epistemic troubles and possibilities.

In the succeeding text, I will discuss questions such as: how can we deal with the peripheral and the central as part of the same conceptualisation? How does one conduct fieldwork by allowing for loss of control? How might one deal with the periphery as part of anthropological methods for gathering material, and for thinking about this material? How can one discuss ideas of the peripheral in a context of broader epistemological challenges? Why does the peripheral pop up time after time under different disguises in contemporary anthropology? How can one conduct anthropological research that is both focused and defocused at the same time?[3]

The chapter concludes that a cross-eyed, fringe-orientated gaze at the world is good to think with, since it might bring forth otherwise hidden knowledge. Also, it might generate alternative ways of knowing, paving the way for fundamental discussions of a methodological and epistemological nature.

Remoteness

Remote from the urban areas of Denmark, in the marshes, in the Southwestern corner of Denmark lies Tønder. This city of approximately 8,000 inhabitants became a borough in 1243. It was a vital hub for production and trade of cattle, laces, wood carving and silverwork, and also a cultural centre for centuries with a distinct architectonical profile. Furthermore, it has been an important strategical position to hold for the kings, dukes, and princes who fought over the territories of Schleswig Holstein. After the Second World War, it became a city where the Danish welfare state was showcased, especially through welfare institutions: art museum, historical museum, hospital, teacher's training college and other educational institutions, barracks, police station, court house, jail, prefect, land law committee, upper secondary school and a number of primary schools, sports and swimming halls, and theatres and music scenes. It was nicknamed *the city of institutions* (Becker-Christensen 1993). The city has also had a large number of specialised shops, from sophisticated antique boutiques to shoe shops and stores selling Danish design furniture, supplemented by high-end restaurants.

Over the last decades, this scenery has changed. In common with many other provincial cities, Tønder is under transformation, becoming a place in the outskirts (Raahauge 2017). Among other causes, this is due to infrastructural differences; as larger urban areas become connected by way of motorways and airports, the cities that are not connected to this infrastructure become ligated and thereby outskirted. Also, structural reforms of the Danish welfare system that happened around 2007 play a large role in the transformation of the provincial cities of Denmark. A reorganisation has been accomplished of the web of welfare institutions, transferring welfare amenities to larger cities, thereby emptying smaller cities of welfare institutions. The outskirting is also connected to discourses about the province, pointing to places outside larger urban areas as periphery (Askholm and Dalsgaard 2019). Focusing on the relations between space, welfare and the citizens of Tønder, my project deals with the transformations of everyday life in a city where the welfare institutions have been removed or diminished, and where the periphery has become an emerging mode for how to talk about, and maybe also live in, what used to be a city in the province.

I am a native from Tønder, so I have the advantage of having implicit knowledge and also a broad network in Tønder, while at the same time I have the disadvantage of being 'home-blind', as anthropologists often put it. Methodologically, this gives an edgy feeling of conducting fieldwork in a way that is at the periphery of traditional ethnographic practice. This is not the only edgy feeling that I have concerning this project. As I will come back to in the second part of this chapter, the peripheral challenges the project in many ways, concerning the empirical object of Tønder as peripheral as well as the theoretical and epistemological concerns on a larger scale that are present in this project. While conducting home-blind fieldwork in Tønder, I am searching for supplementary lenses, in order to be able to gaze at the field through a filter that could make other types of knowledge about the place visible. Most of all, I want to get into the aspects of my field that go beyond the patterns and notions which might label it too easily and too early. I would like to access the peripherical, not only as a notion to subsume the phenomena and movements in the field, but also as a perspective for the citizens of Tønder of perceiving everyday life and for me of analysing the topic.

While seen through the corner of the eye

As mentioned above, another of my research projects, *Haunted Houses*, engages with the frictions and potentials of peripheral positions. This project explicitly deals with matters that are only perceptible when seen through the corner of the eye, so to say, resistant as it is to sociological reasoning extrapolating to higher societal causalities, opposing anthropological ideas about patterns to be extracted from the material by generalising and seeing the phenomena somewhat from afar. For *Haunted Houses*, I have interviewed hundreds of people in Denmark who have experienced haunting. The original intent was to focus on the spatial side of haunting, but since a wide range of epistemological and ontological questions emerged as the fieldwork progressed, it also became a study of ambiguity, absence and presence. On an empirical level: how do you know what you have experienced (or that it was an actual experience) when you experienced something that you did not know existed (or that you actually know does not exist)? On an analytical level: how do you deal with a field where most of the people that you talk to believe in their experience but not in what they experienced? Where can you place the questions that arise from these paradoxes? They all are anthropological questions, but not in the ordinary sense of the word, since you have to allow for cracks and fissures, not only in the description of what took place and why, but also in the analysis of it all, and the meta-analysis of how to incorporate things that are absent but still present, as actions, imaginaries and contested figures. It would have been easy to relegate this into an explanation, where the actual experiences were thought of as subsuming something else that goes on underneath it, invisible but active on the surface, like Sigmund Freud did in *Das Unheimliche* (1919), or like anthropologists tend to do when explaining patterns and structural premises for actions at an everyday level. Such structural or pattern-oriented analyses are part of the anthropological family silver that I am not on a quest to deconstruct. My point is, that some sides of the world can be better seized by acknowledging the ambiguity of the situation, action or thing, by dealing with among other topics, the peripheral.

In this context, *while seen through the corner of the eye* appears as a methodological approach; it is a quote from one of the people I interviewed. She told me, that she was sitting in front of the TV and then, out of the corner of her eye, she saw this black smoke. It disappeared when she focused on it. That happened more and more frequently. This was only the beginning of a long and elaborate series of haunting experiences of the family (see also Raahauge 2016). People who experience haunting and ghosts narrate about their difficulties explaining their experience, the vagueness of the phenomena, and the lack of control of both the notion and the experience. This lack of control is a premise for both the one experiencing haunting and for the anthropologist, since the field is resistant to an overall analysis. It can only be explored in bits.

These non-controllable and vague aspects, immanent in the haunting project, are also part of the welfare project, albeit not so manifest. As the city of Tønder is transformed from 'the city of institutions' to a city dependent on other cities, the stability of the city is no longer too clear; its citizens think of Tønder as becoming more elusive and edgy in these years. This loss of stability is also a loss of control, for the citizens who are not sure of what will happen to the city, and for the anthropologist who cannot point to the figure of welfare institutions, or other figures for that matter, as a stabilizing part of the city. A defocused lens and a periphery-oriented gaze might be productive in order to see something that captures the city better than labelling it an abandoned city, acknowledging that this would not be the image that the citizens I have been talking to would consider true.

Haunted Houses as well as *From Province to Periphery* call for an alternative gaze, in order to generate awareness of, and ability to acknowledge, the paradoxical and vague sides of the field. Be it due to the fact that people experience what they should not be able to experience, or because the site is under transformation to a bleaker version of itself, in both cases, there is something at stake that has to do with important parts of the field being covered and best to be explored through a peripheral gaze. The challenge is to gaze at the periphery as 'situated at the edge of dominant paradigms', as suggested by the editors in the introduction to this anthology. Seen through the corner of the eye is thus a short cut through which the uncontrollable, unexplainable and often vague aspects of the periphery might be accessed.

Defocused

The shift from being a centre of its own to becoming the periphery of many other places means that Tønder has become increasingly relative to other places, and the defocused state also places the past and the future references in a more manifest position. The relational references point to the golden days of the past, and to the possibilities of the future, and also to the relation to the cities that now host education and work possibilities, institutions, vibrant life etc. and they point to urban hubs such as Hamburg, Aarhus and Copenhagen. Instead of focusing on 'here', 'there', 'past', 'present' and 'future', the defocused aspect might give the advantage of grasping the relations and the fluidity between these points, giving access for exploring the multiple times and places and undefined situations of life. A defocused gaze might help us to be able to navigate different realms and dimensions, and to make room for the complexity that we encounter in the fieldwork. On the other hand, too much complexity can turn into white noise, where nothing is heard because of the unsorted amount of information. It takes the skills of being open, mobile and aware of the qualities of the complexity, and also it demands that you are able to choose what should be part of your ethnographic material. Such a double gesture takes place when encountering the field and when deciding what to take with you. In which way is it important that one of the retired teachers from the secondary school has set up a Facebook site for homeless cats, organising housing, sterilisation and feeding of them? Would it be better to work with the numerous ornithologists attracted to Tønder due to the birdlife of the marshes? And yet, since we strive towards openness and fluidity, the criteria for choosing should be clear.

The defocused aspect also suggests that you might be able to gaze at 'welfare' in ways that are more explicitly linked to Tønder. Since the welfare amenities once abundant in Tønder have been diminished, the state of welfare spaces has become less obvious, thus I have had to wait, to rephrase, and thereby to accept a certain loss of control over my definition of 'welfare space'.

Welfare is spatially connected to welfare institutions, but spaces of welfare are also perhaps to be thought about in other ways – the small talk and the invitation to 'ladies' evenings' in the backstage of the vintage clothing shop that the shopkeeper refers to as 'welfare', the walk on the dikes in the marshland that the retired doctor talks about as another kind of welfare, or the fact that people offer each other a lift in the car to get to the hospital, now 45 kilometres away, maybe these examples could serve as examples of alternative welfare spaces.[4]

This loss of control is a vital engine for conducting fieldwork; when starting out, there was a specific idea about what was in focus, and when, in the middle of it all, it was necessary to let go of this idea, since something else showed out to be relevant. For another reason as well, loss of control is a fruitful part of conducting fieldwork; when focusing too much on what has been defined aforehand, or what is conventionally obvious, it becomes difficult to see the vital qualities of the diffuse, vague sides of life. In this way, loss of control by way of defocusing generates a deep and rich ethnography, as long as it is manageable both to defocus and to focus, when we put the picture together again.

The defocused aspect of the periphery puts the time aspect of being a place under transformation into perspective. Perceived as an elusive field, the substantial transformation that this field undergoes is highlighted, rather than the stable sides of the city. Thus, instead of focusing on the grandeur of the past, the stability of being the oldest borough in Denmark, or on the dense neighbourhoods, communities and friendships that thrive there, it brings in a discussion of the sensation of waiting, and of being in transit between unstable identities. This defocused gaze on the time aspect also underlines the point made by many citizens, namely that the city is no longer a centre of its own. It has got other potentials which they see emerge in this situation. For instance, some of the citizens have talked about the potential of the city as a place of silence and quietness. Others talk about the hidden quality of the city. Yet others point to the history and culture of the city as something that is unique to the place, while some point to the rare landscapes of the marshes. These potentialities are, paradoxically, highlighted by way of the defocused gaze.

Furthermore, the shift from being a place with a heterogeneous to a homogeneous demography is accessible through the defocused gaze. Tønder has been a city of a number of national and regional belongings and languages (Danish, German, 'sønderjysk', 'Schleswig Holstein'ish', 'Platdeutsch' and 'Frisian'). This has become less manifest over the years. Also, Tønder used to be a city of many different work opportunities and education possibilities, due to the blend of farming land and institutions, shops and factories. The disappearance of many of the institutions leaves a vacuum of waiting for new kinds of stabilities, also concerning the variation of the population.

The defocused aspect also opens up for a discussion of the spatial condition of being ligated infrastructurally and of being perceived as a place on the edge of civilisation. Infrastructurally, Tønder is ligated by way of the lack of motorways and frequent train and bus connections. For instance, a man in his fifties who got a slipped disc in his back had to attend a doctor at the hospital in Odense, approximately 150 kilometres away, by bus, train, train and bus, which made it impossible to reach the appointment in time. This is a disadvantage that has only recently become a life condition. Also, this sensation of edginess is manifest among the pupils of the upper secondary school, who think of themselves as ligated and far away from the vibrant life of larger urban areas. Due to the lack of smooth infrastructure they spend hours in busses, driving from place to place, when they attend school or sport, when they go to parties or concerts, or when they go to refugee dwellings in Tønder in order to teach Danish to the refugees that are temporarily housed there. Most of these pupils long to get out of Tønder. Someday, they might return, they say.

A defocused gaze also touches upon the relationship between centre and periphery, and their folding into each other. Furthermore, it touches upon the discussion of centre-periphery as being one of many spatial organizations, some of which do not include edginess, as, for example, dualities, triads, or rhizomes. Tønder used to be a centre with a periphery around it; now, it has become the periphery of other centres, setting the question of what it takes to be a centre or a periphery, and of who decides *what is what*. Tønder used to be talked about as a gateway to Europe, situated four kilometres from Germany, or, as they say in Tønder, two hours from Hamburg. Now, in the discourse of the media, it is typically depicted as an example of outskirts, as one of the most remote places you can find.[5]

Far-away perspectives

In the approach of this anthology, the frictions presented here turned into a striving towards another kind of a methodology, echo-like; the idea of *peripheral wisdom* and *peripheral methodologies*, as well as the question of *ethnographic limits* put challenging fringy aspects to the fore, impelling us to stay defocused in order to see something else.

The peripheral as ambiguous: Between imaginaries and displacement

In *Josephs and His Brothers,* Thomas Mann (1943) states that '*einmal*', or 'once upon a time', refers to both the past and the future. He uses the image of a wanderer at the seafront, who is drawn towards the misty cliff to be seen far away; he is positioned between his now-here and the imagination and drive towards what he wishes to explore out there at the coastal cliff, which he can only get a glimpse of. This idea of seductive imaginaries of displacement is also present in Tønder, where many still remember the vivid city of the past, and where aspects of the future are suggested.

What you see in the corner of your eye arouses a desire to focus. When you focus, disappointment appears, because when in focus, clearness and transparency cause the mystique to vanish. This is the logic of desire of horror movies (Spielberg), of theorists of desire connected to sexuality (Freud and Lacan) and capitalism (Bauman 2002).[6] This logic of desire is also present in my study of haunting (Raahauge 2015c, 2016), as exemplified in the following story.

A woman who as a student worked until late at night experienced the same every night at a quarter past two. The sound of someone who walked the stairs towards her apartment and put a key in the keyhole of her door. She invited guests to stay and experience the sounds, so many people heard them. Her cousin also heard the sounds, and he wanted to get to the bottom of it; therefore he made her sit in the corridor in front of the entrance door together with him until they heard the sounds. Then, he opened the door, and they saw nothing. Only darkness. After that, it was silent for a long time, maybe years, before the sounds came back.

This story is typical for my material, and it clearly states the point: the desire for understanding what is going on makes the event compelling, the act of unveiling the mystery takes away the very qualities that it haunts. It is when you do *not* focus on the centre of the event that you perceive what is going on. The centre of the scene and the method of investigation turns out to be dark and empty, the periphery and the vague sensation of listening with half an ear is fraught of noises and experiences.

This sensation of loss of control was pervasive in my material, for the one experiencing the haunting as well as for the anthropologist. The more I worked with the field, the more it became clear to me that this was not an obstacle, it is rather a method to understand what is going on without labelling it through conventional definitions and explanations. The loss of control has become a guardian against viewing the field through too defined lenses in order to catch a glimpse of the more elusive aspects of the field.

The fact that the haunting is about *hearing* something rather inexplicable is also characteristic of the material (Raahauge 2014). While seeing is conceived as the primary sense of orientation, hearing remains ambiguous; you heard it but there might be several reasons for the sound, or maybe you did not hear it? So, while seeing is distanced and connected to clarity, hearing is intimate and dubious, the explanations vague and contestable.

While vagueness has been a point of fascination of aesthetical approaches and discussions, (Baudrillard 1987; Virilio 1991; Perniola 1996); here, it becomes political in an incidental way (Thrift 2004). The sense of vagueness and elusiveness connected to Tønder has to do with economical and structural dynamics going on throughout multiple scales, globally, nationally and regionally. Also, it has to do with new sets of political values that emerge from the reorganization of the geographical space through structural and infrastructural movements. Elusiveness is connected to displacement, in the sense that smaller cities are displaced by way of this structural reorganization together with wider societal transformations (Avermaete et al. 2015); and, in a more humane way, because people and places of the present refer to the past and to other places through imaginaries (de Certeau 1984).

The peripheral can pose challenges because of its status as a contested and normative notion. To researchers and artists, *periphery* is typically a notion, which arouses a desire to explore ambiguity, to try to unveil what is per se opaque. In my work with space,[7] periphery is in the same high end of notions as for example in-between spaces, white spots, non-places (Augé 1995), gaps, terrain vague (Ørskov 1987), opaqueness, ambiguity, one could go on. The enchantment of notions that seem obscure or off the beaten track is infinite, while at the same time as these notions and phenomena are explored, they are put on centre stage, thus taking away the auratic nimbus they hold.

Back to the field of Tønder, a quality of this site, as of many other peripheral sites, might be that it is not in the centre; Tønder is not connected to the money flow transforming the larger, central areas. This might be thought of as a periphery-quality. The peripheral as a methodological perspective might enhance the gaze for such qualities, in the peripheries and, if lucky, also in the centres. If turning to the reception of periphery in the field, the normativity of the notion is quite different. While notions such as *welfare* is typically understood as 'good', *the periphery* is typically understood as 'bad'. To the citizens of *the periphery*, it means poorer, more boring, more restricted lives with fewer possibilities and a less varied population, together with a derogative discourse about the place you live. There is no haven where notions are purely descriptive, still *periphery* is highly contested, also in comparison with many other notions, which brings matters to a head; how to deal with contested, normative notions that should still serve as part of the analytical framework? And how do we deal with the fact that some notions have seduced us even before we start out working with them? The only way to approach this challenge, as far as I can see, is to accept the fact that this is a normative notion, and try to steer into a way to work with it, so that all the qualities it contains are used to shed light on your field and supplement your discussion of methods, or even, as this anthology does, use it as a focus point of the methodological and theoretical discussions raised.

The peripheral as a focus: The Moebius band

Another challenge is connected to focusing on the periphery. In an everyday optic as seen from its citizens' point of view, Tønder is the centre of their lives. For the inhabitants of the marshlands, Tønder is the only large city in the area, turning it into a local centre. For the German tourists, Tønder is a central tourist site. The important role of Tønder through history also brings the centre-periphery discussion up front. The elaborate, architecturally rich, conspicuous buildings are the obvious reminiscent of its former central role, while at the same time, by their presence they are highlighting the fact that this is no longer a centre. In a more recent past, the welfare institutions that have been relocated to larger cities, used to serve as mini-hubs, a series of centres inside the city. While these centres are now either diminished or absent, the buildings are still there, as a reminiscent of the former welfare city.

As seen from the point of view of contemporary infrastructure, global hubs, larger urban areas, and distribution of welfare amenities, Tønder, as other provincial cities, is definitely perceived as periphery, both in the opinion of the discourse from the outside, and in the eyes of its citizens. Centre and periphery fold in and out of each other in often unforeseen ways, like a Moebius band that turns and twists, now it becomes a centre, now periphery. Also because of that, the theme of the periphery is important, both in connection with the discussion of the relativity of the Moebius band quality of the notion, and when dealing with concrete sites such as Tønder and other provincial cities world-wide that have been abandoned or have turned into peripheral places.

The peripheral as empirical evidence: Veiled ethnographies

During fieldwork, these challenges become concrete, despite their intrinsic elusiveness. It is much easier to ask about and find ways of acting in connection to central places, themes, relations, things or people, than it is to observe or ask the people you are together with to point to or unfold the nature of peripheral phenomena and relations. Periphery is hard to grasp due to its negatively biased definition, something defined by what it lacks, implying a centre, not only as a defining anti-notion, but also as part of it. The peripheral is hard to grasp because it consists of events, relations, actions, figures that do not appear on the radar – bland and vague aspects of everyday life that are difficult to both perceive and explicate. As a result, the peripheral is difficult to work with, yet necessary. Most of the vivid and rich qualities of ethnographic accounts stem from what might be considered peripheral, still it leads to a fuller picture of the field. This importance of peripheral qualities is based on the double movement of being mobile, yet at the same time finding a way to choose what comes in, and what is left out.

This is part of the attraction of the peripheral; in the everyday life lived in the field, an infinite number of observations are made, and at the same time choices have to be made about what is taken seriously as empirical material, and even more seriously as examples in writings, or notions that are recognised as of major importance or even part of a pattern. These choices are based partly on what actually happened in the field, and partly on estimates which are impossible to account for in all details. At the same time, it might become important to point to material that is not obvious; stating the obvious can be avoided, or be supplemented, only through access to peripheral bits of the empirical material. This operation of keeping focus, while still taking in remote bits and pieces is one of the ways that ethnographic descriptions become thick; the peripheral mutates into an important part of ethnographic method, even if it is not always recognised as such. Indeed, the gathering and selecting of data is first of all conditioned by the criteria for recognising what is relevant; the parameters behind this are seldom questioned; for whom, or by what principle, is the material chosen relevant? Or, for that matter, why are some ideas or modes of thinking considered more peripheral than others? This somewhat cross-eyed gaze at both the centre and the periphery of a certain field is important, also because it is the premise of establishing more relevant material out of the observations.

Fieldwork can pose another kind of challenge if conducted in order to explore something that is enmeshed in the field, while at the same time not visible or noticeable as something that you can point to. One of my colleges, Steffen Jöhncke, studied male prostitutes in Copenhagen in the late 1980s. Within a few years, this field had changed from being a visible, accessible network, to become isolated and difficult to access; it was not possible to point to where the male prostitutes were to be found. Due to the fear of AIDS, relations and sites concerned with sexual encounters in the gay community of Copenhagen had changed rapidly from networks where people knew each other to more isolated cells that were difficult to get to know. The same impenetrable quality is also present in my study of haunted houses in Denmark; since ghosts, haunting and spectres are only rarely recognised as a real phenomenon that you can consider part of a rational worldview, those who have had such otherworldly experiences go under the radar; they do not talk about it to others in fear of being ridiculed, and many of them are confronted with the problem of having experienced something that they do not conceive of as possible. *Why me?! I do not believe in ghosts, but I believe in my experience*, are quite common utterings in my interviews.

This obscurity of the field is also present in Tønder; the recent decrease in welfare institutions has brought networks of social relations that are no longer connected to institutions, and therefore less easily accessed for the anthropologist as well as for the people who live in the city. These vague, implicit networks with no core, and no central meeting place, are difficult to find, which turns them into white spots of the field. This kind of vagueness displays a technical difficulty for conducting fieldwork, and, more profoundly, it means a lack of control for the fieldworker, because you are not sure where to look or what to look for. This kind of methodological challenge is common in the daily life of anthropologists, and the classical work methods of conducting fieldwork entails a technique for overcoming this problem; participant observation and its inherent work method of accepting loss of control, waiting, staying and getting bored, while tiny details surface and point in different directions, often showing pathways to some partial network or small relation here and there, and often giving way for the emergence of fragments you would not have noticed if not challenged by the lack of centres and giving access to new ways of observing that you would not have perceived had you not been in a position of waiting.

Epistemological problems: On the limits of anthropology

Having opted for fieldwork and slow participant observation as the way to deal with vagueness in the field and in your gaze on the field, there is another critique which is important to raise: the critique of empirical facts gathered through ethnographic fieldwork raised by the anthropologist Richard Baxstrom. In his article *Knowing*

Primitives, Witches, and the Spirits: Anthropology and the Mastery of Nonsense (2014), Baxstrom argues that the gaze of the anthropologist is informed beforehand; when knowing what to look for (in the case of Tønder, effects of becoming peripheralised, former or diminished welfare sites and relations), you do not see what is real to the people that surround you (in the case of Tønder, ambiguous or not obvious vague places and peripheral states). The technique of anthropology is to conduct fieldwork in order to extract the right empirical pieces of information. Baxstrom compares this technique to the methods of the witch trials of the 16th century: the system (based on principles drawn up in advance) decides what is considered real (to the theological experts partaking in the trial at the witch craze, or to the anthropologist today), not the phenomena that surround us (part of the field). This critique of the primary anthropological road to knowledge is hard to counter.

In *Specters of Marx: The State of the Debt, the Work of Mourning, and the New International* (2006 [1993]), Jacques Derrida approaches the same problem from the perspective of terminology, by establishing a 'hauntology', aimed at criticising the ontology of Western philosophy. This rigid definition-ridden monolith is not capable of understanding the phenomena and processes of the world it seeks to describe, so in order to permit the floating, changing world we inhabit into the language of philosophy, Western ontology should be replaced by a 'hauntology'.[8] Bruno Latour, in *Why Has Critique Run Out of Steam?* (2004), also addresses these fundamental questions; he deals with the methods of social scientists and points out that concrete parts of everyday life are explained as either facts (this is due to cognitive processes, biological facts, etc.) or fairies (this is due to the way the world is understood in that particular place). Both of these explanations work by explaining away the concrete phenomena, things, actions etc. that are part of the world, instead of taking them seriously.

From Baxstrom's critique of anthropological striving for empirical evidence with a bias, through Derrida's critique of Western philosophy's quest for notions that might subsume a world that escapes these very notions, to Latour's critique of social scientists' urge to explain the world by abstracting the concreteness of everyday life into facts or fairies, these critiques are close to the discussions raised with the notion of peripheral wisdom. What might be understood through twisted evidence that obscure what is right in front of you, abstract stable categories that are in the way, or facts and fairies that lead you astray, could become something else, when filtered through notions such as peripheral, because it provides us with a sidelong approach. Not that this notion, or for that matter notions such as in-between space, white spot, non-place, gap, terrain vague, non-site, ambiguity, etc., would be a safe road towards knowledge, but it is worth finding out what you might be able to see, when you try not to look straight into the matter, while trying rather to see it from out of the corner of your eye.

Peripheral problems? Unfocusability, seductiveness and desire

The elusive, edgy, defocusing imaginary of 'once upon a time' emerges in places like Tønder, rising in turn some unexpected desires and imaginaries about 'authenticity'. In 2014, Tønder marshlands and the city of Tønder became a

UNESCO world heritage site. Now, it is a giant museum piece, rare and unique. Tønder itself is a display of Frisian styles of building and of city structures from the middle ages onwards. Although the landscape is man-made, it is thought of as authentic and natural. This is why funds have put millions of Danish Kroner into a grand project converting the area into a nature-tourist site, with Tønder as an authentic old city as part of the experience. The city might have become a periphery due to the loss of welfare institutions and infrastructure, but after this, it has been destined to become part of a site for nature-tourism, it is going to get a para-authentic new life. This is yet another kind of periphery, and a new kind of peripherical thinking: due to the desire for authenticity aroused by the silent, hidden, subtle, secretive aura of the peripherical city and landscape, the Tønder marshes is going to be branded and lifted into the simulated authenticity of becoming a tourist recreation area. Out of desire for the pristine aspects of the periphery, the area is becoming a periphery of itself: when the tourist-identity becomes the major identity, the peripherical identity becomes a periphery even of its own self. What used to be a city of the welfare state is about to become a city of private welfare Maecenas. It is a story of authenticity lost and regained, through being periphery, and perhaps transformed into a para-periphery. It is also a story of becoming an object to be gazed at by a double oblique glance - by locals and by visitors.

One thing is that the field of Tønder might be centre as understood through one aspect (for example, being the place where people live their lives), and at the same time periphery as perceived from another aspect (for example, the periphery of not being part of the urban areas of Denmark), another thing is that it is an impossible task to keep the periphery as your focus; the peripheral *becomes* central, by way of your gaze. This impossible, implicit quality of the peripheral has the problem that it dissolves before our very eyes when we look at it; we might be studying a peripheral site, and, while respecting the periphery as both a mode of exploration and an object to explore, we place it at the centre of our studies, and even worse (or better), we push it towards becoming centre or just central, because we explore it. In other words, it becomes fancy, interesting, relevant, desirable, seductive because it is recognised as peripheral. Or might it be possible to 'stay with the peripheral', as the introduction proposes? We might try to. Haunting is experienced as an isolated cell, not as a part of everyday life. Thereby the haunted is placed in-between two realms, the realm of the familiar and the realm of the strange. This position is central to the experience and for the analytical gaze. Staying with the peripheral is a matter of staying in this fluid state between different realms, points, times and places.

The seductive power of the peripheral lies in the quality that it cannot be accessed as a whole or focused on in a straight, stable way, it cannot be understood through firm analytical notions or frameworks, it cannot be accessed easily through ethnographic fieldwork. Furthermore, it paves the way for relevant questions about the frictions of the framework (the presence of absent places or relations), the relativity of the subject matter of periphery (Moebius), the white spots of vague fields for fieldworking (Jöhncke), or the truth of the empirical material that comes from fieldwork (Baxstrom). At the same time, peripheral thinking thrives from the kinds of thinking that strive to be centralising, transparent and strong, just like experiences of haunting become intense on the background of everyday life's controlled and recognisable experiences. Also, the peripheral is seductive, due to its *unfocusability*, it is there only in fragments and as an ambiguous field or perspective, seen through a glass darkly, distorted or obscure; at the same time, this property of the peripheral is the engine for all the challenges that have been discussed until now. For this reason, the peripheral is difficult to perceive, understand, explain, work on, and also for this reason it is desirable to do so.

Notes

1 The research project *Spaces of Danish Welfare* (2017–2022), situated at The Royal Danish Academy of Fine Arts, the Schools of Architecture and Design in Copenhagen is a collaboration between architects and anthropologists, funded by the Independent Research Fund Denmark. It deals with the transformation of Danish welfare systems as seen from a spatial point of view. My project explores the rather recent spatial configuration 'the periphery'. Currently, I am conducting fieldwork in Tønder (Raahauge 2015a, 2015b, 2017). The research project *On the Limits of Reason* (2007–2012) of the University of Copenhagen focuses on the way people deal with encountering the limit of their reason in different fields. My project explores haunted houses in Denmark; the study of haunted houses is ongoing although formally the overall research project has ended (see also Jöhncke, Raahauge and Steffen 2015).

2 The session *Peripheral Wisdom* at the EASA conference in Stockholm in 2018 is the starting point of this chapter, not only as an article that has this origin in this context, rather this became part of my search for alternative ways of addressing my topic and my fieldwork; it was a possibility to be included into a network that strived to focus on the peripheral, on the aspects of the field that are present by way of their absence or their ambiguity. This aspect has been vital to me, since the start of my fieldwork about *Haunted Houses* in 2007.

3 A caveat is worth addressing, namely that peripheral thinking might sometimes lead to relevant findings, yet now and then, it might just lead you into a cul-de-sac.

4 This would, admittedly, bring the notion of welfare out of its stable definitions concerned with the distribution of 'welfare' from the state through institutions, and the interpretation and action of the civic society of these welfare amenities by way of the large amount of associations that exist in Denmark (about the Danish welfare state, see also Kaspersen 2013; about the idea of welfare and its connection to architecture, see Avermaete, van den Heuvel and Swenarton 2015).

5 Remoteness is adjacent to periphery, as it deals with the quality of being out of focus and by way of that relevant. In 2017, the multidisciplinary conference *Remote. Rethinking Remoteness and Peripherality* on Svalbard dealt with these themes.

6 Freud, Lacan and Spielberg deal with desire as a general theme in their work, for that reason they are not given specific references. Bauman, on the other hand, explores modernity, postmodernity, consumerism, while focusing on desire as adjacent to these themes, an example is in his work *Society under Siege* (2002).

7 In the Royal Danish Academy of Fine Arts, my daily work is situated among architects and designers leading to other fields, ways of thinking and modes of acting than what I used to be surrounded by, when working at the Department of Anthropology of the University of Copenhagen. Still, we share the interest in periphery and other such fringy notions.

8 This challenge is obvious in my work on haunted houses; nobody knows what it is, still it is a common thing that it takes place – 'it' being subsumed by the notion *haunting* which is a residual character for the non-recognisable experiences of the

people I have talked to (Raahauge 2015c, 2016), and it is also present while working with the periphery, due to the vague, ambiguous quality of the analytical notion as well as the empirical material that it produces and is produced by.

References

Askholm, Anne Sofie and Kathrine Dalsgaard 2019. 'Vandkantsvinkler. Antropologiske blikke på fortællinger fra og om "udkanten"'. *Debat. Antropologi og Medier. Jordens Folk* 54 (1): 25–39

Augé, Marc 1995. *Non-places. Introduction to an Anthropology of Supermodernity*. London: Verso.

Avermaete, Tom, Dirk van den Heuvel and Mark Swenarton (eds.) 2015. *Architecture and the Welfare State*, Oxon: Routledge

Baudrillard, Jean 1987. *Amerika* (Amérique). København: Akademisk Forlag.

Bauman, Zygmunt 2002. *Society Under Siege*. Cambridge: Polity Press.

Baxstrom, Richard 2014. 'Knowing primitives, witches, and the spirits: Anthropology and the mastery of nonsense'. *Republics of Letters: A Journal for the Study of Knowledge, Politics, and the Arts* 3 (2): 1–22.

Becker-Christensen, Henrik 1993. *Byen ved grænsen. Tønder 1920–1970*. Aabenraa: Institut for Grænseregionsforskning.

de Certeau, Michel 1984. *The Practice of Everyday Life*. Berkeley: University of California Press.

Derrida, Jacques 2006 (1993). *Specters of Marx*. New York: Routledge.

Freud, Sigmund 2003 (1919). *Das Unheimliche*. London: Penguin.

Jöhncke, Steffen, Raahauge, Kirsten Marie and Steffen, Vibeke (eds.) 2015. *Between Magic and Rationality: On the Limits of Reason in the Modern World*. Copenhagen: Museum Tusculanum Press.

Kaspersen, Lars Bo 2013. *Denmark in the World*. Copenhagen. Hans Reitzels Forlag.

Mann, Thomas (1933–1943) 2000. *Josef og hans brødre* (Joseph und seine Brüder/Joseph and His Brothers). Copenhagen: Gyldendal.

Perniola, Mario 1996. *Kunsten som neutral mutant* (L'arte come mutante neutro). Copenhagen: Det Kongelige Danske Kunstakademi.

Raahauge, Kirsten Marie 2017. 'Towards the outskirts'. In *Forming Welfare*. J. Rosenberg Bendsen, K. Lotz, K. Vindum, M. J. Jensen, D. Simpson and K. M. Raahauge (eds.) København: Arkitektens Forlag, 172–189.

Raahauge, Kirsten Marie 2016. 'Ghosts, troubles, difficulties, and challenges. Narratives about unexplainable phenomena in contemporary Denmark'. In *Belief Narratives*. (Guest editor R. Hiiemäe). *Folklore. Electronic Journal of Folklore* 65: 89–111

Raahauge, Kirsten Marie 2015a. 'Into Tønder: Field specific in the marshlands'. In *The Tønder Project: Observations*. Copenhagen: The Royal Danish Academy of Fine Arts, 7–17.

Raahauge, Kirsten Marie 2015b. 'Out of Tønder: Lost fields in the marshlands'. In *The Tønder Project: Design Projects*. Copenhagen: The Royal Danish Academy of Fine Arts, 7–11

Raahauge, Kirsten Marie 2015c. 'The ghost in the machine'. In *Between Magic and Rationality: On the Limits of Reason in the Modern World*. Jöhncke, Steffen, Vibeke Steffen and Kirsten Marie Raahauge (eds.) Copenhagen: Museum Tusculanum Press, 315–343.

Raahauge, Kirsten Marie 2014. 'Gengangerlyde (Ghost Sounds)'. In *De dødes liv (The Life of the Dead).* Ole Høiris, Ton Otto & Ane Bonde Rolsted (eds.). Århus: Aarhus University Press & Moesgård Museum, 125–131.

Thrift, Nigel 2004. 'Intensities of feeling: Towards a spatial politics of affect'. *Geographiska Annaler* 86B (1): 57–78

Virilio, Paul 1991 (1980). *The Aesthetics of Disappearance.* Los Angeles: Semiotexte.

Ørskov, Villy 1987. *Den åbne skulptur og udvendighedens æstetik.* Essays. København. Borgen.

9 Fooled into fieldwork

Epistemic detours of an accidental anthropologist

Francisco Martínez

Epistemic de-centring

Certain stories of failure can stalk us wherever we go, reverberating and giving form to our professional identity as (accidental) anthropologists. Field accidents situate us in a condition of negative capability, making it difficult to know how to go on while facing our limits of comprehension. They also decentre us from our original plan and from our object of study, generating dynamics of disorder and epistemic detours.

In this chapter, I engage with a set of field accidents and failures and unresolved questions in my research experience in Georgia. Normative approaches would simply dismiss the learning and argue that these encounters lacked systematic engagement and ethnographicness. Yet, following the proposal of this volume to step into peripheral paths to knowledge, I show that fieldwork is not necessarily guided by an understanding of what significance or relevance are, nor does it have to follow well-planned techniques that involve systematic methods for assembling data.

Fieldwork is destabilising rather than instrumental, thus it can hardly be determinate and result-oriented. Here, it is proposed as an epistemological position, characterised by openness to be surprised and to fail, and by the acknowledgement that there are different ways of 'knowing reality'. The awareness of our limited knowledge makes possible an excess of ideas and of relations, and lead us to unfamiliar territories and to questions that were not previously mapped. It is in this sense that entails an oscillating movement through multiple spatial and temporal frames – producing questions to be answered out of the field, and material to be analysed with tools and concepts not always available in the present.

This kind of learning is beautifully shown by Anton Chekhov in a letter written to his friend Suvorin in Sakhalin Island: 'I saw everything, so the problem now is not what I saw, but how I saw it' (1999: 171). Building up on Chekhov's ideas, we could say that mine was an ethnography merely half-seen and of things situated on the outskirts of my comprehension, certainly not understood to the end. The referred stories of failure appeared to be beside the point, neither originally casted as ethnographic, nor planned within a conventional methodological frame. How I gained access to local knowledge and what I learned with these events was not seriously ethnographic, but profoundly anthropological (Ingold 2007),[1] thus complicating the relationship between research experiences and knowledge production.

Besides reconsidering the accidental nature of anthropology as a discipline, some other questions answered in this chapter are: How could we incorporate the accidental wisdom generated in the field into anthropological analyses? Which are the similarities and contrasts between the fieldwork of journalists and anthropologists? And what commitments do anthropologists have in the field, and what kind of bonds do we make because of those commitments?

Half-consistency

In February 2010, I visited Abkhazia as a special correspondent of the *El Mundo* newspaper to attend the ceremony in which Sergei Bagapsh re-assumed the presidency of the separatist republic in the Caucasus. I had been working for the newspaper for eight months, and was based in Istanbul. As I speak Russian, and the correspondent in Moscow, Daniel Utrilla, had enough territory to cope with, it seemed like a good idea to extend the domains of my office and also to visit a region I had heard of and read about so much during my time living in Russia.[2]

I entered Georgia through the Turkish border (Sarpi) and stayed in Batumi for a couple of days with two colleagues. We then visited Poti, a port on the Black Sea that has gained strategic importance due to the new energy infrastructures related to the oil and gas transported there from the Caspian Sea. Finally, we took a *marshrutka* to the Enguri River. In my fieldnotes, I wrote that people talked a lot about Mikheil Saakashvili, then the president of Georgia, yet they often referred to him in ambivalent ways: handsome and intelligent, but too polemical and cocky. I also noticed a great number of potholes on the roads and cows freely crossing them, which generated some considerably disruptive driving.[3]

Once in Sukhumi, the capital of the breakaway region of Abkhazia, we stayed in a cheap hotel, about 20 minutes walking distance from the centre. Still affected by multiple wars, there was not much on offer for accommodation back then in Sukhumi: a pricey hotel (Ritsa) for diplomats, businessmen and international delegations, a students' dorm, and then the Vesna, where we stayed, which, despite undergoing a recent renovation, had no Internet. In my time there, I held, for instance, an interview with the newly appointed prime minister of Abkhazia. The headline of the interview, as published by the newspaper, was: 'Independent is the one who knows how to assume independence and is able to defend it.' Among the notes compiled from the interview, I found:

> Sergey Shamba recriminates to his secretary for not having offered us tea, as we were waiting for him to finish with the delegation of Russian astronauts visiting Sukhumi. Shamba receives us in his former office of the Minister of Foreign Affairs, which shows furniture of Soviet design in the typical Soviet autumn colours (a particular coat of green and brown). He began the interview with a contemplative gaze, yet at the end of it, he stared at me while answering questions about Kosovo and Chechnya.

(Figure 9.1)

Figure 9.1 Sergey Shamba. Francisco Martínez

But what makes these observations and records of conversations simply journalist notes, and not fieldnotes themselves? Is it so that notes not taken to end up in an ethnography should not be considered as fieldnotes, or are we instead discussing issues of personal reflexivity, ways of approaching informants, appreciation of the social and cultural locatedness of knowledge, and research design and protocols? My answer would be that fieldnotes do not simply allow an instrumental thickening of the analysis; while they are also distinct because of being open to the possibility of several valuations by a range of people and at different times, thereby creating an unpredicted surplus of ideas, meanings and interpretations to be mined years later – richer than what the researcher was aware at the time of data collection (Strathern 2004: 5; also Marcus and Okely 2007).

For instance, after re-reading another of my notes for preparing a journalist report, I discovered something that I did not note back then, namely the half-consistency of many of the things I was perceiving then, starting with the very independence of Abkhazia – a fact that some might believe, others might not, and some others in turn might only half-believe (see Navaro-Yashin 2012). See this note, for example (Figure 9.2):

> We go from Gali to Ochemchira, a city that the Georgian army did not expect to lose but was indeed lost, like what also happened to Gali and to the Kodori valley. Here in Ochemchira, the remains of a destroyed amusement park appear as an open wound from the war, left visible still as in the case of the burnt parliament in Sukhumi. It is hard to say if the houses are half-built or half-destroyed.

Gia, our hired driver, is half Abkhaz half Georgian. He lost his whole family during the siege to Tqvarcheli: 'We ate once a week and we went to fight every morning. After a while, you take it as normal'. He regrets: 'So much politics and, as always, it is normal people who end up suffering. After the war everything was very hard, both for the Abkhazians and for the Mingrelians. People are already fed up with politics, they just want to live in peace'.

Abkhazia's landscape combines mountains and valleys with access to the sea and fertile fields. The south, however, is ghostly broken, crowded with burned and abandoned houses. We enter one of them, which is currently being rebuilt with the help of the Danish Refugee Council. Segrevan Kobalia is the father of the family and, while they finish rebuilding the house, he lives with his wife in a 5 m² cabin. The wife prefers not to say her name, and explains: 'We found the house burned, but I can't accuse anyone. The war burned it' … Another similar cabin is located on the right, in which her daughters with her sons-in-law and grandchildren live altogether. 'Where am I going to go? I have my house and my family here; And what am I going to do in Georgia? I have no property, I could not survive there', laments Kobalia. The family receives a monthly pension of less than 15 euros from Tbilisi, and yet, even if we insist on asking about politics, they refuse to talk more on the topic (they cannot talk of what has abandoned them).

Figure 9.2 Ochemchira. Francisco Martínez

The insights provided here might be still on the way of becoming ethnographic material, even if they were not written by someone identified as an anthropologist but as a journalist. These insights show, however, a different reflexivity and indirectness than that of a journalist. Different professions take different things for granted and also engage with contradictions differently, showing distinct ways of seeing and knowing the world (Shore and Trnka 2013). For instance, anthropologists demonstrate a high degree of responsibility towards the informants and also commitment to (and accountability by) everyone involved in the research. However, journalists practice a different approach to sources in the name of the 'public's right to know', the assumed role of the watchdog of society and an alleged commitment to 'the truth' (Awad 2006). Also, journalists' doings show different ways of making sense, of listening and of drawing facts together, as well as more wariness of the dangers of subjectivity than anthropologists (Bird 2010). Further, compared to anthropologists, journalists have a different writing time because of their urgent deadlines and the need for quick delivery – as if it were a commodity (Hannerz 2004). Such divergence in the use of time in journalism and anthropology writing eventually generates different effects of distance or coevality, affecting matters of representation (Fabian 1983).

As an answer to the acceleration of news, an abundance of information and a sense of redundancy in contemporary media, a rather immersive slow form of journalism has emerged in the last decade – slow not in terms of how the story is told, but of how it is *handmade*. In Tbilisi, I met with Paul Salopek, a National Geographic fellow (and winner of two Pulitzer prizes) who was walking around the world, retracing the footsteps of our ancestors, in a journey on foot across four continents (over 34,000 kilometres). I had the chance to spend several evenings with Paul at Nodar's Newsroom café, while I also travelled with him for a few days, learning that his observations (after having worked as a foreign correspondent in Africa, the Balkans, the Middle East, Central Asia, and Latin America) could be way more anthropological than mine, despite my academic training in this discipline.[4]

Robbed into the field

Nowadays, there are hundreds of options for accommodation in town; however, ten years ago it was still a time of cyber-cafés and Sukhumi was a place where young people had a sense of 'temporal marginality' (Frederiksen 2015). Indeed, in town there were just two public places with an Internet connection: the central, fancy hotel previously referred to and a cyber-café. Immersed in finishing my report for the newspaper, I failed to notice a group of youngsters slip under the desk and steal the bag containing my laptop, photo-camera, passport and wallet. Once I noticed it (too late, as they had already vanished with my stuff), I called Maxim Gundja (then acting minister of foreign affairs and the man I had interviewed the day before), who invited me to his office. For a week, I was using his desk phone to call official authorities in Moscow, Istanbul and Tbilisi to let me cross the border and receive a German safe-conduct pass to get out of Georgia. Half-jokingly, Gundja invited me to stay longer in Abkhazia, get a local wife and work for the Ministry of Foreign Affairs (they needed Spanish-speaking diplomats).

The public broadcaster of Abkhazia, Apsua TV, reported the robbery and asked the locals to 'at least' give back my documents to the police (something they actually did, albeit a month later). One of the explanations put forward by Apsua TV was that Georgian provocateurs had attacked a Spanish journalist in an attempt to damage their international image. I had to stay there for a week, exploring different options to flee from Abkhazia despite not having any documents (while also hoping that the robbers would appear again, after having capitalised on my laptop, wallet and photo-camera). One of my travelling companions, Marc Morte, decided to change his travel plans and stayed with me, covering my costs until the situation was resolved. The condition of negative capability made us surrender to a state of receptiveness, able to tolerate anxiety, and to be in uncertainty – without the need to understand what is going on (Bion 1970).

We were in a standby situation, and yet many things continued to happen to us; we travelled around the country, and once back to Sukhumi we were often checking trash bins in the parks and on central streets in the hope of finding some of my documents. I met twice with the head police officer. The first time, and after my detailed description of the scene, he showed photos of over a hundred young men who could be potentially suspects of the robbery. I could not recognise any of them. Feeling like I was part of a crime film, I seemed to be embodying a nightmare. The second time I met the head police officer was a day before my departure. Then, I questioned the officer's will to help effectively. He became very upset and said that the country was still affected by the recent wars, that I should have known where I was coming to, and that they had to deal with other issues, not just my robbery. It made me feel immature and unprepared for what I was doing.

Now, ten years later, I re-read some of the emails I exchanged back then with some colleagues. For instance, after informing the editor in chief of my newspaper about my robbery, he replied with two brief emails (12 February 2010): 'You have 3200 characters for the report plus 900 characters for a support box. Your "Soviet" phones don't work'; adding half an hour later: 'Can we help you with something? Can you send what I have asked you?' I also exchanged some emails with Utrilla (the correspondent of my newspaper in Moscow), saying to him: 'I will learn something from this' (15 February 2010). Originally, the email seemed to say that I would be more attentive while travelling to certain zones; yet, looking back, what I meant is that this event was impelling me to make certain decisions, such as quitting the (stressful and precarious) profession of journalism. Indeed, a year later I began a PhD in Anthropology, and the robbery turned out to be unexpectedly crucial to my academic career.[5]

On Tuesday 16 February, I finally crossed the Enguri River, which functions as a *de facto* border between the two states, an invisible frontier that does not appear in maps but greatly affects the life of two neighbouring cities, Gali and Zugdidi. Once I was in the *de facto*-controlled Georgian territory and had presented all the required documents, the official guards made a phone call and asked us to wait there for 15 minutes. The guards gave no explanations but invited my companion and I to get into the cabin and have a cup of tea with them. They even ordered Misha, the driver of our *marshrutka* (minibus), not to leave without us. Then, without introducing themselves, a TV crew arrived and began to ask questions while recording us on their TV cameras. After I refused to participate in the suspicious show, they vigorously took on Marc, who said that my laptop and documents were stolen in a café in Sukhumi, 'a normal situation that could have happened anywhere'.

Marc went to Armenia, while I took Misha's *marshrutka* to Tbilisi, where the Spanish honorary consul (Mikheil Akhvlediani) met me, fed me and cheered me up with stories about the royal Bagrationi dynasty. When I took a taxi and said to the driver that I was Spanish, he replied that he had just seen on TV how 'the Russians had kidnapped a Spanish journalist in Abkhazia' to avoid the journalist showing how bad the living conditions were on the other side of the Enguri River. Once I arrived at a hostel, I checked my mail; Marc had written, saying 'We have to repeat this experience' (17 February 2010). Also, an officer from the delegation of *Transparency International* in Tbilisi wrote to invite me to visit their office and speak about what had really occurred since there were two contradictory versions of the same incident. Only then did I realise that the taxi driver was talking about me, since Imedi TV and the Georgian Public Broadcaster had reported that two Spanish journalists had been arrested and had their belongings confiscated by the Russian army. The report showed my companion talking, albeit with a Georgian voiceover that did not accurately translate his words (in fact, saying almost the opposite).[6]

That was also when I met Nikoloz Gambashidze ('Nik') for the first time. I remember very well the tension around that moment. As I had no wallet, I asked my brother to buy my airfare from Georgia. Yet, once at the airport, I was told that the ticket was not valid. The German safe-conduct pass would expire at midnight, in less than an hour, so in desperation I called Joan Puig (a Catalan living in Tbilisi with whom I had had a couple of drinks that evening) to come and pay my airfare in situ. Joan arrived with Nik a few minutes before midnight...[7] Five years later, Nik became my 'Lazarus' in Georgia. In my nine months of fieldwork, we went on more than twenty excursions, all over the country. Nik studied history and worked as a guitar teacher and in a communications office, yet in the early 2000s he had to reinvent himself as a taxi driver in order to be able to pay for the higher education of his children. Nik talked naturally about these life meanderings, and when I asked about the extent to which a person can become other than what he is, Nik replied that he was affected by circumstances that lie beyond individual control (Martínez and Agu 2016).

Rumour has it that when Nik was younger, he liked to smoke weed. My friendship with him makes me reconsider, though, what is to be shared (and concealed) about Nik in this chapter, and, overall, on the need to be opaque in certain instances while writing an ethnography by practicing a 'measured economy of disclosure' (McLean and Leibing 2007: 13). What we can disclose about Nik, however, is his passion for 1970s music, particularly Pink Floyd, Led Zeppelin, Deep Purple and The Beatles. During our trips, Nik recalled the difficulties involved in getting hold of these bands' LPs back in the Soviet era. Often, he also remembered the glorious European days of Dinamo Tbilisi, when the football team played in the UEFA tournaments and defeated clubs such as Liverpool, West Ham and Feyenoord. Nowadays, Nik is a fan of *el Barça*, and after the great games of this Catalan club and of Messi, he repeats 'Big victory!' (in English).

He claims not to understand the lyrics of the songs of his favourite bands, but 'the pleasure I get from listening to them cannot be wrong'.

Nik took Joan as one of his own, almost like a kin member, despite not speaking a common language and talking through body gestures and signs, and repeated expressions such as 'Big victory!' I wonder what was *gained* in such inventive dialogues based on incomplete understanding and distorted communication, instead of what was lost in them (Crapanzano 2014). For a decade they met almost every day, when Nik drove Joan to his office, while they also met for dinners, for excursions and to watch football together. Most of Nik's clients are Europeans, the majority of whom are associated with the EU mission. Nik has a calm demeanour and talks like a true cosmopolite, aware of what is going on in the world, knowing about different notions of taste and value, and showing a sophisticated understanding of things. However, he has left his country on only two occasions (a few days each to Turkey and Russia). As Nik confessed, he believes that if he is away from Tbilisi for more than a week he might fall ill. He has friends who emigrated abroad in the terrible, chaotic 1990s, and Nik has been repeatedly invited to visit them. Indeed, he likes to imagine visiting them, but he is too busy making ends meet, saving money, taking care... trying to construct livable lives for himself and his family. It could also be that his imagining replaces the actual possibility of travelling abroad; since, as in the case of The Beatles' lyrics, imagination takes him further.

Personally, I think that Nik does not want to go abroad because he is afraid that what he might encounter could be worse than what he had imagined all these years. Also, in Tbilisi Nik is a master, an urban *capo*, knowing the city like the palm of his hand. And I am not talking about merely cartographic knowledge, but, more importantly, about being street-smart, knowing tricks, gestures, sidepaths and all that does not appear on the maps, nor adheres to any script. As shown by urban ethnographer AbdouMaliq Simone in his research in Jakarta, Hyderabad and Freetown, peripheral wisdom can be understood as a particular oscillation between opacity and transparency, openness and closure, and refusal and engagement, challenging the systemic logics and grammars aimed at defining what that knowledge is, and opening up the interstices, as 'a space for multiple compensations' and improvised living (Simone 2019: 116) (Figure 9.3).

In 2010, Nik had an old Mercedes, but more recently he was driving a hybrid Japanese car with right-hand steering and the radio in the Japanese alphabet. He is used to a world in which things are not the way they are supposed to be, being familiar with ambivalence and lack of meaning. One of the few solid certainties of Nik's life is the Georgian Orthodox church. After a painful, personal episode that ended up well, albeit one which I am not allowed to share, Nik devoted himself entirely to this faith and he now respects all Orthodox fasting periods and demonstrates a profound religiosity. Still, he shows himself as culturally open, crafty and with a charming sense of non-travelled cosmopolitanism. However, debates on LGBT rights in the country make him very upset. Indeed, talking about this topic has been the only time I saw Nik agitated, saying that 'After all, Georgia is Georgia, and Europe is Europe'.

The last time we met, Nik took me to his summer house with his son. On the way back, each of us had to choose our favourite Pink Floyd song. 'Now we can finally call each other friends', he said.

Figure 9.3 Nik. Francisco Martínez

But is it so that in the periphery, one is impelled to make new friends, and when in the centre only allies? Geopolitics might unfriend neighbours, turning them into enemies; but the opposite case might also happen: friendship can be fortified in unfriendly contexts. Then, people with no blood ties can be ready to help and support one another, generating an extended notion of fraternity despite, or rather because of, sharing difficulties, struggles, or a sense of peripherality (Frederiksen 2013). As part of human survival, friendships evolve not at the expense of pain but are instead tied together with self-defence and the work of getting on from day to day, sharing each other's resources in hard times (Terrell 2015). These are stories of mutual support, of hospitality, loyalty and solidarity, dissolving boundaries and dichotomies. Yet in peripheries, friendships can also be experienced in a rather ambivalent way, having less to do with emotions than with personal favours and doubt. In these situations, friendship can be performed not only as a role but also as a status, being eventually associated with notions of male honour, as well as becoming an instrument of social control (Brković 2017; Khalvashi 2013; Zakharova 2015).

Friendship is a universal sentiment, but it does not happen in a vacuum; rather, it occurs in specific locations and historical times. In other words, friendship takes place and unfolds in time, based on experiences such as sharing hopes, problems, plans, thoughts, joy and material things (Beer 2001). I often consider the extent to which liminal experiences, such as geopolitical border crossing, strife and need of care, whereby equality is embodied and a sense of consciousness and suspension of knowledge are generated (Turner 1973), might make the footprint of friendship stronger, even if not free of utilitarian instrumentality.

Otherwise, friendships developed in the field might also appear as 'accidental communities' (Rosen 2018), bonded together through elements of chance, contingent struggles and ephemeral incidents. When conducting fieldwork, we are persons in-between, holding double responsibilities, both to our professional community of practice and to our community of informants (Jaarsma and Rohatynskyj 2000). The anthropologist is a subject that knows with and through others; yet our ways of being in-between dovetail with our methodology, in both the analytical sense,[8] and the empirical dimension.[9] Also, specific ways of being in the field as well as specific relations between places, times and people eventually affect what can be known; that is, the quality of being knowable (Holbraad et al. 2018).

Missed chances

How far can the consequences of our errors and accidents reach in the field? In my time in Abkhazia, I managed to publish several reports and interviews in *El Mundo*. Some of the proposals that were not accepted by the newspaper were pitched to other journals or re-written and published in other languages.[10] However, due to the accidental circumstances and my need to leave Georgia quickly, I missed the chance to interview the former president of Georgia and former minister of foreign affairs of the Soviet Union, Eduard Shevardnadze, who died four years later. I also lost most of the photos and videos I made in the field, as well as most of the notes written about a group of young emigrées engaged in recovering Abkhazian folk music. I remember their mixed feelings about the expectations of returning to the country of their ancestors, and the difficulties of integrating into the new Abkhazian society, suffering from material shortage and having to learn Russian as their lingua franca (Figure 9.4).[11]

I managed to find some notes, for instance those of my conversation with Cemre Jade, a professor at Sukhumi State University, who came from Turkey. She compared this return to that of the Jews to Israel, yet acknowledged that 'some have returned back to Turkey after a few months here. Those who come with many expectations do not adapt – the conditions are difficult. There is no hot water, there is no heating. However, more and more arrive every day. I have been here three years now, and to me, it compensates for the difficulties.' Before arriving, Cemre was manifestly anti-Russian; after three years here, however, she had moderated her position: 'The diaspora has as much right to complain about the ongoing Russification as those who live here to try to improve their living standards through Russian investments. But Moscow should still apologise for the genocide of the nineteenth century.' The two main waves of emigration occurred around 1860, when Tsarist Russia conquered the Caucasus, and in the 1930s under Stalin. 'That was centuries ago, the times have changed and now the Russians help us', argued Nart Gechba, who had recently arrived from Jordan. Iban Bakik also came from Jordan, and thinks that 'it is not the same to see our country in photos than to live here. I advise people to come and see the actual situation and then decide whether to stay or not' (Figures 9.5 and 9.6).

In the field, I was not aware of the relevance and research potential of the people I was meeting. For instance, when I interviewed Viacheslav Chirikba, I focused on

Figure 9.4 A group of young emigrées. Francisco Martínez

the rare Basque–Abkhazian dictionary he had written (arguing that these two languages had the same roots). However, I ignored that Chirikba was about to become the new minister of foreign affairs, after Maxim. I had the same feeling of having missed a chance a few years later in Tbilisi when I failed to interview a man whose job was to guard ping-pong tables in a public park next to the stadium of Dinamo Tbilisi, and charge us (the players) for it. As I learnt while playing with him, that was his only income. I went there to play table tennis for quite a while. Yet immersed in gaming (mostly with my friend Alex), I did not arrange a proper interview with this man, whose job is to capitalise on something that, in principle, belongs to everyone. Indeed, one day, when it started to rain, the man simply left the park and Alex and I could play ping-pong for free for several hours. Of course, in the pauses between matches, we did talk, but I did not care to take notes as I could not prevent the potential relevance for my research of this encounter. The problem, however, is that once I returned to talk to him properly, months later, he had vanished – along with the ping-pong tables. A year later, and then two years later, I came back and he was not there anymore.

Rather than simply experiential, being in the field is equal to a journey that goes from knowing to not-knowing, gathering new questions in your pocket and challenging the preestablished significance and meanings of things; it serves to make you aware of your own epistemic limits, of what you ignore and of the fragility of the things that we construct. In some cases, fieldwork impels us to

Figure 9.5 Chirikba. Francisco Martínez

opt for longer paths instead of taking the expected straight ones, which lead 'to endless questions about the value of ethnographic analysis of any kind' (Holbraad et al. 2018: 4).

As noted in the introduction to this volume, the peripheral also shows a particular openness to the unknown and accidental, and a complex oscillation between engagement and withdrawal. We can thus think the peripheral as an de-centred standing, instead of a counterpoint. It is situated at the fringe of dominant paradigms, inhabited as a zone of questions, empirically multiple, emergent, mysterious, conflicted, vexed, ambiguous and conditional.[12] Nonetheless, the periphery, as *terra ignota*, is not always a beyond, but it can also be the in-between – found in the interstices, in the grey zones of interacting, showing a complex, oscillating relation between the abstract and the concrete, between the rupture and the continuity, often manifested 'as a collapse of distinctions' (Frederiksen and Knudsen 2015: 13), not always knowing what is the beginning and the end.

Accidented anthropologist

This chapter echoes an accidental anthropology, built upon a confessional tone and sense of failure. It reflects on the intrinsically uncertain character of fieldwork, often risky and messy, resisting plans and making unclear where the field ends and begins. Indeed, these stories carry both instances of success and failure, exploring the peripheral as an epistemic fringe, characterised by discontinuity,

Figure 9.6 Me and the ping-pong guard playing. Alex Bieth

the suspension of knowledge and a need of reinvention – three of the basic features of any liminal condition (Turner 1973).

In *The Accidental Anthropologist* (2006), Michael Jackson narrates how his involvement in academia has not been a clear route, but more of an accidental one determined by contingent factors and decisions and threshold experiences. After acknowledging that he does not really understand his own life trajectory, Jackson adds that for reasons he cannot fully fathom, he was always coming back to anthropology – finding in this discipline 'a mission and a refuge' (Lévi-Strauss 1962: 58). One of the key points that Jackson seems to make is that his personal openness to the accidental and the peripheral conditioned his trajectory into the discipline, which took place through unexpected incidents and dislocations. We can also argue that rather than learning anthropology, one *ends up* an anthropologist. For that adventurous deviation, one does not have to avoid failures in the field, but only accidents from which it is impossible to recover.

Accidents and failures are taken to involve a mistake and to have meaning, which is not always the case. This is noted, for instance, by Lee Ann Fujii (2015), who argues that accidents are not merely an intrinsic part of fieldwork but are also constitutive of data.[13] After presenting five stories from her field research on local violence in Rwanda, Bosnia and the US, Fujii proposes 'accidental ethnography' as a mode of attention to the unplanned moments that take place outside our research plans, as a methodology of gathering valuable 'nondata'. Frank Pieke (1995) also discussed how the haphazard conditions under which fieldwork is conducted might turn out to be crucial for our interpretative insights, turning unexpected events into opportunities. In his case, the protests of the Chinese People's Movement in Tian'anmen Square, Beijing, in May 1989 made obsolete his carefully designed research plan. Then, after changing his initial plan and switching all his attention to the protests, he discovered the unexpected risks of this decision in being asked to become a human shield and putting his Chinese academic counterparts in a vulnerable situation.

Several publications show an increasing interest in how accidents are not necessarily a failure but simply a piece of empirical material. Based on his fieldwork in Taiwan, François Bouchetoux (2014) analysed methodological failures that generate nausea and feelings of shame and guilt. In his view, reflexivity is the strategic device through which anthropologists cope with the awkwardness, boredom and miscommunications of fieldwork. There are more inspiring examples of how to incorporate the accidental into our research. For instance, Dariusz Jemielniak and Monika Kostera (2010) have gathered nine stories from organisational ethnographers to speak about different gaffes and slips that have occurred during their fieldwork. Interestingly, these tales had been excluded from their final texts, instead taking success stories as more relevant for the chosen topics. However, as the informants acknowledge, these errors had important consequences of for the construction of the ethnographer's identity and of research narratives. Another example reflecting on the research plans that do not go too far or never began is the volume *The Lost Ethnographies* (2019), edited by James Smith and Sara Delamont. This project shows how ethnographies that didn't work still shed light on how ethnography works. In the field, as they argue, nothing is ever wasted, and we might *gain* to learn things despite situations going awry or plans falling apart.

In this chapter, I try to interpret similar situations by reflecting on what kind of learning they entailed for me, as a researcher. Accidental episodes that were not central to research appeared, however, as highly relevant components of anthropological knowledge-making. Incidents, on hold situations and inattentiveness to the ethnographic relevance of the learning can be thus an important part of any construction process in anthropology.[14] The novelty brought by peripheral methodologies might be, therefore, the researcher's openness to embrace the unknown and hazardous, as well as to incorporate accidental, uncontrolled experiences to our ethnographies.

Conclusion: Remaining on the way to knowledge

In a continuous dialogue that goes back and forth to past events, this chapter discussed how we become anthropologists in relation to certain places, informants and events. It developed as a series of episodes that combine empirical and analytical reflections on research accidents in which it was unclear what could come out from the experience and even how to proceed in the field. I accounted for a series of accidental experiences that opened up unexpected professional reconsiderations and analytical possibilities about how anthropologists conduct their professional works and lives. By putting accidents and failures at the centre of analysis, I have tried to understand how research experiences mature with us, providing a methodological engagement with my epistemic troubles, as well as an analysis of the peripheral and the accidental in the field. As Jackson (2006) foregrounded, not-knowing can be cultivated as a way of being on the way to knowledge and accidents practiced as a form of learning. It could be, however, that we remain on hold, or incidentally deviated from the straight institutional line, certainly not progressing as planned, and yet intensively in the field.

Despite rarely being acknowledged in ethnographies, moments of perceived failure and negative capability show, however, relevance to understanding the production of anthropological knowledge. The insights included here are not yet ethnographic, as the research was not originally conceived as ethnographic.[15] They work, nonetheless, to contextualise the productive potential of accidents and failures in the field and in learning, as well as what they reveal and teach despite implying stepping out from the expected ways of knowing. Here, failures are taken as speaking of the insecurities, detours and self-doubts that accompany the research process, and also as a way of reflecting on episodes that shape our professional careers at-cross-purposes.

All these are relevant epistemological and disciplinary concerns that address the subjective dynamics of data collection in a way that allows analytical questions to emerge from field accidents. We could conclude by speculating upon the concept of a *de facto* fieldwork, in contrast to a *de jure* one – to distinguish between those practices that are disciplinarily recognised as belonging to the method, yet fail to acknowledge how fieldwork exists in reality; and those field experiences that were not originally designed as ethnographic, yet contribute to generating relevant anthropological knowledge (in the confines of what is recognised as data and of fieldwork itself).

Ultimately, what the chapter shows is the elasticity of what we understand as the field – we, anthropologists, often talk about the field, but it is not entirely clear what we mean by that, partly, because we always end up creating it. In my case, I ended up falling into an anthropological field accidentally, by remaining on hold, and without being aware of the content and contour of my research. With the years, this field has been expanding (as I go along with new life and professional experiences), growing in density, and, in some cases, becoming messier and vague.

Notes

1 Anthropological insights are elaborated through fieldwork, yet not always based on systematic, instrumental techniques. As Tim Ingold insists (2007), anthropology is not simply ethnography, and ethnography is not merely an anthropological technique. In his view, these two activities have different objectives and also produce different types of narratives. Yet Ingold's concern (and complaint) does not merely concern the differences between the two, but, more importantly, about the contraction of anthropology into ethnography. He has also criticised the tendency to attribute 'ethnographicness' to all our encounters in the field, undermining the ontological commitment of anthropology as a discipline, which is characterised, in his view, by a 'long-term and open-ended commitment, generous attentiveness, relational depth, and sensitivity to context' (Ingold 2014: 384).

2 The Caucasus (as a location) and Europe (as an ideal) are still the main others of the Russian identity.

3 Nine years later, I wrote an essay accounting for the different types of holes in Georgia and reflecting on the kind of effects that they generate – enabling and defying human agency simultaneously, keeping people on hold and perpetuating a particular order, as devices for connecting and disconnecting (Martínez 2019c).

4 Once we departed, Paul kindly wrote an essay for an exhibition I co-curated; here an excerpt of his text: 'The Republic of Georgia was a primitivist painting... The country people were crookedly built, too: swollen-handed and weathered. The women wore gumboots and strata of faded sweaters … a handmade society… In Georgia I gripped door handles made of baling wire. I warmed myself at wood-fired stoves hand-snipped from sheet metal. At one roadside spring, someone had poked a well-whittled stick to a dented tin cup: a custom-made dipper of such exquisite balance and proportion that it added pleasure to the act of drinking… Azerbaijan has been shaped by a single resource for more than a century: oil. The Azeri countryside was tidier. Villages were more grid-like. (One of the first things to vanish in affluent post-industrialized landscapes is the curve.) … The houses were professionally engineered and squared, and finished with blown stucco. Doorknobs were machined, mass-produced. The doors closed flushly within precise, factory-made frames. People dressed in newer and better-fitting clothes. It was nearly impossible to find dirt roads to walk on: ribbons of pavement unspooled over the least hamlet capillary in Azerbaijan. Azerbaijan had been reshaped by machines for other machines—steamrollers working for cars' (Salopek 2016: 159–160).

5 There is something that always precedes fieldwork, as well as also a *during* and an *after* temporality in anthropological research too (see Chua 2015).

6 See the article then written by Transparency International: http://transparency.ge/en/node/568

7 Writing this passage made me feel like a fictional character, as if I were a sort of Harry Houdini (an early anthropologist himself), driven to prove (and showcase) my escaping capacities to sceptics.

8 Investigating relations through relations (see Strathern 2020); focusing upon the discrepancy between the de facto diversity of practices and the ideal, normative formats (see Miller 2007).

9 A transformative, transcendental experience is constituted through interactions and recognition (Pina Cabral 2017)

10 In English, Italian and Russian, besides Spanish, being published in the *Osservatorio Balcani e Caucaso, Mediterráneo Sur, and Russia Beyond the Headlines* An example of this is my report about the IDP's in the Gali region: https://www.rbth.com/articles/2011/04/14/we_have_to_say_we_are_abkhazians_so_we_do_12732.html

11 In Turkey, there are around two million Circassians (Northern Caucasians), of which over 500 000 are Abkhaz. The diaspora is also present in Jordan, Syria and Israel, and the de facto government of Sukhumi has been trying to attract them back (not just Abkhazians, but also Cherkeshes, Kabardinos, Shapshugs).

12 Elsewhere, I have presented myself as an expert in peripheries, discussing different notions of disciplinary and personal peripherality. As I have written, the experience of peripherality does not imply a previous condition of centrality. Also, the use of peripherality rather depends on the researcher's background, interest and aptitudes, 'To be at the margins is a circumstantial condition that requires particular muscles, such as openness to risks and collaborations with unexpected epistemic partners, and also the ability to resist or adapt to rapid changes and ruptures... getting to know the tricks that help to mobilise resources and overcome discontinuities' (Martínez 2019a: 184).

13 Relevant for 'what they suggest about the larger political and social world in which they (and the researcher) are embedded' (Fujii 2015: 525).

14 Moreover, we should consider failure not merely as an endpoint but also as a new beginning, a liminal point of assessment, interrupting the expected flow of things (Miyazaki and Riles 2005; Appadurai 2016; Ssorin-Chaikov 2016: Martínez 2019b).

15 The material provided is not the result of a well-planned research, but rather the outcome of happenstance observations in which I was not in control of things, nor knowing what to know. Even so, these insights provide a surplus of anthropological ideas. Nonetheless, even if the analysis of these insights might contribute to discussions about borders, friendship and politics at the margins of a globalised world, this study does not try to prove anything in particular; rather, it fathoms the possibility of turning stories into data by accounting for several dead-ends and new beginnings.

References

Appadurai, Arjun 2016. 'Failure. Introduction'. *Social Research* 83 (3): xxi–xxvii.

Awad, Isabel 2006. 'Journalists and their sources: Lessons from anthropology'. *Journalism Studies* 7 (6): 922–939.

Beer, Bettina 2001. 'Friendship, anthropology of'. In *International Encyclopedia of the Social & Behavioral Sciences*. Neil J. Smelser and Paul B. Baltes (eds.) Amsterdam: Elsevier, 5805–5808.

Bion, Wilfred 1970. Attention and Interpretation. London: Tavistock.

Bird, Elizabeth 2010. 'The journalist as ethnographer?: How anthropology can enrich journalistic practice'. In *Media Anthropology*. E. W. Rothenbuhler and M. Coman (eds.) Thousand Oaks: Sage, 301–308.

Bouchetoux, François 2014. *Writing Anthropology: A Call for Uninhibited Methods*. New York: Palgrave Macmillan.

Brković, Čarna 2017. *Managing Ambiguity: How Clientelism, Citizenship, and Power Shape Personhood in Bosnia and Herzegovina*. Oxford: Berghahn.

Chekhov, Anton 1999. *Life and Thought: Selected Letters and Commentary*. New York: Northwestern University Press.

Chua, Liana 2015. 'Troubled landscapes, troubling anthropology: Co-presence, necessity and the making of ethnographic knowledge'. *Journal of the Royal Anthropological Institute* 21 (3): 641–659.

Crapanzano, Vincent 2014. 'Must we be bad epistemologists? Illusions of transparency, the opaque other, and interpretative foils'. In *The Ground Between–Anthropologists Engage Philosophy*. V. Das, M. Jackson, A. Kleinman and B. Singh (eds.) Durham: Duke University Press.

Fabian, Johannes 1983. *Time and the Other*. New York: Columbia University Press.

Frederiksen, Martin Demant 2013. *Young Men, Time, and Boredom in the Republic of Georgia*. Philadelphia: Temple University Press.

Frederiksen, Martin Demant 2015. 'Temporal marginality'. In *Hopeless Youth!* F. Martínez and P. Runnel (eds.) Tartu: Estonian National Museum, 107–109.

Frederiksen, Martin Demant and Ida Harboe Knudsen 2015. 'Introduction: What is a grey zone and why is eastern europe one?'. In *Ethnographies of Grey Zones in Eastern Europe*. I. Harboe Knudsen and M. D. Frederiksen (eds.) London: Anthem, 1–23.

Fujii, Lee Ann 2015. 'Five stories of accidental ethnography: Turning unplanned moments in the field into data'. *Qualitative Research* 15 (4) 525–539.

Hannerz, Ulf 2004. *Foreign News: Exploring the World of Foreign Correspondents*. Chicago: University of Chicago Press.

Holbraad, M., S. Green, A. Corsín Jiménez, V. Das, N. Bird-David, E. Kohn, G. Hage, L. Bear, H. Knox, and B. Kapferer 2018. 'FORUM what is analysis? Between theory, ethnography, and method'. *Social Analysis* 62 (1): 1–30.

Ingold, Tim 2007. 'Anthropology is *not* ethnography'. In *Proceedings of the British Academy*, vol. 154. London: Oxford University Press, 69–92.

Ingold, Tim 2014. 'That's enough about ethnography!' *HAU: Journal of Ethnographic Theory* 4 (1): 383–395.

Jaarsma, Sjoerd R. and Marta A. Rohatynskyj (eds.) 2000. *Ethnographic Artifacts: Challenges to a Reflexive Anthropology*. Honolulu: University of Hawaii Press.

Jackson, Michael 2006. *The Accidental Anthropologist*. Dunedin: Longacre.

Jemielniak, Dariusz and Monika Kostera 2010. 'Narratives of irony and failure in ethnographic work'. *Canadian Journal of Administrative Sciences* 27: 335–347.

Khalvashi, Tamta 2013. *Peripheral Affects – Shame, Publics and Performance on the Margins of the Republic of Georgia*. PhD Thesis, University of Copenhagen.

Lévi-Strauss, Claude 1962. *Tristes Tropiques*. London: Hutchinson.

Marcus, George E. and Judith Okely. 2007. 'Debate section: "How short can fieldwork be?"'. *Social Anthropology* 15 (3): 353–367.

Martínez, Francisco 2019a. 'An expert in peripheries: Working at, with and through the margins of European anthropology'. In *Changing Margins and Relations within European Anthropology*. F. Martínez (ed.) ANUAC. Journal of the Italian Association of Cultural Anthropology, 167–188.

Martínez, Francisco 2019b. 'Insiders' manual to breakdown'. In *Repair, Brokenness, Breakthrough: Ethnographic Responses*. F. Martínez and P. Laviolette (eds.) Oxford: Berghahn, 1–16.

Martínez, Francisco 2019c. 'What's in a hole? Voids out of place and politics below the state in Georgia'. In *Repair, Brokenness, Breakthrough: Ethnographic Responses*. F. Martínez and P. Laviolette (eds.) Oxford: Berghahn, 121–144.

Martínez, Francisco and Marika Agu. 2016. *Aesthetics of Repair in Contemporary Georgia*. Tartu: Tartu Art Museum.

McLean, Athena and Annette Leibing 2007 *The Shadow Side of Fieldwork: Exploring the Borders between Ethnography and Life*. Malden: Blackwell.

Miller, Daniel 2007. 'What is a relationship? Is kinship negotiated experience?' *Ethnos: Journal of Anthropology* 72 (4): 535–554.

Miyazaki, Hirokazu and Annelise Riles. 2005. 'Failure as an endpoint'. In *Global Assemblages*. A. Ong and S. J. Collier (eds.) Malden: Blackwell.

Navaro-Yashin, Yael 2012. *The Make-Believe Space: Affective Geography in a Postwar Polity*. Durham: Duke University Press.

Pieke, Frank N 1995. 'Accidental anthropology. Witnessing the 1989 Chinese people's movement'. In *Fieldwork under Fire. Contemporary Studies of Violence and Survival.* C. Nordstrom and A. Robben (eds.) Los Angeles: University of California Press, 62–79.

Pina Cabral, João 2017. *World: An Anthropological Examination.* Chicago: HAU Books.

Rosen, Matthew 2018. 'Accidental communities: Chance operations in urban life and field research'. *Ethnography* 19 (3): 312–335.

Salopek, Paul 2016. 'Border of desire: The geopolitics of bricolage'. In *Aesthetics of Repair in Contemporary Georgia.* F. Martínez and M. Agu (eds.) Tartu: Tartu Art Museum, 158—161.

Shore, Chris and Susanna Trnka (eds.) 2013. *Up, Close and Personal. On Peripheral Perspectives and the Production of Anthropological Knowledge.* Oxford: Berghahn.

Simone, AbdouMaliq 2019. *Improvised Lives: Rhythms of Endurance in an Urban South.* Cambridge: Polity.

Smith, James and Sara Delamont (eds.) 2019. *The Lost Ethnographies: Methodological Insights from Projects that Never Were.* Bingley: Emerald.

Ssorin-Chaikov, Nikolai 2016. 'Soviet debris: Failure and the poetics of unfinished construction in Northern Siberia'. *Social Research* 83 (3): 689–721.

Strathern, Marilyn 2004. *Commons and Borderlands: Working Papers on Onterdisciplinarity, Accountability and the Flow of Knowledge.* Oxford: Sean Kingston.

Strathern, Marilyn 2020. *Relations. An Anthropological Account.* Durham: Duke University Press.

Terrell, John Edward 2015. *A Talent for Friendship.* New York: Oxford University Press.

Turner, Victor 1973. 'The centre out here: Pilgrims' Goal'. *History of Religions* 12 (3): 191–230.

Zakharova, Evgenia Y 2015. 'Druzhba i rodstvo v kvartalakh Tbilisi: imperativy i praktiki' [Friendship and Kinship in Tbilisi Neighborhoods: Imperatives and Practices]. *Etnograficheskoe obozrenie* 5: 100–116.

Conclusion

Catching a glimpse of peripheral wisdom

Lili Di Puppo, Martin Demant Frederiksen and Francisco Martínez

Out of the corner of one's eye

It is in assembling the different contributions to this volume and seeing how they interweave and resonate with each other that we slowly catch a glimpse of what we have called 'peripheral wisdom' and the methodologies that can help us to approach it. The way in which accidental experiences, unexpected moments, floating impressions and sensations interweave freely and give rise to new associations is also a quality of peripheral wisdom that can be found in many of the texts in this volume. Catching a glimpse, seeing things 'out of the corner of one's eye' (Raahauge, Waltorp & ARTlife Film Collective) and the 'sideways glance' (Feder-Nadoff) appear as a particular mode of (anthropological) attention that brings us closer to moments, tonalities and textures of life and of the world that would otherwise disappear or remain hidden, were we not suddenly to become aware of them and of their *presence*.

The quality of this awareness lies precisely in the fact that it happens unexpectedly; we are caught unaware by moments or phenomena, as occurs in Raahauge's haunting stories. Something furtive, subtle and unknown suddenly grabs our attention while awakening in us what we might call a dormant mode of attention and being. This state of awareness or mode of attention mirrors the phenomena, moments and experiences that awaken it, in the sense that we find it difficult to name the possibilities of knowing that we sense in ourselves. Why does it appear difficult to name and grasp this knowledge? What form of knowledge is peripheral wisdom? Peripheral wisdom appears as something furtive, in movement, like the Greek *mētis* (Klekot), as difficult to take hold of and to possess (it cannot be *had*, as Feder-Nadoff says), as something that is unfolding in unconscious ways (Arantes and Di Puppo) and as a loss of control (Raahauge).

Peripheral wisdom is a form of knowledge that is interwoven with unknowns; it manifests itself precisely on the line between knowing and not knowing. It can be a knowledge that we did not know we had, of something that inexorably escapes us, but which at the same time appears to be deeply intimate (Di Puppo). The presence and *preservation* of the unknown thus stands forth as a necessary condition of knowing; the unknown is a necessary ingredient in allowing this particular mode of perception to unfold. The unknown also appears as *un-reflected* in the sense of being an unconscious and intuitive form of knowledge, a form of knowledge that either remains dormant or lies dormant, suddenly awakening, but not always in a perceptible way. This form of knowledge can thus be resistant to reflection, as in the knitting knowledge described by Arantes. Peripheral wisdom can also appear as a form of knowledge that suddenly takes possession of us, appealing to a hidden state of being. Floating experiences and modes of perception that may be too subtle to really be taken hold of can themselves manifest in states of drifting away (Nolas and Varvantakis), when we abandon ourselves to the moment and its richness. A state of receptiveness, or even defencelessness (Di Puppo), may seem more propitious to the manifestation of this mode of knowing. The porous, permeable state of receptiveness, of a dreamy abandonment, recalls Amira Mittermaier's reference to the state of being 'acted upon' and its valorisation in religious 'stories of dreams, visions, apparitions, spirit possession, prophecy, revelation, the miraculous, and, more broadly, stories that involve elements of surprise and awe' (Mittermaier 2012: 250).

The state of drifting away, of immersing oneself in a moment or an experience, alerts us to the meaning or dimension of *being present*. The subtle moments, memories and floating impressions that appear in some of the texts often disrupt the traditional methods of fieldwork, raising questions such as *What is the 'field', ultimately? What is 'presence'? What is it to be in the field, to be there, present? What are we present for?* These questions resonate in Nolas and Varvantakis's and Di Puppo's texts (see also Rethmann 2007; Dalsgaard and Nielsen 2016; Martínez 2019), as they relate how unexpected *immersion* in the present moment or happening can sometimes require the renouncement of conventional fieldwork methods. The sudden awakening of childhood memories by a dish or a book (Nolas and Varvantakis), or the experience of surrendering to the moment in a ritual ceremony (Di Puppo), raise the further question of what (in)attentiveness consists in.

Traditional ethnographic research demands focused attention in which the researcher is simultaneously preoccupied with research questions, methodological canons and disciplinary constrictions. But how can the researcher really be *there*, in the present moment, in the company of his/her interlocutors, alert to them and open to the sensations that emerge in this space? How can the researcher be attuned to changes to the atmosphere, sudden shifts of perception, to the possibility that other dimensions might open up? Drifting away in fugitive memories – ones that make their presence deeply felt (Nolas and Varvantakis) – or the sensation of a space's opening up and the intuition of a power's being present (Di Puppo) can thus be experienced as *being there*. By surrendering to these sensations, we become fully aware of the subtleties and nuances of field experience. By contrast, more focused attention may correspond to disengagement with the richness and unexpectedness of the present moment and its multiple sensations.

Reflecting on narratives of ghost stories in Denmark, Raahauge notes how her informants recalled in some of their stories that the experience of a ghostly presence suddenly slipped away when focus was placed on it. Thus the experience of this presence happens 'out of the corner of one's eye', in one's peripheral vision or oblique gaze. When attempting to face the ghost (as in the story of a man who decisively opens a door after hearing steps in a corridor), one faces emptiness. Raahauge says of her informant, who felt a presence while watching TV: 'out of the corner of her eye, she saw this black smoke. It disappeared when she focused on it.' She further comments on the story: 'This impossible, implicit quality of the peripheral has the problem that it dissolves before our very eyes when we look at it.' Raahauge's ghost stories suggest the impossibility and undesirability of focused, sharp vision, which finds its parallel in the problematic of *explaining away* supernatural phenomena. Supernatural phenomena such as ghosts that defy reason are often explained away by relating them to known phenomena (see also Mittermaier 2019).

As Robert Desjarlais (2018) has shown, such experiences may also exist beyond the realm of the supernatural as phantasmal presences: imagined or improbable flows or currents that are not easily explained. This poses challenges for researchers who are expected (by themselves or by others) to offer clear explanations of the phenomena they encounter. Paul Stoller (1994) refers to this as the tendency to 'dust off' phenomena in an effort to figure out what lies beneath, warning that in this process we risk losing sight of what is potentially the most significant aspect: the dust itself.

Seen from this perspective, as is also apparent in the texts by Raahauge and Frederiksen, to 'explain away' is to risk losing what is really there. Both prefer to engage with things that simply happen, invisible but active, as the product of silent transformations. This approach to the social, which does not appear on the radar, resonates with François Jullien's observations about the propensities of things (Jullien 1999). To capture how things silently tend towards an end, he proposes indirect, timely and selective engagement, allowing things to happen, paying attention to the fissure in order to detect slow transformations – those that happen quietly, 'without warning, without giving an alert, "in silence" without attracting attention, and as though independently of us' (Jullien 2011: 3).

Etymologically, the verb *to explain* relates to the notion of 'flattening' (from the Latin *planus*) and of outing (*ex*). Focused vision can appear one-dimensional or flat in that it seeks to suppress the blurriness of phenomena or experiences and the possibility of other dimensions of knowledge and (non-)manifestations. The demand for sharpness and clarity also appears in the TV professionals' request for a 'clear story' in Waltorp and the ARTlife Film Collective's attempt to make a documentary movie about their lives. The Afghan women who, with Waltorp, make up the ARTlife Film Collective prefer to engage with the more indistinct and mundane dimensions of life, the *blandness* of which can be experienced as smooth and soothing. This resembles Lisa Stevenson's observation, regarding the relation between fact and image, that 'desire/feelings/experiences express themselves in images, not to hide themselves, but because those desire/feelings/ experiences *are*' (Stevenson 2014: 45, emphasis in original). As such, images do not necessarily have hidden meanings but are styles of existence that lose their affective hold if they are 'unraveled or unwrapped into a series of facts' (ibid.).

Thinking about the *imaginal realm*, or the *mundus imaginalis*, that we encounter in the work of philosopher Henry Corbin (and to which Waltorp and the ARTlife Film Collective allude in their discussion of the *flow of images across realms*), we find another dimension of how the *image* relates to knowledge. He warns against equating the imaginary with the *unreal*, with 'something that is and remains outside of being and existence' (Corbin 1999: 1).[1] The *active imagination* as an organ of perception 'lifts us up' to another mode of being and knowing, the two dimensions being interrelated. By contrast, the focused vision and the ideal of clarity that it contains imply distancing and detachment: in order to 'see' phenomena, we take one step back. As several chapters in this volume show, however, this act of distancing may amount to a loss of *what is really there* in the sense that phenomena that lie beyond our analytical reach nonetheless make their presence felt in our research.

Intimacy, the invisible and the expanding field

Some of the experiences and phenomena that appear in the contributions to this volume may be precisely too loose and intimate *to be seen* or reflected through the act of distancing that underlies focused vision. Raahauge thus remarks on *vision* when commenting on haunting stories: 'while seeing is distanced and connected to clarity, hearing is intimate and dubious, the explanations vague and contestable'. While intimacy, as a dimension of the kind of peripheral knowledge we may encounter in the field, may appear to be 'less clear', it does not make our experiences 'less real', as in Di Puppo's experience of a ritual ceremony, which happened with her eyes closed.

Arantes's difficulty capturing her knowledge of knitting provides another example of how intimacy can open up a further dimension of knowledge beyond the ideal of clarity contained in *vision*. Her knowledge of knitting appears to be too close and intimate to be captured; by being so close, it becomes invisible. She is able to approach this knowledge only by sharing it with her novice sister-in-law and through the discussion of her fieldwork diaries in a group. It is thus through her diaries, another intimate and often hidden part of the research process, that she is able to catch glimpses of this knowledge. Diary-writing appears as an unconscious voice in fieldwork, in a sense a more domestic and intimate part of the research. It may take place at the kitchen table after a long day of fieldwork, consisting in unformed, interwoven notes and fragments. Diary-writing is thus attuned to the intimacy of knitting and the way in which the knowledge it contains cannot be grasped immediately but is rather hidden in the interstices of sentences.

The dimension of intimacy shows how peripheral knowledge can also be linked to the *unspectacular*, the domesticity and cosiness of home (Arantes), the bland and mundane (Waltorp & ARTlife Film Collective) or the hazardous and inadvertent (Frederiksen). Intimacy also appears in the childhood memories conjured up by a book or a well-loved dish, which cause Nolas and Varvantakis to drift away to an *elsewhere*. Intimacy conveys the multidimensional quality of knowledge in the sense that the strange and the unknown can often be found in the most intimate of places. Hence, it is the familiarity of the settings in which they make their presence felt (a bedroom or a living room) that makes the manifestations of ghosts so unsettling in Raahauge's recounting of her informants' stories. These ghost encounters in the most intimate of places – the home – again suggest the intimate connection between the known and the unknown. The strange does not need to be sought in far-off lands, those belonging to anthropology's original imaginary; indeed, it often resides in the closest of places. Di Puppo's experience of a ritual ceremony is also an opening to the fathomlessness of one's interior.

Intimacy is linked to *immediacy*, the unmediated quality of the experiences and moments encountered by the authors in this collection.

Rather than constituting a form of scientific detachment and distancing, a peripheral mode of attention appears in the form of *dislocation* (Waltorp & ARTlife Film Collective) or *disorientation*, even *transportation* or elevation to other dimensions (Di Puppo) and other time-spaces (Nolas and Varvantakis). A peripheral mode of perception makes us navigate different realms or find ourselves in the space between knowing and unknowing. This in-between appears in Raahauge's observation about the wanderer image in Thomas Mann's *Joseph and His Brothers*: 'a wanderer at the seafront, who is drawn towards the misty cliff to be seen far away; he is positioned between his now-here and the imagination and drive towards what he wishes to explore out there at the coastal cliff, which he can only get a glimpse of. This idea of seductive imaginaries of displacement is also present in Tønder.' The imaginary, the glimpse of a horizon, has the effect of displacing one's being and allowing one to evade, for a moment, the place in which one is (Nolas and Varvantakis). Instead of seeing these other dimensions and realms as mere fantasy, 'only' dreams to be forgotten in the work of research, we feel a drive to further explore them rather than close the door to them. We may also feel the desire to establish new relations between theory and practice (Cerwonka and Malkki 2007), in some cases problematising them in our attempt to be 'nearer' to people's 'felt realities' (Desjarlais 1997: 12), by way of staying within the shadows of things or experiences (Frederiksen).

As an example, Waltorp and the ARTlife Film Collective ask, 'What happens when we let ourselves be taken over in the field? It is a move resisting premature analytical closure; resisting the masterly and expertly at the expense of attuned listening.' Attuning to the field, letting ourselves be taken over in it, involves resisting the urge for analytical closure so as to let the subtle knowledge we encounter unfold at its own pace (Di Puppo). A space between different realms opens up through presence, our not knowing distinctly where we are, as the question loses its meaning. Varvantakis is transported back to his grandmother's kitchen when he senses the flavours and tastes of a dish, renouncing focused attention for another mode of being present. The experience of the line between knowing and not knowing interrogates our perception of the field. Are we creating the field as a construct that does not quite hold together, or are we perpetually discovering it by sensing how it extends in all its vitality, losing sense of where it ends and begins (Martínez)?

Rather than the flat surface created by centred, focused attention, the field may appear to be living and to become animated in an evasive making, giving us glimpses of new realms of knowledge, impelling us to reconfigure the traditional, anthropological idea of encounter, and questioning the need to domesticate the unknown, exotic and alien into common verbal knowledge (Cox, Irving and Wright 2016).

Preserving the unknown

Many of the contributions to this volume speak of the need to *preserve*: to preserve the unknown and the dissonant (Frederiksen, Di Puppo), the cracks and fissures (Raahauge), the incompleteness (Feder-Nadoff), the blandness or greyness

(Waltorp & ARTlife Film Collective). More fundamentally, these authors are asking the question of how to preserve the *realness* of our experiences and their immediacy rather than substituting them for something else. Analytical closure can be seen as a premature move that does not allow the experience to live on (Di Puppo); the experience of the field simply exists in the absence of analysis, in an ethnographic not-yet (Martínez).

How do we sense the 'realness' of these field experiences – experiences which may seem to be lost precisely when we try to engage in the work of the mind (Di Puppo) and extract meaning out of them (Frederiksen)? Why does the analytical labour – similar to an alchemical transformation but in reverse – appear to rob these experiences and phenomena of their vitality, richness, and ultimately their 'realness'? There is a sense that the vitality of experiences can be preserved only if their mystery, their intimate connection to an unknown, is also preserved. What we may obtain, if we engage in analysis, appears literally to be a *pale reflection*, a substitute. Frederiksen refers to the 'shadow world of meaning' when quoting Sontag's observation that 'to interpret is to impoverish' (Sontag 2009: 4).

What the chapters in this volume bring to the fore is the fact that 'realness' does not necessarily lie in clarity, sharpness of vision or the coherence of analytical interpretation. Experiences that do not leave a clear imprint – a traceable form or explanation (Raahauge, Di Puppo) – nonetheless linger on, even though there may be no tangible thread linking us to them. The question of a clear imprint, of a clear form and sharp or focused vision, relates to the question of representation that we also find in the ARTlife Film Collective and Waltorp's resistance to conveying their experiences in the form of a 'clear story', a conflict. We also find it in the question of dramaturgy in Frederiksen's text: the problem, for anthropologists, of getting the story *too* right or making it too logical. Raahauge refers to the *loss of control* experienced in the field as a method, as 'a guardian against viewing the field through too defined lenses in order to catch a glimpse of its more elusive aspects'. The clarity of representation, its form and the control it implies, suppresses the immediacy of experience and the puzzlement that it entails. As Raahauge (2016: 106) also observes regarding the ghost phenomena she encountered in her fieldwork on haunting: 'the inexplicable phenomena might be thought of as a door into new and puzzling, yet powerful worlds. This is related to the double nature of both presence and absence they manifest – an absence of explanation, of cohesion, of meaning, and of control, combined with a presence of intense, personal sensations and possible new horizons.'

The intensity of experience, its intimacy (Nolas and Varvantakis, Waltorp & ARTlife Film Collective, Di Puppo), makes it impossible to discard it. The intensity and indefinite quality of these fieldwork moments reorder our epistemic hierarchies and what we view as 'relevant' by interrogating the possibility of sorting out events, experiences and phenomena according to 'relevance' (Martínez, Frederiksen). As Raahauge further notes, '[i]t is when you do *not* focus on the centre of the event that you perceive what is going on. The centre of the scene and the method of investigation turns out to be dark and empty, the periphery and the vague sensation of listening with half an ear is fraught with noises and experiences.'

Tim Flohr Sørensen observes how 'certain phenomena, located at or beyond the margins of knowledge, are not necessarily the result of a deficiency in the data, methodology or epistemology' (2016: 742). In *An Anthropology of Nothing in Particular*, Frederiksen (2018) purposely refuses to fall into meaning and to explain, contextualise or even make sense of the stories gathered in the field. Traditionally, anthropologists have tended to exclude their own ignorance in the final monograph, even if not knowing or lack of meaning may have been a key element in how the fieldwork unfolded. Instead, Frederiksen chooses to fully embrace the ambivalence of the nihilist relations going on around him in Georgia, presenting fieldwork as a rather confusing activity, characterised by waiting for something that never shows up and a meaning that never comes around.

Knowledge by subtraction

The absence of anywhere to hold on to constitutes the vantage point of the peripheral. A quote by Woodham included in Waltorp & the ARTlife Film Collective's chapter evokes the sense of dislocation generated by peripheral vision (or sensation): 'It is this hidden verb that helpfully conjures to mind the experience of peripheral vision: from the corner of one's eye, a flash appears – a spark so intriguing that it *carries the perceiver away* from what they were doing or the place to which they were going. In this sense, the agency of the periphery lies in its capacity to pick us up and spirit us off: it is not a static point which occupies the edge of a frame – rather, it is the very motor of our on-going self-dislocation; it is that which takes us away from our centre' (Woodham 2018: 4). Raahauge further explores the advantage of a *defocused*, peripheral vantage point as the possibility of navigating different realms and time-spaces: 'Instead of focusing on "here", "there", "past", "present" and "future", the defocused aspect might give the advantage of grasping the relations and the fluidity between these points, giving access for exploring the multiple times and places and undefined situation of life in the periphery.' The desire to espouse the movement and nuances of the field, of navigating between different realms of knowledge, excludes the possibility of a fixed, stable centre.

Our methodology for approaching what we call 'peripheral wisdom' is not that of proposing alternative epistemological or ontological standpoints in opposition (or as alternatives) to Western epistemology. This would result in our again being caught in fixity. Rather, the peripheral methodology can be understood as states of being, attentiveness and perception such as *circling around* and *suspension*. Instead of defining peripheral wisdom, naming it, drawing its contours, *focusing* on it, we circle around it, in the sense of entering the movement that it engenders and sensing the intensity of the experiences that we associate with it, dislocated and disorientated.

Circling around something that appears out of place, attuning to shifting phenomena, sensations: this peripheral knowledge is not something that we can claim to possess; rather, it takes possession of us. The mobility of the peripheral vantage point can be found in the Greek *mētis*, discussed by Klekot in relation to pottery. It can also be found in the subtle organ of perception, the heart (*qalb*), which Sufis polish in order to reflect the divine light (Di Puppo). The movement and fluctuation of this higher knowledge appears in a quote by the scholar of Islam Alexander Knysh (1993: 58), in which he refers to the Sufi medieval scholar Ibn Arabi's doctrine of Divine manifestations: 'to discover the "true" nature of God and His relationship with the World, the observer must renounce his rational outlook and give himself to the veridical "direct vision" (*shuhud*) and intuitive "direct tasting" (*dhawq*). This new, higher knowledge can only be achieved by the human heart (*qalb*), an Arabic word whose lexical connotations point to "motion", "fluctuation" and "transformation". The heart "moves", "fluctuates" and "transforms" persistently following the outward "movements", "fluctuations", and "transformations" of the Divine Reality.'

Suspension, as a mode of attention, involves staying on the indefinite line or in the space that opens up between the known and the unknown, lingering on it. As Raahauge (2016: 96) observes regarding her informants, who have experienced ghost phenomena: 'The narratives often question the reality of the experience, and in that way the narrator is in a position of suspense, waiting for a possible next experience to confirm the reality of the first one.' The diaries, which help Arantes to come closer to the knitting knowledge that she has mastered but does not possess, can also be seen as notes in a state of suspension – fleeting, unformed, a more immediate knowledge prior to interpretation. This state of suspension can further be seen as a state of unlearning, a prerequisite for making way for the unknown, the accident, the surprise in the field (Martínez). As Waltorp and the ARTlife Film Collective ask, 'How to let knowledge *unfold* and embrace modes of attention that entail unlearning?' Unlearning entails engaging in knowledge *by subtraction*, leaving the pockets or 'holes' of the unknown, preserving the mystery, surrendering to the moment and leaving the mind behind (Di Puppo) (Fader-Nadoff refers to *blind-visuality* in the work of forgers in Mexico). It is not knowledge *by accumulation* (Ingold 2011, 2017) that seeks to turn experiences, events and phenomena in the field into mere material to be incorporated in a work of research.

Knowledge by subtraction is the acknowledgment that we do not know; sometimes, all we can say is that 'something happened'. As Frederiksen says regarding the inadequacy of trying to interpret the events surrounding a Georgian wedding: 'The drama, in this particular case, consists of occurrences where something "simply happens".' Raahauge says something similar about ghost phenomena: 'Something happened to someone' (Raahauge 2016: 95). Similarly, in her experience of the ritual ceremony, Di Puppo notes: 'I know that something happened in me, a power that made me bow.' A surplus of ethnographic detail for the sake of showing that 'we were there' (Di Puppo) or a surplus of meaning (Frederiksen) appears inadequate, as it only distracts from the experience or the event. By seeking to preserve the unknown, our peripheral methodologies are in search of a new language, one more evocative than explanatory, for example in the shape of a non-discursive flow of images (Waltorp & ARTlife Film Collective) or a poetic form (Di Puppo).

The *resistance* to analysis and interpretation of the phenomena and experiences we encounter in the field also raises the question of the nature of the field and how we approach it. In particular, it puts into question the view of the field as a (cultural or social) context to the extent that the moments, experiences and phenomena that appear in this collection may seem precisely to be out of place and out of context. The field is often thought of as a place of contextualisation for analytical categories and concepts. However, the experiences, moments and phenomena in this collection instead evoke *dislocation* (Nolas and Varvantakis, Di Puppo), dissonance and improvisation (Frederiksen), the disorientation and suspension of knowledge (Martínez, Raahauge). Recounting experiences of ghost phenomena, Raahauge (2016: 97) says that her informants feel 'as if the ghost and the one experiencing it do not share the same context'; the ghost experience appears as 'a fragment that needs some kind of framework in order to become understandable; it is as if it is out of context on purpose' (ibid.).

Di Puppo's experience of a ritual ceremony brings into question precisely the possibility of incorporating such experiences into a framework, making them understandable. They seem to be inevitably beyond any one context, surpassing what one might call context as they open the way to new dimensions. Experiences of this kind appear as fragments from another world; they hint at other associations, other dimensions. Reflecting on his archaeological research in the *seemingly* abandoned Holmegaard Glassworks, Tim Flohr Sørensen talks about the way in which objects resist his analytical efforts (Sørensen 2017). He talks about *trusting* the archaeological traces he encounters and letting objects or constellations of them direct and transform his gaze. In her archaeological work in a storage house in Eyri, Iceland, Þóra Pétursdóttir (2014) also talks about *learning to turn to things*. The entanglements and constellations of objects that could change overnight in the abandoned archaeological sites mirror the unexpected associations that we encounter in our field experiences. They alert us to the presence of improvisation (Frederiksen), to the potential of new, emerging associations, such as those that arise in the flow of images presented by Waltorp and the ARTlife Film Collective.

Rather than leading to a sharpness of vision, the peripheral methodologies we discover in our field experiences can be thought of as leading to a *sharpness of attention*. The Greek *mētis* that appears in Klekot's text on pottery is knowledge in movement, a knowledge that espouses the shifting quality of a moving world, but it is also full alertness, the capacity to be fully aware of the present moment. As much as Varvantakis drifts away in dreamy abandonment when savouring a dish during his fieldwork (one that unexpectedly brings him back to his grandmother's kitchen), the details that the dish brings to mind are potent in their liveliness. While peripheral wisdom is about engaging with indistinctiveness and discontinuity – the inherent vagueness of phenomena and field experiences, which seem to hang between the known and the unknown – it also brings about vividness and sharpness in the mode of attention that results from it. It is akin to seeing things anew, in a perpetual discovery of the world. When engaging with associations and constellations that appear incoherent, out of place, or with subtle moments and experiences that may appear to lack 'relevance', we become fully engaged in our field, fully alert to the way things present themselves to us. This state of alertness is also humility in the presence of the unknown and of the enduring mystery of the world we encounter.

Note

1   Corbin further distinguishes between allegory and symbol: 'Every allegorical interpretation is harmless; the allegory is a sheathing, or, rather, a disguising, of something that is already known or knowable otherwise, while the appearance of an Image having the quality of a symbol is a primary phenomenon (*Urphänomen*), unconditional and irreducible, the appearance of something that cannot manifest itself otherwise to the world where we are' (ibid.: 18).

References

Cerwonka, Allaine and Liisa Malkki 2007. *Improvising Theory: Process and Temporality in Ethnographic Fieldwork*. Chicago: University of Chicago Press.

Corbin, Henry 1999. *Swedenborg and Esoteric Islam*. West Chester: Swedenborg Foundation.

Cox, Rupert, Andrew Irving and Christopher Wright (eds.) 2016. *Beyond Text?: Critical Practices and Sensory Anthropology*. Manchester: Manchester University Press.

Dalsgaard, Steffen and Morten Nielsen 2016. *Time and the Field*. Oxford: Berghahn Books.

Desjarlais, Robert 1997. *Shelter Blues: Sanity and Selfhood among the Homeless*. Philadelphia: University of Pennsylvania Press.

Desjarlais, Robert 2018. *The Blind Man: A Phantasmography*. New York: Fordham University Press

Frederiksen, Martin Demant 2018. *An Anthropology of Nothing in Particular*. Winchester: Zero Books.

Ingold, Tim 2011. *Being Alive*. London: Routledge.

Ingold, Tim 2017. 'Evolution in a minor key'. In *Verbs, Bones, and Brains*. Agustín Fuentes and Aku Visala (eds.) Notre Dame: University of Notre Dame Press.

Jullien, François 1999. *The Propensity of Things Toward a History of Efficacy in China*. New York: Zone.

Jullien, François 2011. *The Silent Transformations*. London: Seagull.

Knysh, Alexander 1993. Orthodoxy and heresy in medieval Islam: an essay in reassessment. *Muslim World* 83: 48–67.

Martínez, Francisco 2019. 'Doing nothing: Anthropology sits at the same table with contemporary art in Lisbon and Tbilisi'. *Ethnography* 20 (4): 541–559.

Mittermaier, Amira 2012. 'Dreams from elsewhere: Muslim subjectivities beyond the trope of self-cultivation'. *Journal of the Royal Anthropological Institute* 18: 247–265

Mittermaier, Amira 2019. 'The unknown in the Egyptian uprising: Towards an anthropology of al-Ghayb'. *Contemporary Islam* 13, 17–31.

Pétursdóttir, Þóra 2014. 'Things out-of-hand: The aesthetics of abandonment'. In *Ruin Memories: Materialities, Aesthetics and the Archaeology of the Recent Past*. Bjørnar Olsen and Þóra Pétursdóttir (eds.) London: Routledge, 335–364.

Raahauge, Kirsten M 2016. 'Ghosts, troubles, difficulties, and challenges: Narratives about Unexplainable phenomena in contemporary Denmark'. *Folklore* 65: 89–111.

Rethmann, Petra 2007. 'On presence'. In *Extraordinary Anthropology: Transformations in the Field*. Jean-Guy Goulet and Bruce G. Miller (eds.) Lincoln: University of Nebraska Press, 36–52.

Sontag, Susan 2009 (1961). 'Against interpretation'. In *Against Interpretation, and Other Essays*. Susan Sontag (ed.) London: Penguin Books, 3–15.

Sørensen, Tim Flohr 2016. 'In praise of vagueness: Uncertainty, ambiguity and archaeological methodology'. *Journal of Archeological Method and Theory* 23 (2): 741–763.

Sørensen, Tim Flohr 2017. 'Art and archaeology: Looking at Holmegaard glassworks'. *Journal of Contemporary Archaeology* 4 (1): 141–147.

Stevenson, Lisa 2014. *Life Besides Itself: Imagining Care in the Arctic*. Oakland: University of California Press.

Stoller, Paul 1994. 'Conscious ain't consciousness: Entering the Museum of Sensory Absence'. In *The Senses Still: Perception and Memory as Material Culture in Modernity*. Nadia Seremetakis (ed.) Chicago: The University of Chicago Press.

Woodham, T (2018). 'Foreword: Peripheries'. *Moveable Type*, Vol. 10, 'Peripheries'.

Afterthought

Notes on the peripheral, in a plague year

Robert Desjarlais

The face of London was – now indeed strangely altered: I mean the whole mass of buildings, city, liberties, suburbs, Westminster, Southwark, and altogether; for as to the particular part called the city, or within the walls, that was not yet much infected. But in the whole the face of things, I say, was much altered; sorrow and sadness sat upon every face; and though some parts were not yet overwhelmed, yet all looked deeply concerned; and, as we saw it apparently coming on, so every one looked on himself and his family as in the utmost danger.

Daniel Defoe, *A Journal of the Plague Year*, 1722

I write this from a periphery. One of several, in fact. To be more precise, and without finding any security in such precision, I write from a studio apartment in a building set along a side street in Vesterbro, one of the outlying neighborhoods of Copenhagen, Denmark. Beyond the city centre, this particular area rests on the edge of the former meatpacking district, since transformed into an open-air arcade of shops and restaurants. The doors of most of these establishments are closed just now. It's unclear when they will open again.

I write peripherally, in a time of uncertainty and anxiety and ever-shifting viral Reproduction Rates, RO 2.5, 1.07, 1.33. There is a virus circulating the world, COVID-19. It has made its spectral way across the globe, and is now lighting upon most corners of the world. While news of the Corona outbreak is on everyone's mind, it's terrifically unclear where the microbes might be at any given moment, whether or not they are in the air that one passes, or breathes in, or if it's clinging to the doorknobs and elevator buttons that mark a trail back home.

Many people wonder if they've already had the virus. There was the flu-like ailment and lingering cough they had back in January, or the sore throat in February, which went away as mysteriously as it arrived. Or that delirium fever that one night, gone by morning. Most continue to worry that they might fall ill with the infection, with death as a possible outcome. It's scary.

I write from certain telling peripheries of space and time. I dwell on the margins of family, friendship, institutional power, within circuits of life and death. I am far from the action. My existence so far hovers well beyond the so-called front lines or any virulent 'hot spots' in the world. I have not been near a hospital or health clinic, or any testing centres. I've heard no ambulance sirens sounding desperately through the streets. I've seen no dead bodies piling up, or kept in temporary storage facilities (though I've heard of the mass graves). I'm not sure even where I should go if I were suddenly to fall ill with a fever and sore throat, or lose my sense of taste and smell. Still, it's as if it's around me now, unseen, lingering in the streets below.

The virus is sneaky. Largely invisible and unpredictable, immeasurable, it sneaks up on people, hits them hard. Levels them. There's no respite for some. Others say they experience no symptoms at all. There's quite a range, which adds to the perplexity.

No one knows what the long-term consequences of the infection will be for those who survive it. No one knows for sure if, once you've had it, and supposedly have the resultant antibodies in your blood, you are then forever immune from further infections. But some of those who have recovered from the illness now find comfort in the likelihood that they have immunity, and they go about their days in ways more at ease than others.

No one knows what will happen, or what things will be like in a month or year from now. No one knows whether or not the virus will return with a vengeance in the fall, or next year, or the next. Anyone who tells you anything for sure is a fool.

They are now predicting 'wavelets' of viral infections this summer, affecting urban centres like waves ascending onto a shoreline and flowing into the surrounding marshlands.

I arrived in Copenhagen at the start of March. There was distant news then of outbreaks in Seattle, and in the New York City area, along with the intense fight to stop the spread of the virus in China, Hong Kong and South Korea. But in Europe and North America it was nothing like it is now. Within days Italy caught on fire, and then Spain, and soon after – with the country's leaders and health experts fearing the worse – the schools and universities in Denmark closed down. Within days shops, restaurants, and cafés had shut their doors as well. Now, when I bike through central Copenhagen I pass through a ghost shell of the city, and I try to imagine what life was like here before the shut-down, or how it might be like once again.

The building from which I write provides lodging for 'ex-pats', namely women and men from elsewhere who have come to Denmark to work or study. Most are here for just a few months or so. Some have young children with them. The structure's hallways and stairwells are vacant most of the time. I had come here from New York, where I most often reside. Each night I read the news from that city and state and try to comprehend what it's like to be there now. The high rates of infection have plateaued, but there's still that massive plateau. It appears that most people are staying at home, concerned about going outside. Most wear masks there, now, or so I gather, from images seen on-line.

All that is far away from here. Others have it much worse, compared to many of us now in Denmark. We're able to go outside when we want to. Few people were masks. It's like the apocalypse has happened and all the people are still around. That doubleness is an odd reality to take in.

When I fall asleep at night I enter into a sweet oblivion. Any dreams are elsewhere. Once I wake it all comes crashing down again. It's as if news of the virus comes from outside the apartment and glides through the windows along with the morning light. Often I check the news before sitting up in the bed. Holding a smartphone in my hands I scroll through the headlines of online newspapers, dispatches from New York, India, Great Britain, Hong King, China, Sweden, Singapore, Mexico, you name it. The virus is everywhere. It has entered into all aspects and fault lines of human existence. Travel bans. Overburdened hospitals. Death in care homes. Isolation and loneliness. Virtual teaching, and schooling at home. Increased rates of drinking and abuse. Health disparities. Unemployment lines and statistics. Unpaid migrant workers stuck far from home.

The virus is also nowhere precise and singular and tangible.

I have come to call this the 'viral sublime', without any hard thinking on that – sublime in the way that the virus and its effects are at once everywhere and nowhere, and how it exceeds the ability of a single mind to grasp its workings, its spread through the world, the countless ways people's lives and deaths have been affected. Sublime as in inspiring awe, and a correlated incapacity to comprehend the allness of it. It's impossible to fathom the full extent of its damage, the tolls exacted, its many obscure pathways, or what the near or distant future will bring. And the numbers keep increasing. It's overwhelming – and fascinating, those many interlacing dimensions of a plague. And viral, too, these operations in body and mind. Wavering thoughts and imaginings of the virus move about like the contagion itself, as imagined. Cytokine storm is an apt term, medically, and phenomenologically.

'It's madness', writes a friend, far away in space and time.

'What is happening across the globe is so surreal', writes another.

Viral shredding. Self-quarantine. Social distancing. Sheltering in place. Herd immunity. Contract tracing. Corona shaming. Ghost games. Ground glass opacity. These are the idioms of the day, words to live and fret by.

CONFRONT YOUR DISCOMFORT reads a sign made of block letters printed onto sheets of paper and taped to the glass windows of a nearby shop.

The apartment where I'm residing seems safe. There is the phantasm of safety, at least, for I feel a sense of security and apartness when I return home after being outside. The door locks tight, and once I take off my coat, gloves, and wash my hands, I feel that this space keeps me free of any contaminants, for as long as I remain there. But who knows. It could be around here, somewhere. On the kitchen counter, perhaps, or seeded onto the set of keys I carry with me. Unseen microbes might have snuck in with me when I returned home after getting coffee this morning – I had forgotten to wash my hands straight off. I only thought of that after taking a few sips from a paper cup. So there you go. Nothing is clear.

I look out my window quite often and see people across the way, similarly hunkered down, couched within their own peripheral knowings. I try to imagine what their days are like, what's on their minds just then. On slight occasions we see each from afar but we never acknowledge the other's presence.

It's like the city is composed of a thousand peripheral knowings. There's much more than that, actually, in the world at large, 'these manifold peripheralities' (Arantes). Everyone has a slight side view and partial grasp of what's involved, as they try to find their way. In these zones of uncertainty, in emergent time, no one anywhere has a clear and comprehensive sense of what's going on. Everyone is in their own little Zoom quadrant of knowledge and perception. Each day brings new moments of unlearning, not-knowing, and epistemological and ontological limits. Systems of medical care, knowledge, technology, commerce, and power are fraying at the edges. The centre is not holding. Non-mastery, indeed. I doubt that anyone truly feels that they are a master of everything or anything just now. No masters of the universe, as in decades past. Any precise sense of mastery is an illusion. And yet one still strives for it, in small moments, of writing, knitting, crafting, making, walking, talking, reading, drinking, or watching films that stream into the solitude of one's nights. Across the way there are children playing in a playground, kicking a ball around, and a child's first steps, her mother walking closely, proudly, behind. Small moments of grace. And then there's the Nordic sunlight, soft, clear and subtle, gaining in strength each day.

Peripheral knowing is a signal method for these uncertain times. Or for any other time, as the fine contributions to *Peripheral Methodologies: Unlearning, Non-Knowing, and Ethnographic Limits* make clear. This outstanding compendium rightly delineates 'the vague, contradictory, unfinished, superficial, and eccentric' as both subject and method of anthropological inquiry. With such shifting focuses on zones of uncertainty, on everyday un-makings, on unordinary encounters and wayward affects, on scenes of shadow, opaqueness, and off-focus vagueness, on singular events and temporal openness, on incomprehensible insights and perceptions, 'unknowing' and 'eccentric knowledge' (Feder-Nadoff, Klekot), on the strange or incommensurable in the affective, embodied logics of social life, on moments of non-knowledge and non-mastery and the limits of explanatory language and rational thought – with all this, pathways of anthropological work open into fertile new terrains of thought and reflection. There is something especially timely and salient in the tracts of concept and language that the authors of this volume's essays advance, each in their own singular ways. The writings by Lili Di Puppo, Martin Demant Frederiksen, Francisco Martínez, Melissa Nolas and Christos Varantakis, Lydia Arantes, Ewa Klekot, Michele Feder-Nadoff, Kirsten Marie Raahauge, Karen Waltrop get at keen textures and shadings of the peripheral (with Paul Stoller's foreword offering a sage reflection from this ethnographic storyteller). With these texts, specific, tentative sensibilities and methodologies arise for research, thought and writing. Certain encouragements are at hand, as well, or so I read these pages. Go beyond clarity and precision. Hold fast to the right to opacity. Search for wisdom in odd and sporadic moments, in the uncanny, and in domains not usually thought to hold wisdom. Cultivate a negative capability in going beyond conventional modes of representation, narration and analysis. Mine (unapologetically) the subjective, the isomorphic, and accidental. Preserve the unknown and dissonant. All of this is much-needed advice and perspective.

To which I would add the gentle encouragement, seek out the phantasmal, trace out its spectral workings and haunting reverberations, tend to the micro-phantasms that thread through everyday life.

With such reflections I return myself to certain peripheral moments that have captured my own thoughts and imaginings of late, and these, likewise, in incidental, incomprehensive, non-masterful ways.

- as with that afternoon hour, in one of the first day of the shutdown, while I walked along a sidewalk in Vesterbro: I watched as a young man delicately removed his bank card from a telling machine and, with precise gestures with his fingers, wiped down each side and surface of the card with a snow-white cloth.

- or in those first days after the university and other places had closed, but a few cafés were still open: I would go there in mornings to work, with others doing much the same while seated a few metres apart away, each of us going about our tasks while, it seemed, we all knew we were doing something slightly transgressive, and risky.

- or that day when I read about some expert's research study of the slight but altogether significant wind currents that swirl about in the wake of someone walking past or running nearby; since then, when I walk in any of the city's streets, trying to keep the proper distance from others, I try to calculate, with no actual sense of precise calculations, how the virus might circulate in the air swirling past that healthy-looking jogger who just ran by me, or the couple that walked too close to my own two-metred space in the city, the air between us all too transparent. Risk calculation.

- or the other morning, as I set out for a walk: while standing at a street corner, waiting for the signal to turn green, I noticed a man across the way, his body decked out in gloves, winter scarf, jacket with the hood pulled over his head, and a mask and dark sunglasses that hid his face, as if he wanted no part of himself in direct contact with others, which led me to wonder – and wonder only – what concerns led him to protect himself so fully.

- or the empty packets of paracetamol tablets I found one day while cleaning the apartment; they were hidden underneath a counter, the once-there contents of which led me to wonder if the previous tenant of the flat had suddenly come down with a fever and, worried for her health and safety, had quickly returned to a family home in another land.

- or of how one can go without thinking about the pandemic for hours at a time, while engaged with some task, and then awareness of its cruel force quickly slips back into consciousness; it's surprising to find that one can actually forgot about it for a while, while feeling guilty for having done so.

- or the planes of diffusion that can emerge when one is on one's own for several days at a stretch, and coordinates of time and space, selfhood and language start to lose their bounded tightness and one risks falling into a fugue of crumpled subjectivity and unmade beds.

- and then to step outside and suddenly talk with another living being, in person, in a three-dimensional flow of time beyond the flat façade of a computer screen, this can almost be like a religious experience, a visceral encounter with the vital presence of another; somehow it's the eyes of the other that are most alive.

I find now, without much peripheral wisdom of my own, that such sporadic perceptions and musings are in accord with what the authors of *Peripheral Methodologies* so astutely convey to their readers: that it's with such moments, and others, that much can be gleaned about the way life is lived these days, and a robust and generative anthropological method can be made of such uncommon attentiveness. As Di Puppo, Frederiksen, and Martínez put it in the conclusion to this collection, 'Something furtive, subtle and also unknown suddenly grips our attention, while awakening in us what we can call a dormant mode of attention and of being'. As with the intricate, compelling subjects of the essays in the volume, these tangents and asides similarly suggest the peripheral methodologies of everyday life. While such chance encounters and obscure possibilities and fleeting modalities of thought and sensate perception might not be at the centre of most research studies or domains of discursive thought, they say a lot about what it's like to perceive, think, feel and imagine in the contemporary world, be it in a plague year, or any other time.

Copenhagen
May 2020

(Un-)Index

body-full-mind 82

casting on 68, 87
cunning eccentricity 84

de-centred 2, 169

entanglements 100, 173
exploration 82, 131, 142, 157

field-accidents 146

glimpses 165

half-consistency 146
Hasard (fr.) 31

idiom 45
infra-knowledge 1
intermediary ix
intimacy 27, 75, 168
isomorphic articulation 115

maybe nearly 31

negative capability ix, 1, 145
no one knows 177

occasional stirring 45, 57
out of sight 131

phantasm 176

the between x
thissing that 131
tongue-eyed 101

unnecessary 22, 25

vitality 54, 170
vulnerability x, 96

words birds 17

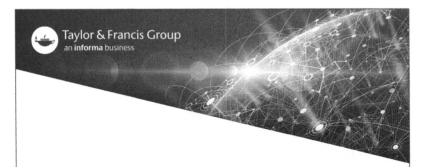

Printed in the United States
by Baker & Taylor Publisher Services